D1478495

Mindreaders

Theory of mind, or "mindreading" as it is termed in this book, is the ability to think about beliefs, desires, knowledge and intentions. It has been studied extensively by developmental and comparative psychologists and more recently by neuroscientists and cognitive psychologists. This book is the first to draw together these diverse findings in an account of the cognitive basis of "theory of mind", and establishes the systematic study of these abilities in adults as a new field of enquiry.

Apperly focuses on perceptions, knowledge and beliefs as paradigm cases of mindreading, and uses this as a basis from which more general lessons can be drawn. The book argues that an account of the cognitive basis of mindreading is necessary for making sense of findings from neuroscience and developmental and comparative psychology, as well as for understanding how mindreading fits more broadly into the cognitive system. It questions standard philosophical accounts of mindreading, and suggests a move away from the notion that it consists simply of having a "theory of mind".

This unique study into the cognitive basis of mindreading will be ideal reading for academics and advanced students from the diverse disciplines that have studied theory of mind in particular, and social cognition more generally.

Ian Apperly is currently a Reader in psychology at the University of Birmingham. He studied natural sciences at Cambridge University, and completed his PhD at the University of Birmingham.

Mindreaders

The Cognitive Basis of "Theory of Mind"

Ian Apperly

Psychology Press
Taylor & Francis Group

HOVE AND NEW YORK

Published in 2011
by Psychology Press
27 Church Road, Hove, East Sussex BN3 2FA

Simultaneously published in the USA and Canada
by Psychology Press
270 Madison Avenue, New York, NY 10016

Psychology Press is an imprint of the Taylor & Francis Group, an Informa business

© 2011 Psychology Press

Typeset in Times by Garfield Morgan, Swansea, West Glamorgan
Printed and bound in Great Britain by TJ International Ltd, Padstow, Cornwall
Cover design by Andy Ward
Cover photo © eva serrabassa/iStockPhoto

This publication has been produced with paper manufactured to strict environmental standards and with pulp derived from sustainable forests.

British Library Cataloguing in Publication Data
A catalogue record for this book is available from the British Library

Library of Congress Cataloging-in-Publication Data
Apperly, Ian.
   Mindreaders : the cognitive basis of "theory of mind" / Ian Apperly.
      p. cm.
   ISBN 978-1-84169-697-3 (hb)
1. Cognitive psychology. 2. Philosophy of mind. I. Title.
   BF201.A66 2010
   153–dc22
                                                            2010019000

ISBN 978-1-84169-697-3 (hbk)

Contents

Here, as he looked at the table, at the malachite cover of her blotter, and an unfinished letter lying on it, his thoughts suddenly underwent a change. He began to think of her, of what she was thinking and feeling. For the first time he really pictured to himself her personal life, her ideas, her desires; and the notion that she could and should have a separate life of her own appeared to him so dreadful that he hastened to drive it away. This was the abyss into which he was afraid to look. To put himself in thought and feeling into another being was a mental exercise foreign to Karenin. He considered such mental exercise harmful and dangerous romancing.

(Leo Tolstoy, 1954, pp. 159–160)

List of figures

Preface and acknowledgements

Before I left to begin my PhD in 1995 my undergraduate supervisor gave me a good piece of parting advice: "Don't work on theory of mind – the bubble is about to burst." What he correctly diagnosed was a tailing off in the 15 years of frenetic research activity that had followed seminal papers on the ability of chimpanzees, typically developing children and children with autism, to reason about the knowledge, beliefs, desires and intentions of others. It was not so much that all of the interesting problems had been solved, but that key theoretical positions had become firmly entrenched, and there were just so many experiments that nobody could keep all of the details in their head at once in order to make sense of them. This, at least, was my excuse. I half listened to my undergraduate supervisor, and spent five very interesting years studying theory of mind in "older" children, which at the time meant 5- to 7-year-olds rather than 3- to 4-year-olds. But although my participant group was unusual, and although this somewhat avoided the "neurotic task fixation" of the literature on younger children, this work was squarely in the existing tradition of research on conceptual development. And as predicted, there was a sense that many researchers were growing just a bit bored with endless talks and endless papers on theory of mind.

What was difficult for anyone to foresee was that research on theory of mind, or "mindreading" as I shall call it in this book, would be rejuvenated in just a few years. Impetus for this change has come from at least three distinct disciplines. Firstly, just as many researchers were converging on the view that chimpanzees could not mindread there came a series of studies with much more positive evidence, not only in chimpanzees, but in other species, including distant relations of humans, such as birds. Secondly, evidence that infants might pass suitably adapted mindreading tasks has shaken the long-standing conclusion that the preschool years are the main period of change in mindreading abilities. Thirdly, the trickle of pioneering papers on the neural basis of mindreading in the mid nineties has grown rapidly into a tide by joining with the new research programme of "social neuroscience". Meanwhile, research on young children has continued to make advances, just a little more quietly than before.

Although these developments are very exciting, there is a curious absence in the literature on mindreading. Despite the many hundreds of papers on the abilities of human brains, children, infants and clinical populations, and non-human animals, there remains very little research on mindreading in human adults. This is curious since, in comparable topics, such as spatial cognition or number cognition, cognitive psychological research on how adults think about space or number provides the core model for understanding what children must develop, what brains must process and what might be different about the cognition of clinical populations or non-human animals. It is almost as if researchers investigating mindreading are building the walls of a tower but omitting to put in the floors.

Before I put off too many potential readers, I am not suggesting that existing research is wrong-headed when viewed on its own terms. As will become clear, I shall draw heavily on this work throughout the book both for inspiration and for a wide range of empirical findings. What I shall argue, however, is that besides being a worthy project in its own right, investigating the cognitive basis of mindreading, including studies of adults, provides critical connections between research in each of the sub-disciplines in which mindreading has typically been studied. Making such connections leads to a range of novel empirical questions and empirical predictions for many different areas of research on mindreading. Moreover, findings that appear very puzzling when viewed from the perspective of one sub-discipline, such as infants' success on tasks that seem very difficult for 3-year-olds, might be less puzzling if viewed in the broader perspective of the mature system.

My interest in the cognitive basis of mindreading grew out of my PhD work on children's development. With Liz Robinson I examined children's ability to think about the particular ways in which people represented information, and how this constrained reference and description when talking about what they thought, or interpreting what they said. This forced us to think about mindreading as an on-line process, rather than just a set of concepts or a body of knowledge that children needed to acquire, and it stretched the limits of what it seemed possible to achieve with the tasks typically used in research with children. It seemed natural to look for inspiration in research on adults, where there were many methods available for studying on-line cognitive processes. What I found surprising was that nobody had used such methods to study mindreading in adults, and more surprising still was the realization that despite all of the work on development, this meant that we actually knew rather little about what mindreading abilities children eventually developed. I have been very lucky to have a number of collaborators – especially Dana Samson – who were willing to share their invaluable expertise to address this question, and to have a head of department, Glyn Humphreys, who was willing to back our rather speculative ventures.

It is inevitable that a book of this kind will not do justice to the full range and depth of careful experimentation and clever theorizing that exists in the literature on mindreading. As a developmental psychologist by training I am particularly aware that this is true for the variety of accounts that have set out to explain how children's mindreading emerges from earlier, simpler processes. This book does not present an alternative to these accounts of development. It does aim to present a different, broader perspective on mindreading. Among other things this should have implications for how children develop these abilities, and I hope that this gain justifies my abridgement of many interesting and important ideas.

I owe many people thanks for making this book possible. Liz Robinson planted the idea in my head, where, for some time, it looked set to stay. I am grateful to the publisher for being patient, my friends for not reminding me too often, and the School of Psychology for granting me the sabbatical that eventually gave me time to write. Being much more used to collaborative work, writing as a single author is strange, and brings with it an uncomfortable sense of laying claim to ideas that I know are not wholly my own. This goes in particular for Dana Samson and Steve Butterfill who have been co-conspirators in the development of so many of the ideas presented here, and whom I cannot thank enough.

Sarah Beck was an invaluable sounding board throughout the process, and with an office adjacent to mine, bore the brunt of many problems over endless coffee. Even after this she generously gave her time to provide feedback and encouragement on draft chapters, as did Steve Butterfill, Charlotte Easter, Kevin Riggs, Dana Samson and Laura Shapiro.

Finally, I thank my partner, Laura, who made me read *Middlemarch* before I started.

1 Introduction

What is "mindreading"?

I know what you're thinking. Just in case you've come here by mistake let me be clear that there is nothing mystical about the kind of mindreading I shall discuss. But even without mysticism there remains a good deal that is interesting, surprising and, at times, mystifying, about our everyday ability to "get inside the heads" of other people and think about what they know, want, intend and believe.

Reasons for interest include claims that mindreading is uniquely human (e.g., Penn & Povinelli, 2007; Saxe, 2006), that it is at the heart of key cognitive processes for social interaction and communication (e.g., Grice, 1989; Sperber & Wilson, 1995), and that impaired mindreading may be part of the explanation for a variety of psychiatric and developmental disorders such as schizophrenia and autism (e.g., Baron-Cohen, 1995; Frith, 2004). Reasons for surprise include the discovery of apparently sophisticated mindreading abilities in human infants and some non-human species (e.g., Call & Tomasello, 2008; Emery & Clayton, 2009) alongside apparently poor mindreading abilities in human children (e.g., Carpendale & Lewis, 2006; Doherty, 2009), and sometimes in human adults (Apperly, Samson & Humphreys, 2009). And mindreading is mysterious because there are genuine conceptual puzzles about how it is even possible to know the minds of others. Most obviously, we do not have direct access to what other people know, want, intend or believe, but must infer these mental states on the basis of what they do and say. Although this is clearly something that we actually do on a regular basis, how we do it raises some significant theoretical and empirical questions that have only been partially addressed in the literature. My overall aim is to justify the reasons for interest in mindreading, but to suggest that some of the surprises and some of the mysteries are the result of the literature conceptualizing the problem of mindreading in a rather narrow way.

By way of illustration, researchers have often asked me "Why are you studying adults? Don't they already have a theory of mind?". This question seems very telling about the issues that have dominated research on mindreading. Firstly, the vast majority of work to date has focused exclusively on *when* children are able to reason about mental states such as beliefs, desires and intentions and what factors affect this development. Secondly, many researchers hold that the development of mindreading consists of acquiring abstract mental state concepts, and that these concepts constitute a "theory" about how the mind works. This has led to "theory of mind" becoming the predominant term for mindreading in the academic literature (though "folk psychology", "mentalizing" and "social cognition" are also common). More importantly, this has led to the view that once such concepts are present – and this presence is evidenced by young children's success on simple tasks that require reasoning about beliefs, desires, etc. – psychologists can pack up their toolkits and move on to another problem; there is really nothing further to explain.

I find this baffling. Most cognitive psychologists only study adults, but appear to hold down their jobs despite the fact that young children already have a wide range of cognitive abilities, including aptitude in "conceptual domains" such as number, space, time or physics. The general pattern is that the literatures on adults' cognition not only have lives of their own, but also provide the model of the system that children are developing. Surely there is no reason for mindreading to be an exception?

The emphasis on concepts in the literature on mindreading also gives a deceptive impression of simplicity. It feels like we know what we mean when we credit a child who passes false belief tasks with the concept of belief, but do we really? It should make us nervous that there is little consensus in the theoretical literature on what it means to have a concept. And do we really suppose that unless a child passes a test suggesting that she has a given mental state concept then she is quite insensitive to the way in which behaviour is governed by mental states? Or that once a child does pass such a test there is nothing further for her to learn? Probably most researchers of mindreading would baulk at such black and white characterizations of their views, but common habits of thought in the literature nonetheless proceed along these lines. Witness the fact that the very great majority of work on mindreading concerns the abilities of 3- to 5-year-old children with little attention to younger children and still less on older children and adults. I shall argue that research on mindreading – including research on children – would benefit from a broader perspective on the kinds of data and participant groups that may be of interest and on the kinds of cognitive process that may be at work. We can keep many of the insights behind conceptual change accounts of the development of mindreading, but also accept that having key mental state concepts might be neither the beginning nor the end of mindreading abilities.

So I take as my starting point the fact that we live in a world populated by agents whose behaviour can be understood by supposing that they have mental states (beliefs, desires, etc.) that interact according to psychological laws (e.g., people act to satisfy their desires on the basis of their beliefs).[1] If we take this as the problem domain of mindreading then our question is, what cognitive processes enable us to operate successfully in this domain of agents? Part of the answer to this question is surely that at least some organisms – adult humans at the very least – reason in a sophisticated way about the causes and consequences of mental states *as such*.

But this is unlikely to be the full answer, even for adult humans. To see why, briefly consider another domain, that of normal objects (i.e., non-agents) whose behaviour can be understood by supposing that they have physical characteristics (mass, velocity) that interact according to physical laws (e.g., an object maintains its velocity unless acted on by a force). Some of the cognitive processes that enable human adults to operate in this domain clearly involve reasoning about physical characteristics and physical laws, and such reasoning can be very sophisticated. But what happens when we catch a ball? Of course, a suitably educated adult with sufficient time could make reasonable estimates of the relevant physical parameters, derive a prediction about the ball's trajectory and their own capacity to move, and work out the point of intersection where a catch would be possible. But this is demonstrably not how people catch balls[2] (e.g., McLeod, Reed & Dienes, 2003), or even how they arrive at everyday intuitions about the behaviour of balls[3] (e.g., Hood, 1995; Hood, Carey & Prasada, 2000; McCloskey, 1983; McCloskey et al., 1983). In fact, when operating in the domain of physical objects, people appear to have a wide variety of tricks and strategies, rules of thumb and specialized cognitive processes. These enable useful work in the domain but do not necessarily operate over conceptual representations of forces and physical characteristics, or at least not the same ones as would have been learned in physics classes. It seems plausible that the same will be true for mindreading.

Why "mindreading"?

Readers already familiar with the literature will know that most researchers talk about "theory of mind" rather than "mindreading". I have done the same in publications, because this is what everyone expects, but it always chafes, for two reasons. The important one is that the term is enormously tendentious because it implies that mindreading consists in having a theory about how the mind works. In fact this is, at best, just one theoretical possibility among many. And for my purposes it unhelpfully suggests that "theory of mind" is something that one *has* rather than something that one *does*. The more trivial reason is that "theory of mind" is linguistically awkward. It is bad enough as a sort of compound noun for describing a putative psychological faculty, and much worse as an adjective to describe "theory of mind processes" or "theory of mind brain regions", and as for inflection, if I have a theory of mind do I really want to be a "theory of minder"?

Since I shall have to use the term a lot, I propose to talk about "mindreading" instead. I prefer the term because it is theoretically neutral, yet captures something of the character of the problem. When we read text we not only process the words in front of us but also make elaborated inferences about the meaning behind them, which go far beyond what is on the page. When we mindread we often have to process perceptually accessible social stimuli, and we always have to make significant further inferences to arrive at the underlying thoughts, desires, knowledge or intentions that we cannot directly perceive. Others have opted for other terms, such as "social cognition" or "social understanding" (e.g., Carpendale & Lewis, 2006), but these are much too broad for my purposes. I shall keep returning to the point that there is a very great deal more to social cognition than mindreading alone, and this is discussed in many other sources that I shall refer to along the way. But mindreading is the topic of this book.

Epistemic mental states as a case study

We have very rich mental lives. I have already mentioned beliefs, knowledge, desires and intentions, and we could keep going for some time charting further kinds of epistemic, emotional and motivational states. A full account of mindreading will ultimately require an explanation of how we navigate a social world of agents who have all of these mental states, not only for completeness but because different mental states combine together as the causes and consequences of behaviour. However, we are not only very far from having the evidence required for a full account, but there remains a good deal of work in conceiving the form such an account should take. Since my aim is to examine the cognitive basis of mindreading in greater depth than is typical in the literature, this comes, for the time being, at the expense of examining a broad range of mental states. My simplifying strategy is to limit most of my discussion to epistemic mental states such as perceptions, knowledge and belief. Rightly or wrongly, these occupy the centre of the literature on mindreading, giving me the largest evidence base to draw upon. My hope is that the account developed for epistemic mental states can serve as a model for the broader family of mental states, and ultimately for a fully integrated account of mindreading.

Normative models and philosophical theories

From its inception the modern study of mindreading has involved close collaboration between psychologists and philosophers. When Premack and Woodruff (1978) asked whether the chimpanzee has a "theory of mind" it was the commentaries of three philosophers (Bennett, 1978; Dennett, 1978; Pylyshyn, 1978) that led to paradigms involving perspective differences – such as the false belief task (Wimmer & Perner, 1983) – becoming the workhorses of empirical studies for the next thirty years. Some of the most prominent psychologists in the field have had strong interests in philosophy of mind, and full-time philosophers of mind have continued to play an important role in the development of empirical research (e.g., Carruthers & Smith, 1995; Davies & Stone, 1995a,b). It is philosophy of mind that supplies the normative model for mindreading. Agents (you and I) hold attitudes (e.g., seeing, knowing and believing) to propositional mental states (e.g., It is raining, again). The mindreader's task is therefore conceived as reasoning about such relationships. As you see me leave my house you may predict my next action – that I will return to fetch an umbrella – if you can judge that I will see that it is raining, that I know that this will make me wet, and that I believe there is an umbrella back inside the house. As we shall see in later chapters, the literature is dominated by questions about how children become able to reason this way, and whether non-human animals ever do so.

Philosophy of mind also supplies the two dominant theoretical accounts of how mindreading is possible. According to so-called "theory-theories" mindreading depends on us having mental state concepts and principles that describe their interactions (Davies & Stone, 1995a,b). This contrasts with "simulation theories", according to which mindreading may not require a fully specified theory of the mind if only we could use our own minds to model (i.e. simulate) the minds of others.

However, although philosophy of mind has made many positive contributions to the study of mindreading, I think it is also partly responsible for the topic becoming rather hidebound. Although the debate between theory-theory and simulation-theory may have given us a useful sense of the different flavours that mindreading might have, it has been remarkably poor at generating empirically testable predictions for propositional mental states such as seeing, knowing and believing.[4] Although there are particular cases that seem to favour one theory or the other, nobody has yet come up with a generalizable test, or set of criteria, that could be used to discern whether a given mindreading problem was solved by simulation or by theorizing (e.g., Apperly, 2008; Stich & Nichols, 1997). I am not the first, and probably not the last, to wonder whether experimental psychologists might be better off without these theories. At the very least that we might do well to set them aside while we pursue empirically tractable hypotheses, and perhaps return to them later to see if they offer us any further insight into what we have found. This is the strategy that I shall pursue here.

I do not propose to be as gung-ho about the normative model, which characterizes mindreading as the ascription of attitudes with propositional content to agents. It will be a working hypothesis that we do in fact mindread in something like this way at least some of the time, and that it is important to know how we do so. However, I do not want to be tied exclusively to this characterization, firstly because I suspect that our very best mindreading abilities might only approximate to the assumptions of the normative model, and secondly because I suspect that much of the work of everyday mindreading – and possibly all of the mindreading of infants and non-human animals – is achieved in ways that deviate very substantially from the normative model. This theme will be picked up in more detail in the second part of the book.

Mindreading perceptions, knowledge and beliefs: The structure of the book, and how to read it

My interest, then, is in what cognitive processes make it possible to operate successfully in a world of agents who have perceptions, knowledge and beliefs. Although surprisingly few studies have tackled this question directly, the existing literature on adults, children, infants, atypical development, cognitive neuroscience and non-human animals provides much useful information to help construct an account. My aim in the first part of the book, from chapters 2 to 5, is to identify a set of questions about the cognitive basis of mindreading, and use these to conduct a very selective review of these literatures. Much more complete reviews and assimilations of different branches of the literature have been conducted elsewhere, and I shall draw attention to these as I go along. The unique features of my review will be the breadth of evidence considered and the focus on what can be learned about cognitive processes. In the second part of the book, in chapters 6 and 7, I shall draw together these different strands of evidence to develop a schematic account of the cognitive basis of mindreading. I shall then explore implications of this account for the study of mindreading in children, adults and non-human animals.

This structure means that readers who are most interested in the theory could skip ahead to chapters 6 and 7. Chapter 6 begins with a distillation of evidence from earlier chapters, and this may be sufficient, if you are willing to take my word for it. However, much of the evidence comes from very recent studies conducted in different corners of the literature. There remains a great deal of controversy about how they should be interpreted, and I discuss these debates together with the detailed findings throughout chapters 2 to 5. I hope that many readers will find it worthwhile to engage with these details because, ultimately, it is this evidence, and the patterns that emerge across diverse tasks and participant groups, that really justifies the effort of taking a new look at mindreading in the later chapters.

A cognitive psychologist's wish-list

Cognitive psychology does not have a universal taxonomic system for characterizing cognition. But to give some structure to my discussion of the literature I shall distinguish between questions about representations, processes and architectures for mindreading. These dimensions are clearly inter-related, but different cognitive processes nonetheless vary with substantial independence on each.

What are the representational characteristics of mindreading? Is mind-reading "special"? In what sense does mindreading depend on a specific set of concepts? Does mindreading pose unusual representational problems? Is the representational basis of mindreading domain-specific (that is to say, specialized for the purpose), or is it domain-general (that is to say, the same representational resources serve other cognitive functions)? What role does language play in mindreading?

What are the processing characteristics of mindreading? Is mindreading effortful? Does it make significant demands on scarce cognitive resources for working memory, inhibition or other aspects of "executive function". Is it "fast" or "slow"? To what degree is mindreading automatic? Will mind-reading always occur in the presence of certain stimuli or will its occurrence depend on context?

What are the architectural characteristics of mindreading? Is mindreading a unitary faculty? Are there distinct sub-components serving different functions (such as processing perception versus knowledge)? Is there a hierarchy with different systems for simple mindreading and more complex mindreading, using different representations and processes? If so, what information passes between them? How is mindreading integrated with other cognitive processes such as communication or action planning? Might cognitive processes for communication or action planning have their own "on board" system for mindreading, so that a given mindreading function (such as processing perception) is performed more than once by separate systems that do not talk to each other?

It is not that these questions have never been asked before in the context of mindreading. All of them have. And, indeed, some people think they have been answered already. It is not uncommon for researchers to simply state that mindreading depends on a specialized cognitive module that is innate, fast, automatic and domain-specific (e.g., Leslie, 2005; Sperber & Wilson, 2002; Stone, Baron-Cohen & Knight, 1998). Curiously, others are similarly trenchant in the view of the development of mindreading as a protracted process that depends on a series of conceptual insights gained through domain-general learning and reasoning (e.g., Gopnik & Meltzoff, 1997; Perner, 1991; Wellman, 1990). Clearly, these contradictory interpreta-tions derive, in part, from contradictory theoretical commitments about the nature of cognition in general and development in particular. But I think they also result from questions about the cognitive basis of mindreading cropping up piecemeal as the by-product of questions about the nature of mindreading in children or non-human animals, the neural basis of mind-reading, or the functional basis of some other process such as communi-cation. I want to ask these questions in a more systematic way, using them to interrogate different fields of the literature for relevant evidence. My aim is to construct something closer to a coherent picture of the cognitive basis of mindreading (chapter 6), which I shall then use to cast light back on the existing literatures that I have drawn upon (chapter 7).

Unspoken problems at the heart of mindreading

So far, so good. My aim is to understand the cognitive processes that make it possible to mindread perceptions, knowledge and beliefs, and we should be able to make progress in this direction by applying a cognitive psychologist's questions to the existing literature on mindreading. I want to keep this structure for the first half of the book. But it may be useful to have some further questions in the back of the mind because of their importance for the second half. These questions concern two related problems that are not much discussed in the literature on mindreading, but which seem important for developing a cognitive account.

The first problem is that the proposed functions of mindreading appear to make contradictory cognitive demands. Consider the following examples, both of which appear to require mindreading. As a member of the jury in a court of law, your job is to judge the guilt or innocence of the person in the dock. Thinking about the defendant's mental states will clearly be critical to this judgement. Did they see the victim spoon the white powder into their tea? Did they know that the white powder was poison not sugar (e.g., Young, Cushman, Hauser & Saxe, 2007)? Did they leave the white powder next to the kettle with the intention that the victim should put it in their tea or were they just careless? Did they know that the poison would kill the victim rather than just make them sick? Of course, this is just one fanciful example. But if we scale up from the complexity already inherent in this simple example, and consider the range of cases that are tried in courts of law it is clear that a juror must be extremely flexible in their mindreading abilities. A case could concern any conceivable person in any conceivable set of circumstances where almost any conceivable information might turn out to bear on the judgement of guilt or innocence. Such flexibility is not expected to come easily. Indeed, we expect jurors to take their time to assimilate the relevant information, to think about it carefully, and to discuss it with fellow jurors before reaching an opinion. These characteristics seem common across a wide range of other situations. Viewed this way, mindreading would seem to be as flexible as any general reasoning process, and as potentially demanding of limited general processing resources for memory and executive control.

On the other hand, consider the case of playing a competitive sport like football. The success of passing the ball depends on whether or not opponents nearby the path of the ball will be able to see it in order to intercept it, and of course on whether the receiving player on your team is in a position to take account of what you are doing. Faking a pass in order to trick an opposing player to commit themselves in the wrong direction seems to depend upon deliberately giving them a false belief about your intentions. Realizing that an opponent cannot see your team mate behind them who is waving for the ball clearly confers a competitive advantage. So playing football surely involves some sort of mindreading (and indeed, mind manipulation), but to be of any use at all, these judgements must be made extremely quickly. And in order not to interfere with other on-going processes involved in playing the game, it would seem very useful, if not essential, that these judgements were made very efficiently, making few demands on limited general processing resources.

So it seems that mindreading must be as flexible as any reasoning process, but at the same time, fast and efficient enough to guide judgements made on the fly. The problem is that these demands are largely contradictory. That is to say, in cognitive systems flexibility and efficiency tend to be negatively correlated. The difficulty in having one system that is both flexible and efficient is apparent from the high prevalence of "two-systems" accounts in cognition, whereby in a given domain, be it social categorization, number cognition or general reasoning, the contradiction is resolved by having two types of cognitive system that operate in the domain, which make complementary trade-offs between flexibility and efficiency. What this means for current purposes is that, although it is common to talk about mindreading (or theory of mind, mentalizing or folk psychology) as if it were one kind of cognitive process, we should not be too surprised if this turned out to be incorrect. Indeed, in chapter 6, I shall argue for a "two-systems" account of mindreading.

A related point that has also not been confronted very clearly in the literature is that mindreading comes up very hard against some deep conceptual problems in cognitive science. Csibra and Gergely (2007) discussed the "inverse problem" in relation to the task of making inferences about an agent's goals and actions. Put simply, the mindreader who wants to infer an agent's goal (or intention, or belief, etc.) from observation of the agent's action (or to predict the agent's action given their goal) is faced with the problem of many-to-one mappings between goals and actions. A given action could be evidence for any number of different goals, and a given goal could lead to any number of actions. This presents a significant problem for inferences about the relations between observed behaviour and mental states. A related concern is the "frame problem" or the "problem of relevance" (e.g., Pylyshyn, 1987). In the general case, the frame problem is to know what are the causes or consequences of a change in a system whose components are all potentially (though not necessarily) linked. Applied to mindreading, the problem is that an agent may have any number of beliefs (and other mental states), any of which might be relevant when trying to judge what the agent will think or do in a given situation. It follows that even the most conscientious juror with all the time in the world should not be able to judge the guilt of the person in the dock: the problem is computationally intractable.

Clearly jurors do make decisions, and footballers do make passes, and so an important objective of the second half of the book is to discuss how this might be possible.

Notes

1 There is, of course, a longstanding debate in philosophy of mind about whether agents really do have such mental states, or whether assuming that they do is just a parsimonious strategy for explaining and predicting their behaviour (e.g., Dennett, 1987; Fodor, 1975). However, for current purposes this makes no difference because both sides of the debate agree that mindreading involves thinking about mental states, whether these are real entities or useful fictions.

2 A series of studies by McLeod and colleagues suggest that fielders running to catch a ball do not explicitly decide their speed or direction of running (as they would if they computed the solution to simultaneous equations governing their own trajectory and that of the ball). Instead, their running is governed by two parameters recovered from visual tracking of the ball's trajectory: ". . . they [fielders] run so that their angle of gaze elevation to the ball increases at a decreasing rate, while their horizontal gaze angle to the ball increases at a constant rate . . ." (McLeod et al., 2003, p. 244).

3 People's everyday reasoning about falling balls, as well as many other physical interactions, is subject to systematic errors and biases reflecting the use of rules of thumb or "naïve theories". For example, McCloskey (1983) found that when adults are asked to predict what happens to a ball dropped by a moving person, many people judge that it will fall straight downwards from the point at which it is dropped. In fact it will follow a parabolic trajectory resulting from the combination of the forward velocity with which it starts and the downward acceleration due to gravity.

4 A much more convincing case can be made that some mindreading of non-propositional mental states, such as action schemas and emotions, is achieved via simulation (e.g., Goldman, 2006). But it clearly does not follow from this success that the debate between simulation-theory and theory-theory will carve at the joints of propositional attitude ascription, which is the topic of this book.

2 Evidence from children

Although the modern literature on mindreading originated with a question about chimpanzees (Premack & Woodruff, 1978), much of the running since then has been made in studies of human development. Not only is this by far the largest literature on mindreading, but many of the central theoretical themes and most prominent empirical paradigms have arisen out of research on children. The current chapter, therefore, is not just designed to provide evidence bearing on questions about the cognitive basis of mindreading, but also to give important background information for the rest of the book. In this chapter I shall describe evidence from typically developing children aged 2-years upwards, followed by evidence from atypical development. These studies set the long-standing benchmarks in terms of theories, paradigms and, until recently, age of acquisition for children's mindreading.

This literature has been cast in a new light by studies emerging in the last few years that suggest that infants have much more impressive mindreading abilities than previously thought. I shall describe these studies in the next chapter. Although this ordering might seem odd, it is much easier to appreciate why the recent studies of infants are so interesting, surprising and controversial if they can be seen against the background of the literature on older children.

Perspective differences as a key empirical device

In their commentaries on Premack and Woodruff (1978), Bennett (1978), Dennett (1978) and Pylyshyn (1978) cautioned that we could never be sure that an animal (or anyone else for that matter) was taking account of another agent's mental states if the animal's own mental states coincided with those of the other agent. Let's imagine we were nearing the end of a long meeting, and your mind started wandering to the subject of beer. You might think it a minor miracle of everyday mindreading if I suggested that we go to the pub. But you might be less sure of my skills if you then found out that this was precisely what I wanted to do myself. It would be a much better test if I had a blistering hangover, so that going to the pub was the very last thing I would think of doing on my own account. For just these reasons it is common in studies of mindreading to contrive a situation in which the subject (animal, child or adult) has to make judgements about another agent who sees, knows, wants, intends or believes something different from themselves.

Children's mindreading

False belief tasks

In 1994 research on children's mindreading was diagnosed with "neurotic task fixation" (Gopnik, Slaughter & Meltzoff, 1994), and a pessimist might say that much of the literature since then attests to the failure of self-help therapies. Although developmental psychologists have devised many tasks, testing many different aspects of children's mindreading (see, e.g., Carpendale & Lewis, 2006; Doherty, 2009), false belief tasks are by far the most frequently used and by far the most richly interpreted. I shall start with these and work outwards.

Almost all false belief tasks are methodological variants on two basic procedures that set up a perspective difference between the child and the target. These procedures are presented in a child-friendly way by making them into an illustrated story, or acting out with puppets or real actors, but are illustrated schematically in Figure 2.1. In the "unexpected transfer" variant (Figure 2.1a; Wimmer & Perner, 1983), a character (Sally, in this case) sees a desirable object placed in one location (the round box) and then leaves the scene. In her absence a second character (Andrew, in this case)[1] transfers the object from its original location to a new location (the square box). Sally returns, and the child is asked to predict where she will look for the object, or where she thinks the object is, as well as questions to check that the child remembers where the object was originally and where it is now. In the "unexpected content" variant (Figure 2.1b; Hogrefe, Wimmer & Perner, 1986) the child is first shown a box that looks as if it should have one type of content (e.g., a tube of Smarties) and is asked what they think might be inside. Most children say "Smarties". They are then shown that in fact it contains paperclips[2]. Next, the child is told that another child will come and see the box in a minute, and is asked to judge what s/he will think is inside the box before she opens it up.

Wimmer and Perner (1983) originally found that many children judged incorrectly until around 5 years of age, though a more recent meta-analysis of 178 studies (Wellman, Cross & Watson, 2001), which included variations of both unexpected contents and unexpected transfer procedures, suggests that the likelihood of a child giving the correct answer changes more rapidly between the ages of 3 and 4 than between 4 and 5. Importantly, children's errors are not random. Instead, children show a systematic tendency to be egocentric, and respond with the right answer from their own point of view.

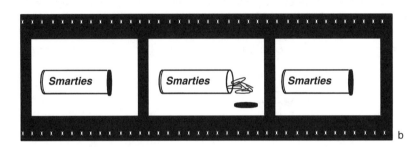

Figure 2.1 Panel (a) shows an unexpected transfer false belief task. Sally places her object in the round box and leaves the scene. Andrew moves the object to the square box. Sally returns to retrieve her object. Participants are asked where she thinks it is or where she will look (correct answer = round box). Panel (b) shows an unexpected contents false belief task. The participant is shown a familiar packaging container, and asked to predict what is inside. They are then shown that in fact there are paperclips inside. Finally, they are asked to predict what a naïve observer will think is inside the box (correct answer = smarties). Figure adapted from Apperly et al. (2005).

Thus, in the unexpected transfer task they judge incorrectly that Sally will look in the object's true location. In the unexpected content they judge that the new child will think there are paperclips inside the Smarties tube.

There have been many attempts to find methodological variants of the task that are easier for children, but in their meta-analysis Wellman et al. (2001) found that most of these had little effect. Even those that did have a reliable effect (such as making it clear that the question was about what the character would think or do *first of all* – Siegal & Beattie, 1991) never succeeded in reducing the age at which children pass false belief tasks by more than a few months. Thus, despite significant efforts to make the tasks simpler and more child-friendly, nobody has yet cured 3-year-olds of their tendency to make errors on false belief tasks. So although there is disagreement about why 3-year-olds tend to make errors (more of which later), there is general agreement that their difficulty is real. And, whether or not 3-year-olds' difficulties are with grasping the concept of belief per se, there is a general presumption that when children do pass false belief tasks we can be sure that they do have this concept.

Mindreading before success on false belief tasks

Using similar methods that require overt judgements from the child, researchers have found evidence that, before they pass false belief tasks, children can reason in quite diverse ways about people's epistemic mental states (as well as other mental states). Flavell and colleagues (e.g., Flavell, 1974; Masangkay et al., 1974; see also Moll & Tomasello, 2006) found that many 2-year-olds and most older children correctly judged that people with different lines of sight might see different things; so-called "Level-1 visual perspective-taking" (see Figure 2.2a). However, many 3-year-olds struggled on a very similar task that required them to judge that people with different

Figure 2.2 Panel (a) shows a Level-1 visual perspective-taking task. Participants must realize that Sally can see the box whereas Andrew cannot. Panel (b) shows a Level-2 visual perspective-taking task. Both Sally and Andrew see the box, but participants must realize that they see it as having different orientations.

lines of sight might see the very same things but in different ways; so-called "Level-2 visual perspective-taking" (see Figure 2.2b).

During their 4th year children can make predictions that people with different beliefs will act in different ways, provided the child does not herself know whether the beliefs are true or false. So if John thinks the puppy is in the shed and Jane thinks it's in the garage, and nobody knows who is right, children predict that John will search in the shed and Jane will search in the garage (e.g., Bartsch & Wellman, 1989). Also during their 4th year children will judge that someone who "has not seen" the object that is hidden in a box will not "know" what is inside the box (Pillow, 1989; Pratt & Bryant, 1990). In fact, explicitly predicting actions from diverse beliefs seems somewhat easier than predicting ignorance on the basis of no perceptual access, but both are easier than false belief tasks (e.g., Wellman & Liu, 2004).

In sum, despite the strong focus on false belief tasks in the general literature, evidence accrued over many years suggests that, well before they pass such tasks, 2- and 3-year-olds (and, in some instances, even younger infants) show some mindreading abilities in relation to what an agent sees, knows and believes.

Mindreading after success on false belief tasks

Just as there is clear evidence that children show mindreading abilities long before they pass false belief tasks, so there is clear evidence that passing a false belief task is no guarantee of success on related mindreading problems. For example, imagine that we embellish the scenario in Figure 2.1a slightly, so Sally peeps through a window while Andrew swaps the object's location (Figure 2.3). Children who could accurately judge Sally's false belief in the original scenario are much less good at judging that Andrew falsely believes that Sally has a false belief (Perner & Wimmer, 1985). One possibility is that such "second-order" false belief tasks require children to understand that beliefs can take other beliefs as their object, and this understanding comes later than a simple understanding of belief. Another possibility is that the conceptual demands of 1st and 2nd order false belief tasks are essentially the same, but that the need to embed one belief under another, and the need to comprehend a more complex story scenario place demands on general memory and executive processes that just make the tasks harder. Consistent with the latter interpretation, attempts to simplify such tasks have enabled much younger children to pass (e.g., Perner & Howes, 1992; Sullivan, Zaitchik & Tager-Flusberg, 1994), though even these revised tasks remain harder than standard false belief tasks, suggesting that there may still be an additional conceptual component.

Other embellishments of the standard false belief task require the child to co-ordinate an understanding of false belief with other mental states. For example, imagine that instead of a desirable object, the object depicted in Figure 2.1a is actually undesirable, and one that Sally would avoid if

Figure 2.3 A second-order mindreading task requires reasoning about one person's thoughts about another person's thoughts. After placing her object Sally leaves the room, but observes Andrew surreptitiously moving the object to the other container. When Sally returns, participants are asked to predict Andrew's false belief that Sally has a false belief about the object's location.

possible. A variant on the usual cover story contrives that Sally must nonetheless open one of the two boxes. Which will she open if she has a false belief about the object's location and a desire to avoid it? Children find it significantly harder to judge correctly in this case than in the standard case where Sally wishes to find the object (e.g., Cassidy, 1998; Friedman & Leslie, 2004; Leslie & Polizzi, 1998; Leslie, German & Polizzi, 2005). Similarly, in the unexpected content false belief task, researchers have asked children to judge the emotional reactions of someone with a false belief. Many 4-year-olds who correctly predict the naïve observer's false belief that there will be Smarties in the box nonetheless judge that he will be sad when he sees the box (he should be happy if he thinks there are Smarties!), and fail to predict his surprise on finding out that there are really paperclips inside (e.g., Hadwin & Perner, 1991; Harris et al., 1989).

The possibility of being false is one distinctive feature of beliefs, but not the only one. Another is that beliefs, along with other mental states, are held under particular descriptions and not others (Frege, 1892/1960; Quine, 1953). This is how Oedipus was surprised to find out that he was married to his mother. Note that Oedipus did not have a false belief. He had not been misinformed and did not think (falsely) that Jocasta was not his mother: this possibility had never occurred to him. Like all instances of perception, knowledge and belief, Oedipus' knowledge about his wife was held only under particular descriptions (including "Jocasta" and "Queen of Thebes") and not others (in his case, including the description "my mother").

Researchers have adapted Oedipus problems to make them suitable for an audience of young children (e.g., Apperly & Robinson, 1998, 2001, 2003; Hulme, Mitchell & Wood, 2003; Russell, 1987; Sprung, Perner & Mitchell, 2007). In our own work we introduced children to an object with two clear identities, such as a die that was also an eraser. One of these identities was apparent just from looking (die) whereas the other required touching (eraser). Heinz the puppet saw the object, but did not feel it, so knew it was a die but not that it was an eraser. We asked children "Does Heinz know that there is an eraser in the box", and to our surprise, found that 5- and 6-year-olds who passed false belief tasks and a variety of checks on their comprehension of Heinz's experience with the die/eraser nonetheless judged that he did know that there was an eraser in the box. In further experiments we told children that Heinz needed an eraser to correct his drawing, and found that they were as likely to predict that he would retrieve the die/eraser (that he did not know was an eraser) as another eraser that he actually knew was an eraser. In fact in a variety of studies using stories or real objects and using verbal or behavioural judgements, including scenarios where false belief and dual identity problems are very closely matched (Apperly & Robinson, 2003), the consistent pattern is that children who pass false belief tasks do not necessarily pass such Oedipus problems.

Oedipus problems may appear arcane, but actually they are very common in everyday life. For example, every child in the school will know "Mr Jones the teacher", but only some children will know him as "the dad of Jenny Jones in Year 3". A child who knows that Mr Jones is Jenny's dad must take care to talk in terms of "Mr Jones" if they want to be understood by their less well-informed classmates. Thus, it is significant that the data on Oedipus problems suggests that even 4- and 5-year-olds don't necessarily understand a fundamental characteristic of mental states; that they represent under particular descriptions and not others.[3]

In sum, nobody who has ever met a 4-year-old, even one who has just passed a false belief task, would really suppose that they have the mind-reading abilities of adults. Nonetheless it is frequently claimed that 4-year-olds' mindreading abilities are at least qualitatively adult-like, meaning that they have the conceptual wherewithal, even if they lack some important knowledge about the world of grown-ups and some finesse in applying the knowledge that they have. Actually, the situation is much less clear: 4-year-olds struggle to understand beliefs about beliefs or the interaction of beliefs and desires; they struggle to see the emotional consequences of beliefs; and they struggle to represent someone's belief or knowledge under one particular set of descriptions.

Now, having briefly introduced the literature on children's mindreading of epistemic mental states I can begin to address some of the questions raised in the introduction about the cognitive basis of these abilities. New studies will be introduced along the way. Many of these focus exclusively on false belief tasks as a measure of mindreading, though I shall also mention studies that use a wider range of tasks. Where it exists, such evidence suggests that the conclusions from studies using false belief tasks generalize fairly well to other mindreading abilities, and I shall work on the basis that this is generally the case.

Does mindreading depend on a specific set of concepts?

Unless we are behaviourists then the short answer to this question is always going to be "yes". But researchers of cognitive development often mean something stronger than a denial of behaviourism when they ask whether a child has a given concept. In the case of mindreading it is common to ask when children understand perceptions, knowledge and belief *as such*. When can they distinguish them from other kinds of thing and from each other? When do they understand how they come about, and how they interact to cause behaviour? From the literature on mindreading in children it appears that there is no easy answer to these questions. It is just not clear whether we should credit a child with a concept of "knowledge" (for example) when she first shows sensitivity to her mum's "experience" at 14 months (as discussed in chapter 3), when she first makes correct verbal judgements about someone else's lack of knowledge at 3 years, or when she first understands Oedipus problems at 6 years. Or perhaps we should assume, on theoretical grounds, that no such abilities would ever have developed unless the child already had a conceptual token for "seeing", "knowing" and "believing" (e.g., Fodor, 1992; Leslie, 1994b)? Surprisingly often, false belief tasks are viewed as the "one true test" of mindreading but this seems wholly arbitrary in the face of the diverse abilities of children at different ages.

Let me be clear that I am not denying that there are genuine changes in children's ability, and that these have a genuinely conceptual flavour. As they get older children not only become better at focusing on the mental states of others as well as their own, and have better memories for what others think and know, but there also appears to be increasing sophistication in the *kind* of judgements that children make. But the literature from children makes the question of whether mindreading depends on a specific set of concepts seem a lot more complicated than it first sounds.

Does mindreading pose unusual representational problems?

Thinking about the perceptions, knowledge and beliefs of others clearly requires that this information be kept separate from one's own perceptions, knowledge and beliefs. Mindreading would be of little use if one lost one's own mind in the process. However, although it seems necessary to keep some kind of log of other agents' perceptions, knowledge and beliefs that is safely partitioned from one's own,[4] this fails, on its own, to capture an important feature of such mental states. The problem is that these mental states are not just isolated facts about the cognitive system of another agent; they are facts that concern the agent's relation to the world as we take it to be. In concrete terms this means that Sally's belief that "the object is in the square box" is not just something we know about Sally. Our thinking must capture the fact that Sally's belief is about a particular object and a particular square box that also feature in our own representation of the world. It is this that captures the fact that Sally's belief is out of step with our own knowledge that the object is really in the round box, and thereby captures the fact that Sally's belief is false.

To one way of thinking, these problems are unique, and solving them is so important that nature has equipped us with specialized innate cognitive architecture for mindreading (e.g., Leslie, 1987, 1994a). Others note that somewhat similar problems are posed by thinking about different times, places and hypothetical states of affairs (e.g., Fauconnier, 1985; Perner, 1991; Peterson & Riggs, 1999), and also non-mental representations such as signs and symbols (e.g., Perner, 1991). I will return to this debate when I collect together the evidence on the cognitive basis of mindreading in chapter 6. For present purposes, these questions mean that we should ask whether children succeed on mindreading tasks at the same time as they succeed on non-mindreading tasks that might make similar representational demands.

False beliefs, false signs and "false" photographs

If mindreading involves reasoning about an agent's attitude to a mental representation (a proposition) then it seems sensible to compare children's mindreading with their reasoning about non-mental representations such as pictures. As for mindreading, children show early signs of understanding non-mental representations, but particular attention has been devoted to non-mental equivalents of false belief tasks. This small area of investigation has a confusing history, but I need to summarize it briefly because the same issues return in my discussion of the literature on atypical development, neuropsychology and neuroimaging.

Essentially, investigators got off to a false start by picking photographs as the non-mental representation to compare with beliefs (e.g., Leslie & Thaiss, 1992; Leekam & Perner, 1991; Zaitchik, 1990). As can be seen in Figure 2.4, it is possible to create closely matched event sequences for false belief and "false" photograph tasks. The initial situation of the object in the square box is either captured by Sally's belief, or by a Polaroid or digital photograph. The object's location is switched to the round box. Children are either asked to say where Sally thinks the object is located or (with the photograph face-down) where the object is in the photograph.[5] Perner and Leekam (2008) summarize 12 studies from 1990 to 2006 that have used these procedures with typically developing children. Although there is some substantial variability across studies, they show no overall difference in performance on false belief and "false" photograph tasks, which is clearly consistent with the idea that 3- to 5-year-olds have a general difficulty understanding representations, not just mental representations like beliefs.

Less encouraging, however, is that where correlations between the false belief and "false" photograph tasks were reported they tended to be small, and whenever age and verbal ability are partialled out they were entirely

Figure 2.4 Panel (a) shows a "false" photograph task designed to match the unexpected transfer false belief task shown in Figure 2.1a. Sally takes a photograph of the initial situation with her object placed in the round box. Andrew swaps the location of the object, and participants are then asked to judge the location of the object in the photograph. Panel (b) shows a similar false sign task. Sally manipulates a sign to indicate where she put the object. Andrew swaps the object's location and participants are asked to judge where the sign shows the object to be located. Figure adapted from Apperly et al. (2005).

non-significant. Worse still, there is an emerging consensus that false belief and "false" photograph tasks are actually poorly matched on theoretical grounds (e.g., Bowler et al., 2005; Leekam & Perner, 1991; Perner, 1991; Perner & Leekam, 2008; Sabbagh et al., 2006). The problem is that "false" photographs just aren't false. The photograph in Figure 2.4a is a perfectly accurate representation of the earlier situation (depicted in the first panel of the figure); it is not "about" the new situation (in which the object has moved), so it is not false. In contrast, Sally's false belief would be a perfectly accurate representation of the earlier situation if her belief was about that situation, but it is not: it is a belief about the object's current location, and as a result it really is false (see Perner & Leekam, 2008 for a more elaborate explanation). Since the photo isn't false,[6] "false" photograph tasks are less well-matched to the demands of false belief tasks than was originally supposed. As we shall see, this does not drastically change the conclusions drawn from studies of typically developing children, but turns out to be much more important in neuroimaging studies and studies of children with autism.

A better match has been achieved by using a sign instead of a photograph (Bowler et al., 2005; Leekam, Perner, Healey & Sewell, 2008; Parkin, 1994; Sabbagh et al., 2006). In the second panel of Figure 2.4b a sign is introduced, the function of which is to indicate the location of the object.[7] The sign is initially accurate, but falls out of step with reality when the object is moved from the square box to the round box. But like Sally's belief, the sign is still "about" the object's real location, so like Sally's belief, the sign is now false. Children's accuracy at judging where the sign shows the object to be is similar to their accuracy when they judge where Sally thinks the object is. Critically, however, their ability to make these two kinds of judgement is also correlated (Sabbagh et al., 2006) and remains correlated even when children's age is taken into account (Leekam et al., 2008). Most impressively, false belief and false sign performance remains correlated even when their performance on a "false" photo task was taken into account, whereas there is no significant correlation between false belief and "false" photo performance when children's performance on the false sign task is taken into account.

In sum, the evidence supports two conclusions. Firstly, "false" photo tasks may be well-matched to the general event sequence of false belief tasks, but they are not well-matched to the need to reason about false representations. Secondly, children's performance on false belief tasks *is* closely linked to their performance on false sign tasks, which *do* require reasoning about false representations but do not involve mindreading. Altogether, this suggests that the representational demands of mindreading on the false belief task are quite specific (they are not fully shared with "false" photo tasks) but they are not fully specific to mindreading (they are shared with the false sign task).

Counterfactual reasoning

Reasoning about false beliefs and false signs might be part of a relatively narrow category of problems involving misrepresentation. Alternatively, they might be part of a broader category of problems that involve reasoning about non-actual situations that are "about" the current situation. For example, counterfactual reasoning (e.g., "what would I have been doing today had I not been writing this book?") requires me to think about a non-actual situation (today I am hiking in the sunshine) and, critically, to think about it as an alternative to the current situation. Contrast this with hypothetical thinking, which lacks the "aboutness" of counterfactual thinking. "If I don't work on my book, what shall I do tomorrow?" requires me to think about a non-actual situation (tomorrow I am hiking[8]), but not as an alternative to the current situation. It is for this reason that researchers have sought to compare children's performance on false belief tasks on the one hand, with their ability to reason about counterfactuals and future hypotheticals on the other (e.g. Riggs et al., 1998; Riggs & Peterson, 2000). This can be achieved neatly within a standard false belief task. To prompt counterfactual reasoning in Figure 2.1a you could ask "Where would the object have been if Andrew had not moved it?". To prompt future hypothetical reasoning you could ask "Where will the object be if Andrew moves it back again?". Using child-friendly versions of these tasks, Riggs et al. (1998; see also Perner et al., 2006; Robinson & Beck, 2000) found that 3- to 4-year-old children performed with similar accuracy on false belief and counterfactual questions, and performance was significantly correlated, even when verbal ability was taken into account.[9] In contrast, very few children made errors on future hypothetical questions, which were significantly easier than matched counterfactual questions. These findings suggest that the representational demands of mindreading on the false belief task are quite specific (they are not fully shared with future hypothetical reasoning) but they are not fully specific to either mindreading or to reasoning about false representations (because they are shared with counterfactual reasoning).

Mindreading processes: Roles for executive function

"Executive function" refers to a set of cognitive processes involved in flexible goal-directed behaviour. They are thought to be involved in working memory, response inhibition, resistance to interference, set-shifting, and planning, and are particularly important in situations that are novel, ambiguous or "ill-structured" (e.g., Burgess et al., 2005; Goel & Grafman, 2000; Hughes, 2002; Shallice & Burgess, 1996). They are strongly associated with frontal brain regions. An anecdotal example may help illustrate what it means for a child to have difficulty with executive function. Bubble painting is a popular activity in British nursery schools. What you do is fill a bowl with a mixture of paint and liquid soap and blow into it with a straw. Placing a sheet of paper onto the resulting mass of brightly coloured bubbles transfers an attractive pattern onto the paper, which mum and dad can stick on the refrigerator. The trouble is that 3-year-olds have already had a great deal of practice at sucking through straws. Bubble painting requires this well-worn action of sucking to be over-ridden in favour of a less familiar action of blowing. Whenever I have observed bubble painting, there always seems to be at least one child who cannot adjust their behaviour in this flexible manner, and so ends up with a mouthful of soapy paint. After they have spat it out, the fact that they can nonetheless tell you what they were supposed to be doing makes this look like a problem with executive control, rather than understanding the task of bubble painting.

Researchers have devised more formal tests designed to capture such everyday difficulties with executive function. Although it is widely recognized that any given task is likely to make multiple executive demands (e.g., Rabbitt, 1997), it is also the case that different tasks tax different functions to varying degrees. Most closely similar to problems with bubble painting are tasks designed to test children's ability to inhibit a familiar, recently performed or desirable action. For example, in the "gift delay" task (Carlson & Moses, 2001; Kochanska et al., 1996) children are told that they will be given an exciting present but that they should look away while it is wrapped. With the child facing away, the experimenter proceeds to wrap the present as noisily and ostentatiously as possible, and later codes from a video how well the child resisted the urge to peek at the present. On the "bear-dragon" task (Carlson & Moses, 2001; Kochanska et al., 1996) the experimenter animates two puppets to play a game of "Simon-says" with the child, who is told that she must follow instructions from the bear (to "touch your toes", "fold your arms" etc.) but ignore similar instructions from the dragon.

Other tests assess children's working memory by asking them to repeat back a short sequence of words or numbers, starting with the last one they were told (e.g., Davis & Pratt, 1996). Still others require children to "task-switch" from sorting pictures on one dimension (e.g., colour) to switching them on another (e.g., shape) (e.g., Zelazo, Frye & Rapus, 1996), to forward-plan a sequence of moves in a simple game (e.g., Hughes, 1998) or to infer a counter-intuitive strategy of pointing away from desirable objects in a game where pointing directly at the objects means that you lose them[10] (e.g., Russell et al., 1991). Performance on all of these tasks shows substantial variability across different children, and significant improvement between the ages of 3 and 5 years, just as children's performance on mindreading tasks seems to be improving.

A moment's reflection on false belief tasks (and other mindreading tasks) suggests that there are many ways in which executive function might be relevant, including keeping track of the event sequence, inferring and holding in mind Sally's false belief as well as one's own knowledge of the object's location, resisting interference between these records, and formulating a response on the basis of Sally's belief rather than one's own knowledge. And indeed, many studies have found correlations between children's mindreading (most often assessed by testing them on multiple false belief tasks) and their performance on a variety of tests of executive function (e.g., Carlson & Moses, 2001; Hughes, 1998). The problem, knowing the complexity of both false belief and executive function tasks, is to discern why these correlations exist. Some help comes from studies that test which executive tasks are more important in correlations with false belief tasks. These indicate that "conflict inhibition" tasks, such as the bear-dragon task described above, correlate with false belief tasks even when performance on tests of children's planning, working memory and ability to delay a response are taken into account, whereas the reverse is not true (e.g., Carlson & Moses, 2001; Carlson, Moses & Breton 2002; Carlson, Moses & Claxton, 2004; Perner & Lang, 2000). But this does not tell us which aspects of false belief tasks are demanding of "conflict inhibition".

There are currently several interpretations of the link between mindreading and executive function in the literature. One suggestion is that executive function is required to handle the entirely incidental demands that mindreading tasks make on attending to and remembering a sequence of events, and interpreting questions (e.g., Bloom & German, 2000). Evidence consistent with this view comes from Carlson and Moses (2001) who found that children's performance on control questions that checked their ability to keep track of the event sequence in false belief tasks was strongly predicted by their performance on a battery of executive function tasks. But the same study found evidence that this was unlikely to be the full story, since children who passed such control trials still went on to show variable performance on the critical questions about false belief, and this variability was still correlated with children's performance on the battery of executive tasks.

"Expression" accounts point out that reasoning about beliefs (whatever the developmental origin of this ability) might make quite specific performance demands. Reasoning about false beliefs may require children to overcome a default assumption that beliefs are true (e.g., Leslie et al., 2004) or to resist any tendency to respond on the basis of their own knowledge rather than what the other person believes (i.e., to avoid a "reality bias" or "curse of knowledge": e.g., Birch & Bloom, 2007; Carlson & Moses, 2001; Mitchell, 1996; Russell, 1996). This proposal has prima facie plausibility, and in later chapters I shall discuss data from adults that are consistent with there being a tendency for interference between information about self and other perspectives. However, it is less clear that this is the limiting step for children's success on false belief tasks.

This is most dramatically illustrated by the results from Call and Tomasello (1999). These authors devised a novel, non-verbal false belief task, which had the side effect of dramatically reducing the possibility of interference from the child's own perspective. The task is shown schematically in Figure 2.5. In a warm-up phase children learn that there is a prize in one of two boxes, and that Sally will help them find it by placing a marker as a clue. On the critical false belief test trial Sally sees in the boxes (so finds out the location of the prize), and while she is away from the scene, Andrew swaps the boxes' locations, so Sally has a false belief about the location of the prize. Sally returns and gives her informative clue. If the child takes Sally's false belief into account then they can locate the prize. The critical issue is that at the point at which children must take account of Sally's belief, they do not themselves know the location of the prize. So they cannot be biased by this information (or at least this possibility is much reduced). Later I shall describe how this manipulation makes a huge difference to the success of a patient with impaired executive function (Samson et al., 2005). However, it made no difference to children, who performed no better on this task than on more standard false belief tasks.

Three further accounts have been suggested. "Emergence" accounts suggest that executive function is necessary for the developmental process of learning abstract concepts such as belief, perhaps by enabling children to

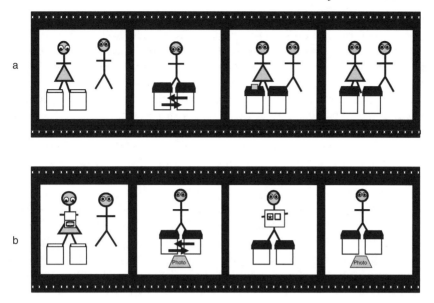

Figure 2.5 Panel (a) shows the non-verbal "low-inhibition" false belief task originally devised by Call and Tomasello (1999). The participant's task is to identify which of the two boxes contains a hidden object. Sally sees where the object is located and leaves the scene. Sally doesn't see Andrew swap the boxes. She returns, and puts a marker on one of the boxes as a clue to the object's location. This clue is helpful, provided participants take account of her false belief. Because participants do not themselves know the location of the hidden object, they do not need to resist interference from this information when inferring that Sally has a false belief. Panel (b) shows a matched false photograph version of this task, described in chapter 4. Again, the participant's task is to locate the hidden object. But this time the photograph serves as a clue. The clue is helpful provided participants take account of the fact that, like Sally's false belief, it misrepresents the object's location. Figure adapted from Apperly et al. (2005).

disengage from the immediate objects of their attention (e.g., Carlson & Moses, 2001; Russell, 1996). "Competence" accounts argue that reasoning about false beliefs requires the capacity (in working memory or other aspects of executive function) to construct mental representations with a certain level of complexity (e.g., Andrews et al., 2003; Frye, Zelazo & Palfai, 1995; Russell, 1996). Until children have sufficient capacity they would be unable to reason about such complex things as beliefs or other mental states. Finally, turning the whole debate on its head, Perner and Lang (1999) argue that since executive function involves top-down control over one's own mental states, perhaps developments in mindreading – turned towards oneself – could be responsible for developments in executive function. This intriguing suggestion clearly deserves further investigation, particularly for the more complex forms of top-down executive control. However, taken at face value, it seems difficult for this theory to explain performance on executive tasks in young children, who would fail most mindreading tasks. It also struggles to explain evidence that earlier executive function predicts later mindreading, whereas the reverse pattern does not hold (e.g., Carlson, Mandell & Williams, 2004; Hughes, 1998; Hughes & Ensor, 2007), or evidence that Chinese children may be significantly more advanced than their American peers in executive function, but not their mindreading (Sabbagh et al., 2006).

In sum, the important conclusion for now is that children's mindreading in general, and reasoning about false beliefs in particular, seems strongly associated with processes for executive function. Such processes are involved in deliberate, effortful control of behaviour and thought. They are domain-general in that they are involved in many activities besides mindreading. And they are in short supply in that engagement in one activity that requires executive function (such as formulating a quick interjection in a meeting) competes for resources with others (such as mindreading to check who may be upset by your off-the-cuff remark). However, the data from children leave the details of the relationship between mindreading and executive function uncertain. Therefore I shall discuss executive expression, emergence and competence accounts again in later chapters as we gain converging evidence from other sources.

The role of language and social experience in mindreading

There is strong evidence that children's success on tasks such as the false belief task is related to their performance on various tests of language (Milligan, Astington & Dack, 2007). What is much less clear is whether some aspects of language are more important than others. Besides direct evidence on the role of language, this research has also generated tasks that are interesting for what they tell us about mindreading more generally, and these have been adapted for studies discussed in later chapters.

Syntax

By far the strongest claims about a specific aspect of language having a role in the development of mindreading have been made for syntax. De Villiers and de Villiers (2000; de Villiers & Pyers, 2002) have long drawn attention to the fact that verbal statements about mental states such as "think" and "know" use a relatively specific syntactic construction: embedded complement clauses. In the sentence "John thought that Aldrin was the first man on the moon", "John thought that. . ." is the main clause, under which is embedded the complement clause "Aldrin was the first man on the moon". This construction allows the truth of the embedded complement clause, which describes John's belief, to vary independently of the truth of the whole sentence. So this whole sentence can be true, despite the fact that the embedded clause is false (it was not Aldrin but Armstrong who was first on the moon). The de Villiers argue that learning this syntactic construction could provide the representational basis for children to think about beliefs, and other such mental states.

Children's understanding of this construction has been tested by reading them short vignettes that involve describing a character's false belief using the embedded complement construction (e.g., de Villiers & Pyers, 2002). Adapting our Sally-Andrew example in this way, we would get a story that told the child "Sally thinks that the object is in the square box, but really it is in the round box". The test question then asks "What does Sally think?". Unlike a standard false belief task, this does not require the child to make any inference about what Sally thinks. All they need to do is attend to the story, briefly hold in mind what they have been told about Sally's false belief, and repeat it back in response to the test question. Nonetheless, this is surprisingly difficult for 3- to 4-year-olds, and not dramatically easier than false belief tasks that do require a belief inference (de Villiers & Pyers, 2002; Flavell, Flavell, Green & Moses, 1990; Wellman & Bartsch, 1988).

Of course, a potential problem is that although children's difficulty might be with embedded complement constructions, it might equally well be with holding in mind information about Sally's false belief (I shall return to such tasks again later). This danger of a circular argument was partially overcome[11] by de Villiers and Pyers (2002) by including other test items that required children to remember something false that Sally *said*. These showed similar results to the false belief items. De Villiers and Pyers (2002) tested the same children on multiple occasions, and found that children's performance on the embedded complements test at an earlier point in time predicted their performance on various false belief tests at a later point in time, whereas early false belief performance did not always predict later performance on the embedded complements task. This suggests that children's understanding of embedded complement syntax may have a causal role in enabling the development of an understanding of belief (though see Perner et al., 2003).

Other evidence supports a role for syntax in the development of mind-reading, but suggests that the relationship may not be specific to embedded complement clauses. Like embedded complement clause sentences, relative clause sentences (e.g., The woman pushed the man who opened the box) require comprehension of an embedded clause that modifies the meaning of the main clause. There is evidence that children's comprehension of such sentences is correlated with their performance on false belief tasks, even when taking account of their comprehension of similar sentences that do not have the same clausal embedding relationship (Smith, Apperly & White, 2003). However, there is also evidence that children's performance on false belief tasks is related to their performance on tests of syntax in general, rather than any particular constructions (e.g., Milligan, Astington & Dack, 2007).

Semantics

Imagine that you don't know which box contains an object that you want. Sally says she thinks it's in the round box. Andrew says he knows it's in the square box. Which do you choose? Picking the right box depends less on comprehending the syntax of Sally and Andrew's statements than on evaluating the semantics of the verbs "think" and "know" in order to compare the relative certainty of Sally and Andrew. Moore, Pure and Furrow (1990) used a version of this task with young children, and found significant improvements between 3 and 4 years of age that correlated with children's performance on a variety of false belief tasks. This highlights the possibility of a relationship between children's mindreading inferences and their semantics for mental verbs. However, this study provides no evidence on causality, or on whether the effect is specific to semantics of mental verbs or semantics more generally. Other studies indicate that children's mindreading is also related to more general measures of semantics (e.g., Milligan, Astington & Dack, 2007; Ruffman, Slade, Rowlandson, Rumsey & Garnham, 2003).

Pragmatics, conversation and social experience

Verbal meaning is more than the sum of syntax and semantics. Even apparently simple sentences, such as "Can I buy you a drink?", can have very different meanings, depending on whether they are uttered between friends in a pub or between strangers in a singles bar. Deriving the meaning behind the message seems to require sensitivity to context – especially social context – and in particular to what the speaker might think or intend (e.g., Grice, 1957). Accounts of pragmatics in adults commonly presuppose the ability to mindread (e.g., Sperber & Wilson, 1995), and this topic will be returned to later. In the developmental literature, the tendency has been to view conversational experience as a particularly rich instance of a general principle; that social interaction is a critical training ground for the development of mindreading.

Much evidence indicates a link between children's conversational experience and their mindreading abilities. Harris (2005) argues that a critical role for conversation is in highlighting perspective differences between the child and their interlocutor, a prediction borne out in a training study by Lohmann and Tomasello (2003). Evidence of the influence of something broader than the mere presence of conversation comes from findings suggesting that parents' propensity to think about their children as having independent mental states is associated with better mindreading in their children (e.g., Meins et al., 2002; Ruffman, Perner & Parkin, 1999). And children's performance on mindreading tests is significantly related to their number of siblings (especially older siblings; Perner, Ruffman & Leekam, 1994; Ruffman et al., 1998), and to the number of older children and adults with whom they regularly interact (Lewis et al., 1996). Summarizing a large number of studies, Dunn and Brophy (2005) suggest that the amount of conversational experience, the degree to which that experience includes talk about mental states, the degree to which such talk is relevant in context, and the quality of the relationship between the child and their interlocutor, all appear to have effects on children's current or subsequent mindreading abilities.

The precise means by which such experiences bear on the cognitive basis of mindreading is not usually spelled out in such research. Most commonly it is seen as enabling the acquisition of mindreading concepts (such as "thinks" and "knows"), either by providing a rich evidence base for inducing these abstract notions, or by introducing these concepts on an interpersonal level that is later internalized by the child (for a discussion see Astington & Baird, 2005). However, others see an emphasis on abstract concepts as a mis-statement of the problem of mindreading, resulting in part from the literature's neurotic fixation on a small number of tasks that are supposed to diagnose the presence of such concepts. Nelson (2005), for example, argues that children's task is to become members of "a community of minds". This involves becoming enculturated into a communal system of values and beliefs; a process on which language gives critical leverage (see, e.g., Fernyhough, 2008 for a related view). These ideas are interesting, though not specified in detail, and Nelson does not put her ideas to work in terms of on-line cognitive processes. Nonetheless, in chapter 6, I shall suggest that ideas of this kind may be part of a solution to the "problem of relevance" that is at the heart of everyday mindreading.

Language as an impediment to mindreading performance

Finally, although the emphasis throughout this section has been on how language and social experience might make a positive contribution to the development of mindreading, it is also important to note the possibility that the requirement to comprehend language might contribute to the difficulty of mindreading tasks (e.g., Bloom & German, 2000). This point will become important shortly, when I discuss research on mindreading in infants. But for the tasks used with young children I think the balance of evidence is against this proposition for commonly used tasks. Attempts to reduce the burden on verbal comprehension made by false belief tasks, and especially 2nd order false belief tasks, have had some success in reducing the age at which children pass (Perner & Howes, 1992; Sullivan, Zaitchik & Tager-Flusberg, 1994). But it is striking that Call and Tomasello's (1999) fully non-verbal false belief task (described above) was no easier for children than a standard false belief task. And anecdotally, my own experience with attempting to present non-verbal video-based false belief tasks to confused and incredibly bored 3-year-olds was a good reminder that language is often what makes tasks comprehensible to children, as well as tolerably fun.

In sum, this section has broadened the discussion of mindreading in two ways. Firstly, two new types of task add a little breadth to the narrow question of what it is that children find difficult about false beliefs. Between 3 and 5 years children not only get better on "standard" false belief tasks that require them to infer an agent's belief, they also improve on non-inferential tasks that just require them to remember the agent's false belief, and on tests of their understanding of the certainty implied by mental state terms like "know" and "think". Secondly, language and social experience appear to be causally involved in the development of children's mindreading. However, to some researchers this relationship appears so inter-twined that it is a mistake to discuss mindreading as if it were a faculty that stood independently from children's increasing social and linguistic experience.

Mindreading and atypical development

Since the very earliest research on mindreading in typically developing children, researchers have also investigated whether impairments in mindreading might be apparent in clinical populations. This work has resulted in significant advances in our understanding of autism, deafness, schizophrenia, and a range of genetic syndromes (e.g., Baron-Cohen, Tager-Flusberg & Cohen, 2000). These findings, and their clinical implications, are reviewed very thoroughly elsewhere. For current purposes I shall focus exclusively on the subset of this research that has direct implications for the questions I wish to ask about the cognitive basis of mindreading.

Autism

Autism is a developmental disorder diagnosed on the basis of impaired social abilities, impaired communication, and non-social behaviour that is inflexible and repetitive (e.g., Baron-Cohen, 1995; Frith, 2003; Happe, 1994a). These behavioural features bear a striking resemblance to the discussion above on the inter-relation between mindreading, language and executive function, suggesting that autism might provide clear evidence on the causal interdependence of these abilities. However, although research on the cognitive basis of autism has yielded some clear headline findings, the detailed picture has usually turned out to be much less straightforward, and actually provides a rather limited amount of clear evidence about the cognitive basis of mindreading (e.g., Happe & Ronald, 2008). The substantial influence that the headline findings continue to have on theory (e.g., Carruthers, 2006; Goldman, 2006; Stich & Nichols, 2003) should, perhaps, be tempered on the basis of these important details.

Perhaps the most prominent headline has come from the finding that, as a group, children with autism perform significantly less well on false belief tasks than children without autism but with similar levels of intellectual disability (Baron-Cohen, Leslie & Frith, 1985). This finding has been widely replicated, and extends to a variety of mindreading tasks besides false belief tasks (Baron-Cohen, 2000). This research clearly indicates that it is possible to have impaired mindreading but still perform relatively well on tests of general intelligence, and has led to claims that an impairment of mind-reading might be a cause of autism.

A second headline is that people with autism often show disproportion-ately impaired language and communication. Consistent with findings from typically developing children, language abilities and mindreading abilities are correlated in children with autism (e.g., Happe, 1995; Tager-Flusberg & Josef, 2005). However, an important complication is the observation that children with autism may require a verbal mental age of 9 years before they pass false belief tasks. This has led to the suggestion that when good language abilities are present, children with autism may solve mindreading tasks, but via an atypical linguistic reasoning strategy (e.g., Happe, 1995). It is unclear, then, whether this evidence supports a general claim that language is necessary for mindreading.

Another headline finding is that children with autism show impairments in executive function (e.g., Happe & Ronald, 2008; Hill, 2004; Hughes & Russell, 1993; Ozonoff, Pennington & Rogers, 1991). This clearly fits with the clinical observation of inflexible and repetitive behaviour. And given the association between executive function and mindreading in typical devel-opment this has also been considered a potential explanation for mind-reading difficulties in autism (e.g., Hughes & Russell, 1993; Russell, 1997). However, as Happe and Ronald (2008) point out, current evidence is decidedly mixed, with evidence of positive correlations between executive function and mindreading performance (e.g., Pellicano, 2007) offset by evidence of executive function impairment in the absence of mindreading impairment (Ozonoff et al., 1991) and vice versa (Pellicano, 2007). A potential explanation for this mixed pattern is that executive function and mindreading have each been measured by a variety of tasks across studies. As described above, both executive function and mindreading are multi-faceted phenomena, and it is far from clear that any "standard" test of executive function will tap the executive processes that are critical for a given mindreading problem. An alternative approach is to compare the performance on a given mindreading task with a matched reasoning task that should make similar demands on executive processes but does not involve mindreading.

Early studies taking this approach found that children with autism who perform poorly on false belief tasks may perform much better on "false" photograph tasks (Leekam & Perner, 1991; Leslie & Thaiss, 1992). Since it was originally supposed that "false" photograph tasks matched false belief tasks in every respect apart from whether or not the tasks had social content, these findings seemed to be very strong evidence that mindreading could be impaired independently of tasks that required structurally identical reasoning. Such evidence was some of the primary impetus for claims that mindreading depends on a specialized domain-specific cognitive module, and not on domain-general executive processes (e.g., Leslie & Thaiss, 1992). However, recall from earlier that "false" photograph tasks are now considered to be less well-matched to the demands of false belief reasoning than originally supposed, because "false" photographs are not false. Other studies using better-matched tasks have since found that children with autism perform at similar rates on false belief tasks, false sign tasks (Bowler et al., 2005) and tests of counterfactual reasoning (Grant, Riggs & Boucher, 2004). These findings accord well with the evidence from studies of typical development suggesting links between these tasks, and with the possibility that these links exist because the tasks make similar demands on executive function.

Altogether then, although it is striking that mindreading can be impaired out of proportion to general intelligence, research on autism does not give good reasons for supposing that mindreading can be impaired out of proportion to all other cognitive processes, such as language or executive function. That is to say, research on autism does not provide support for the hypothesis that mindreading has a strongly domain-specific cognitive or neural substrate, nor does it provide clear evidence on the causal dependence of mindreading on language and executive function. And, the fact that a significant sub-set of people with autism – who have clinical levels of social impairment – nonetheless pass many standard mindreading tasks (e.g., Happe, 1995) should make us cautious about claims that autism is due to a lack of mindreading concepts, or that the presence or absence of these concepts can be straightforwardly diagnosed with laboratory tasks.

Deafness

In contrast to the case of autism, studies of deaf children provide clear evidence to support the view that language is important for the development of mindreading. A critical baseline is provided by the fact that deaf children whose parents are fluent signers (usually because the parents are themselves deaf) show a typical developmental trajectory for language acquisition, and pass mindreading tasks at similar ages to their hearing peers (e.g., Woolfe, Want & Siegal, 2002). Thus, deafness per se does not lead to impairments in mindreading. However, deaf children whose parents are not fluent signers tend to have delayed language acquisition, and, it turns out, also show delay on mindreading tasks (Peterson & Siegal, 2000). As with studies of typical development, it is debated whether this effect is driven by a general delay in language, a more specific delay in the acquisition of specific aspects of syntax, or a reduction in experience with conversational pragmatics (see Astington & Baird, 2005 for relevant discussions). But on any account such findings strengthen the evidence that language acquisition plays a causal role in the development of mindreading.

Summary

Studies of children have been the mainstay of research on mindreading over the past 30 years. Although controversies remain, the basic findings are highly reliable. They suggest that children become able to make progressively more sophisticated mindreading judgements between the ages of 2 and 7 years; these advances are related to developments in language and executive function during the same time period; and disruption to language or executive function may lead to disruption in mindreading.

However, the emphasis on studies of young children runs the risk of missing the bigger picture for at least two reasons. Firstly, theories about mindreading are almost always couched in terms of "acquisition" or "development" in children's early years. This leaves a significant gap in the developmental story from around 7 years to adulthood, which I shall address in later chapters with data from older children and adults. Moreover, this gap means that theories of development in early childhood are not informed by an account of the system that children will ultimately develop. Thus, in chapter 7, I shall discuss the implications of findings from older children and adults for accounts of the development of mindreading in young children.

Secondly, evidence that children's mindreading is strongly related to their developing language and executive function is cast in a rather different light by recent evidence of mindreading in human infants and non-human animals, and it is to this that I turn in the next chapter.

Notes

1 There are many variations on these paradigms with different characters and different scenarios. To highlight the similarities and differences across different types of task I shall frame scenarios in terms of Sally and Andrew as far as possible throughout the book.

2 Tradition dictates that it should be pencils, but we use paperclips because they sound more like Smarties when they rattle around in the tube.

3 Some authors have argued that children have difficulty with Oedipus problems because they struggle with 2nd order mindreading, described in the foregoing paragraphs (e.g., Carpendale & Lewis, 2006; Sprung, Perner & Mitchell, 2007). The idea here is that understanding that "die" and "eraser" are alternative true descriptions for an object already involves reasoning about representations, and reasoning about Heinz's knowledge of one or other of these descriptions therefore involves the 2nd order problem of reasoning about representations of representations. However, this argument runs into two problems. Firstly, children's difficulties are not restricted to judgements about what other people know or do, but extend to judgements about the extension of labels used to name objects with salient alternative identities (Apperly & Robinson, 2002). It is not clear why the latter problems should involve representations of representations. Secondly, on a normative account, understanding representations (such as beliefs and knowledge, and also words, pictures, etc.) entails understanding that they represent under particular descriptions and not others, and so entails understanding Oedipus problems. From this point of view, the arguments of

Carpendale and Lewis (2006) and Sprung, Perner and Mitchell (2007) amount to saying that understanding representations entails understanding representations about representations, which clearly makes no sense. So it seems that either their 2nd order account of Oedipus problems is wrong, or these authors must reject the normative account of what it means to understand representations.

4 Later I shall discuss whether such log-keeping alone might be sufficient to explain mindreading in infants and non-human animals, and some of the abilities of human adults.

5 As with my earlier examples, this description is schematic, and was, of course, embellished in child-friendly terms in the actual studies.

6 Of course, photos can be false. Photo editing software is better than vitamin pills for making anyone look younger. It's just that the procedure used in the studies described here does not create a false photograph.

7 Like photos, signs can also serve the function of indicating non-actual states of affairs. Some thermometers have a bead that indicates the highest point reached by the mercury. We can read this in the cool of the evening as an accurate sign of the midday heat. For this reason, false sign tasks are carefully framed so that the function of the sign is to indicate current reality.

8 And it will probably rain.

9 Like mindreading, counterfactual reasoning admits of degrees. There is evidence that children younger than 3 to 4 years sometimes reason correctly (e.g., Harris, German & Mills, 1996) and evidence that children older than 3 to 4 years struggle on a task that requires them to acknowledge that there is more than one counterfactual possibility (Beck et al., 2006). None of this affects the conclusion I wish to draw for false belief reasoning, which is that there is a close relationship between children's performance on false belief tasks and their performance on tasks that make similar reasoning demands but do not require mindreading.

10 The "windows task" (see also the "less-is-more task" by Carlson et al., 2005) requires children to choose one of two boxes to be taken away in order to keep the other for themselves. The optimal strategy is to give away the less valuable box (the one containing nothing, or the smaller quantity of reward). Three-year-olds find this extremely difficult, and often choose the more valuable box (and thereby lose it) for many trials in a row. This was originally played against an opponent, and was thought to be a test of strategic deception that makes significant demands on inhibitory control (Russell et al., 1991). However, further work has found evidence that the task requires neither deception nor inhibition (e.g., Carroll, Apperly & Riggs, 2007; Russell et al., 1994; Simpson, Riggs & Simon, 2004) but does require the mental flexibility to infer a counterintuitive strategy.

11 I think the circularity is only partially overcome because what someone "says" is intimately related to what someone "thinks". So it remains possible that 3- to 4-year-olds' primary difficulty is with mindreading, and this affects their memory for embedded complements about what someone thinks and what someone says.

3 Evidence from infants and non-human animals

The focus of the last chapter was on children's explicit mindreading judgements, which has provided the main evidence base for thinking about the cognitive basis of mindreading. However, standard interpretations of this evidence have been called into question by a growing body of research on infants and non-human animals. It may seem unconventional to group infants and non-human animals together in a single chapter, but for current purposes I think there are good reasons for doing so. For one, both infants and non-human animals are distinctly lacking in language and executive function. If we observe mindreading abilities in these groups then we can assume that they are not heavily dependent on these resources, and this, in turn, might help us refine our interpretation of the apparent inter-dependence of mindreading, language and executive function in children. Another reason for considering human infants and non-human animals together is that evidence of mindreading in these groups comes from indirect behavioural measures, rather than the explicit judgements that are typical in studies of children. Largely as a result of this, evidence from infants and non-human animals raises similar interpretive questions about what should count as evidence of mindreading. And finally, in other cognitive domains, such as number and spatial cognition, comparisons between infants and non-human animals have been extremely informative about the nature and origins of their cognitive abilities. I think the literature on mindreading is only just beginning to exploit the informative value of such comparisons.

Human infants

Indirect measures

Where someone looks can be a reasonably transparent indicator of what they are thinking about. Behind this appealing gloss is a lot of hidden complexity about how eye movements are synchronized with on-going cognitive processes, what those processes are, and what we can say about those processes from a record of eye movements (e.g., Liversedge &

Findlay, 2000). But for the time being this matters little for the relatively simple studies that have used eye movements, as well as other indirect measures, to investigate mindreading in children and infants.

Initial evidence was not too threatening to the picture emerging from studies of young children. Garnham, Perner and colleagues tested 2- and 3-year-old children on an unexpected transfer false belief task (see Figure 2.1), but in addition to scoring children's judgements about where Sally would look for the hidden object, they also recorded children's gaze direction when the experimenter asked "I wonder where she's going to look?" (Clements & Perner, 1994; Garnham & Perner, 2001; Garnham & Ruffman, 2001). As expected, few of these children judged correctly where Sally would look. However, among the 3-year-olds who judged incorrectly, many showed looking behaviour consistent with a correct answer. These children looked longer at a door from which Sally would exit to approach the box where she mistakenly believed the object was hidden, rather than a second door that led to the box where the object was now hidden. This suggested that they took account of her false belief when they anticipated her behaviour. This was interpreted as early "implicit" awareness of false beliefs, a conclusion supported by evidence that this awareness did little to shake children's confidence in their incorrect explicit judgement (Ruffman, Garnham, Import, & Connolly, 2001). However, the absence of any such effects in 2½-year-olds allowed this evidence of implicit awareness to be viewed as an early stage in the well-established developmental transition in 3- to 4-year-olds' reasoning about false beliefs.

Of course, if implicit awareness is demonstrated in much younger children, it becomes less attractive to view it as an early sign of 3- to 4-year-olds' growing understanding of belief. Using a modified, non-verbal version of Garnham's procedure, Southgate and colleagues (Southgate, Senju, & Csibra, 2007) found that 2-year-olds' looking patterns anticipated that Sally would search incorrectly for the hidden object. Quite sensibly, these researchers did not even test children's explicit judgements, since no study has ever found that 2-year-olds pass standard false belief tasks (Wellman, Cross & Watson, 2001). This study substantially expands the gap between the age at which children show an understanding of false beliefs on measures that require explicit judgements, compared with an indirect measure of behaviour.

Other studies suggest that these effects may not only be observed in eye movements. O'Neill (1996) had 2½-year-olds play with an exciting toy, then placed it on a high shelf, out of reach of the child. During this time the child's mother was either paying attention to the child and the toy, or was not paying attention (she was either out of the room or had her eyes and ears covered). The experimenter then left the room, leaving the child with their mother. Children frequently made requests to their mother to retrieve the toy, but on trials where their mother had not witnessed the toy or its placement on the shelf, children were significantly more likely to point at the toy, name the toy or name its location. That is to say, their request strategy varied according to the mother's knowledge state. Moreover, there is evidence of similar sensitivity to knowledge at 12 to 14 months if the "knowledgeable" mother actively plays with the child and the novel toy, rather than merely being an onlooker (Moll and Tomasello, 2007; Tomasello and Haberl, 2003). And there is evidence that 18-month-olds take account of someone's false belief when acting to help them (Buttelmann, Carpenter & Tomasello, 2009). In all of these cases, infants and young children's behaviour seems to show competence that would not be apparent if they were required to make explicit judgements.

It is also possible to gain insight into infants' cognitive processes by measuring the time they spend looking at different stimuli. In violation-of-expectation paradigms this involves acting out an event sequence where the outcome is either consistent with some underlying principle (solid objects support one another; people search for things on the basis of where they think they are) or violates that principle. If infants discriminate between consistent and inconsistent event sequences (usually by looking longer at sequences that violate the principle) this is evidence that the principle is guiding their expectations about events. In other topic areas violation of expectation paradigms have proved particularly sensitive for revealing abilities in very young infants.

Onishi and Baillargeon (2005) used event sequences closely based on the unexpected transfer false belief task. Fifteen-month-old infants first viewed event sequences that familiarized them with Sally placing an object in one of the two boxes (let's say, the round box), and then reaching to retrieve it. Then, in the false belief test trial (Figure 3.1), Sally places her object in the round box and leaves the scene. In her absence the object moves to the square box. Sally returns and either searches in the round box (consistent with her false belief) or the square box (inconsistent with her false belief). Infants looked significantly longer when Sally's search was inconsistent with her false belief. The opposite pattern of looking was found in a true belief condition where Sally observed the object's movement. In this case, infants looked longer when Sally searched in the wrong box. Together with control conditions, these findings suggest that infants' expectations about Sally's behaviour are sensitive to whether Sally's belief about the object's location is true or false.

These results sparked a great deal of interest and controversy and several alternative interpretations, which are discussed below. But before considering what they may mean, it is important to note that this is certainly not an isolated finding. Using a related method, Surian, Caldi & Sperber (2007) obtained similar results with 13-month-olds. Song, Onishi, Baillargeon and Fisher (2008) found that infants expected Sally's false belief could be corrected if Andrew told her where the object was when she returned to the scene.[1] Song and Baillargeon (2008) found that infants formed similar expectations about Sally's behaviour when she saw a misleading situation

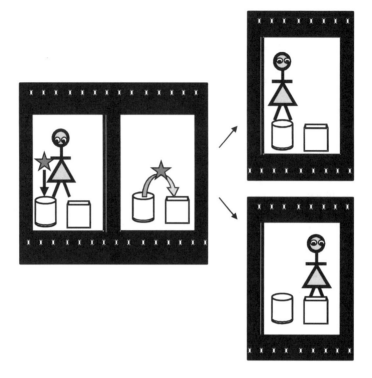

Figure 3.1 Onishi and Baillargeon (2005) devised a violation-of-expectation paradigm to test infants' sensitivity to an agent's beliefs. Sally puts her object in the round box. In her absence the object moves to the square box. If, on her return, she searches in the box that is compatible with her belief about the object's location (top right panel) infants look for less time than if she searches in the box that is incompatible with her belief (bottom right panel).

(analogous to the unexpected contents false belief task) in which the appearance of a box indicated that it contained a doll when in fact it contained a skunk. Violation-of-expectation methods have also found that infants between 12 and 14 months take account of what an agent can or cannot see when interpreting their action (Luo & Baillargeon, 2007; Sodian, Thoermer & Metz, 2007).

Judging from the current proliferation of studies, the abilities of infants uncovered so far may well turn out to be the tip of the iceberg. Although these findings are dramatically out of step with many of those from studies of mindreading in children, it is worth noting that they are consistent with longstanding evidence from naturalistic observation that infants and very young children engage in rich social behaviour with their caregivers that clearly implies sensitivity to the caregiver's mental states (e.g., Dunn, Brown, Slomkowski, Tesla & Youngblade, 1991; Reddy, 1991, 2003). And in the case of simple visual perspective taking, they are not far out of line with results suggesting that infants are sensitive to their mother's knowledge state when communicating with her (e.g., Moll & Tomasello, 2007; Tomasello & Haberl, 2003). In all, there is little doubt that infants show sensitivity to mental states of others in at least some circumstances. The question in all of these studies is *how* infants achieve this sensitivity.

Explanations of infants' abilities

Part of the reason why Onishi and Baillargeon's (2005) findings are so compelling is that their task so closely resembles the false belief task that has been the dominant paradigm in so much work with 3- to 4-year-old children. However, opinion on how to interpret these data is divided. Let me summarize, first of all, conclusions that I think most researchers should agree upon. Infants aged 12 to 15 months have almost no productive language, severely limited receptive language, and capacities for executive function that are different both in quantity and in kind from those available to 3- to 4-year-old children. Thus, the capacities for language and executive function that appear so important for the mindreading abilities of young children cannot feature in an explanation of what infants are doing. If we suppose that infants have mindreading concepts then language and executive function can have had little role in the acquisition of those concepts. And whether or not we suppose that infants have mindreading concepts, whatever information processing gives rise to their expectations about Sally's belief-governed behaviour, it cannot require much in the way of language and executive function.

Innate mindreading concepts?

One way of obviating any need for language or executive function in the acquisition of mindreading concepts is to suppose that these concepts are innate. This conclusion is favoured by Onishi and Baillargeon (2005) and by other researchers who already supposed that "belief" and "knowledge" must be among the fundamental set of concepts that need to be innate (e.g., Fodor, 1992; Leslie, 1987, 2005; Surian, Caldi & Sperber, 2007). However, innateness of mindreading concepts does not explain how they are put to work by the infant to form expectations about Sally's behaviour. Prior to Onishi and Baillargeon's findings, the assumption among these researchers had been that although mindreading concepts were innate, *using* those concepts often made significant demands on executive function. Leslie (e.g., 1994a; Leslie, Friedman & German, 2004) formulates this argument particularly clearly for the case of false belief reasoning, where an innate mindreading capacity – the "theory of mind module" – only serves to generate potential alternative beliefs that might be attributed to an agent. Actually ascribing a particular false belief to an agent requires selection among the possible beliefs generated by the theory of mind module, and this requires an executive capacity that does not develop until 3 to 4 years. Nobody has yet explained how children's reasoning with an innate belief concept requires executive control while infants' reasoning with the same concept does not. Likewise, the fact that the tasks used with infants are non-verbal is, on its own, of little explanatory value. For as we already saw, there is no evidence that removing the verbal demands of false belief tasks makes them any easier for 3- to 4-year-olds. Thus, for the time being, interpreting the infant data as showing that infants have innate mindreading concepts creates as many problems as it solves.

Simpler mindreading concepts?

The discrepancy between children's difficulty with explicit judgements and their success on indirect tests leads Moll and Tomasello (2007) and O'Neill (1996) to interpret their findings more conservatively than the above authors: younger children are not keeping track of their mother's knowledge *as such*; instead they are monitoring her "engagement" (O'Neill, 1996) or "experience" (Moll & Tomasello, 2007). The notions of engagement or experience are not defined in detail, but the idea is that young children track a relationship between an agent (e.g., mother) and an object or situation (an exciting toy) that co-varies with whether or not she "knows" in a useful set of circumstances. Tracking engagement or experience would afford young children some flexibility in interpreting or formulating communicative acts. But these notions would not support judgements about whether or not the agent "knows", and would not conform to normative standards for knowledge formation (i.e., seeing normatively leads to knowing, but does not necessarily lead to "experience" of an object: Moll & Tomasello, 2007).

As I shall go on to describe in this, and later, chapters, I think that it is a move in the right direction to suggest that infants' abilities are distinct from those of older children and adults. However, the biggest problem for these accounts is that they do not make clear *how* it is that "engagement" or "experience" are easier concepts for children to grasp or easier problems for children to process, compared with "perception", "knowledge" and "belief". They offer new words for describing the empirical phenomena, but no theory about how the phenomena actually arise. And without such a theory, they really do not *explain* how infants achieve their surprising sensitivity to mental states without the need for language or executive function.

No mindreading concepts (and no mindreading)?

Perner and Ruffman (2005) offer strongly sceptical explanations of Onishi and Baillargeon's findings, inspired by Povinelli's (e.g., Penn & Povinelli, 2007; Povinelli & Giambrone, 1999) sceptical account of mindreading abilities in non-human animals (more of which below). The more powerful of these is the suggestion that infants have a variety of (possibly innate) behavioural rules that allow future behaviour to be predicted from current behaviour, without going via the intermediate step of inferring a mental state. For example, if the infant had a behavioural rule stating that agents search for an object in the place where they have looked at it, then they would form a set of expectations about the agent's behaviour that matched those shown by the infants in Onishi and Baillargeon's study (Perner & Ruffman, 2005, p. 215). Moreover, Perner and Ruffman extend the same explanation to evidence that older infants and young children are sensitive to an agent's "engagement" or "experience" with a situation (e.g., Moll & Tomasello, 2007; O'Neill, 1996).

It is important to note that this argument is not a mere empirical claim about the kinds of behavioural rules that infants may or may not have, but an argument in principle about the relationship between reasoning about mental states and reasoning about behaviour, and the kinds of evidence that could possibly distinguish between them. As depicted in Figure 3.2, Povinelli and Vonk (2004; see also Perner, 2010) argue that the ability to infer a given mental state from observed behaviour presupposes the existence of a behavioural rule linking observable behaviour (e.g., she looked at the object while it was in the round box) with a resulting, unobservable, mental state (e.g., she thinks the object's in the round box). Equally, predicting behaviour from a mental state presupposes the existence of a behavioural rule linking a given mental state (e.g., she thinks the object's in the round box) with a consequent behaviour (e.g., she will approach the round box to retrieve the object). If this is correct, then inferring Sally's

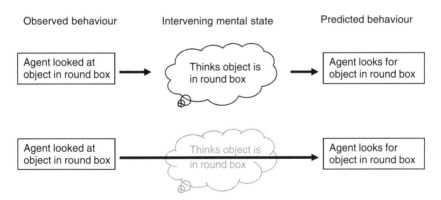

Figure 3.2 Povinelli's sceptical argument about the inferences warranted by studies of "mindreading" in infants and chimpanzees. Both a mentalist account (top panel) and a pure behaviour account (bottom panel) require inferences from observed behaviour to predicted behaviour, but a mentalist account additionally requires the ascription of a mental state. Existing evidence from infants and chimpanzees only shows reliable behaviour predictions from behaviour observations, and provides no direct evidence of mental state ascription. Given this, Povinelli's argument is that the pure behaviour account is more parsimonious and should be favoured.

mental state does not seem necessary because one could just as well map directly from her looking behaviour to a prediction about her search behaviour. Indeed, on this argument it would be unparsimonious to do so. Thus, according to Povinelli (e.g., Penn & Povinelli, 2007; Povinelli & Giambrone, 1999) and Perner and Ruffman (2005) the current evidence from infants does not entitle us to conclude that infants are reasoning about mental states, and moreover, parsimony favours the assumption that they are only reasoning about observable behaviours.

What is the difference between evidence from infants and children?

On a first pass, the argument in favour of behavioural rules seems almost too powerful for comfort. Clearly, what goes for infants ought to go for children, and since the tasks used with infants seem to resemble those used with children very closely, aren't we compelled also to be sceptical about whether 3- or 4-year-olds are reasoning about mental states? This argument was indeed discussed in early research on children's mindreading, but was settled to most people's satisfaction by two kinds of evidence.

Firstly, changes in children's mindreading at 3 to 4 years show coherence over diverse measures. It is not just that they pass a particular false belief task; they pass a variety of such tasks around the same time, in which beliefs are induced via very different kinds of behaviour (e.g., Perner, Leekam & Wimmer, 1987). It would be truly surprising if children just happened to learn simultaneously a whole set of behavioural rules suitable for predicting agents' behaviour on the basis of false beliefs. Moreover, as discussed in the last chapter, at the same time as children pass false belief tasks they pass a variety of other tasks that require similar forms of thinking, but not belief reasoning, such as false sign tasks, tests of counterfactual reasoning, and Level-2 visual perspective tasks. Again, this coherence is inexplicable on a behavioural rules account, but makes sense if children are acquiring a qualitatively new way of thinking that affords all of these reasoning abilities.

Second, as described in chapter 2, children talk about what people think. The important point here is not to suggest that language is necessary for mindreading, or for providing unequivocal evidence in favour of mind-reading over behaviour reading. Rather, talking about what people think is particularly clear evidence that children are ascribing content-bearing mental states. The whole point about behavioural rules is that they afford a direct route from observed behaviour to an expectation about an observed outcome without inferences about mental content as an intermediary. The fact that children talk about mental content – what someone sees, thinks, knows, etc. – seems to suggest that they *are* reasoning about mental content.

Clearly, then, scepticism about whether infants are really representing mental states would be addressed by evidence that their abilities were coherent or evidence that they ascribed mental content. It is too early to judge whether the new evidence emerging about infants' abilities will meet tests of coherence. On current evidence it seems likely that infants may be sensitive to a variety of causes and consequences of beliefs, but there is no evidence that they pass level-2 perspective tasks, counterfactual reasoning or false sign tasks. As for mental content, it is, of course, too much to expect evidence to come from infants talking about what people think. However, in chapter 5, I shall discuss interference effects in adults' perspective-taking that provide evidence for the ascription of mental content without the need for verbal report. And in chapter 7, I shall discuss how such evidence may be brought to bear on the interpretation of evidence of mindreading in infants and non-human animals.

Are we missing a lesson from recent history?

Evidence that infants reason about visual perspective and false belief has been gratefully received by researchers already theoretically committed to the existence of innate concepts. Part of the excitement resulting from Onishi and Baillargeon's (2005) findings, as well as the heat of the subsequent debate, derives from what appears to follow from this nativist conclusion; that subsequent development just involves learning the conditions for the application of these concepts (Onishi & Baillargeon, 2005). However, this rather misses some of the most interesting outcomes from the last 20 years of research on infants' abilities in other conceptual domains.

For example, until the early 1980s there was little evidence that children were able to able to reason about number[2] until they began their earliest counting behaviours at 2 or 3 years of age (e.g., Gelman & Gallistel, 1978). Then, from the 1980s, studies using preferential looking and habituation paradigms began to find evidence that infants were in fact sensitive to number properties, such as the number of items in repeatedly presented sets of stimuli (Starkey & Cooper, 1980), the number of items in a short sequence of events (e.g., Wynn, 1996), and the difference between small and large sets of objects (e.g., Xu & Spelke, 2000). Such evidence led to initial claims that sensitive paradigms had finally revealed that infants had number concepts after all. However, further research revealed that infants could process precise numbers up to a limit of 4 items, and could only discriminate between large sets of different sizes if the ratio of their difference was sufficiently large. The existence of these limits is very informative because they cannot be explained by the nature of numbers per se, and do not appear to be due to limits on infants' intelligence, general processing capacity or executive function (e.g., Feigenson, Dehane & Spelke, 2004).

Although there is much ongoing research and debate about the development of number concepts (see e.g., Carey, 2004; Feigenson, Dehane & Spelke, 2004; Gallistel & Gelman, 2000; Gelman & Gallistel, 2004), there is a reasonable consensus that infants' abilities in the domain of number are enabled by one or more types of process that are relatively specialized for the purpose of extracting and processing information about number. However, these processes are strictly limited in the kinds of information about number that they can handle, and these limits are only overcome once children learn a conventional system of counting and mathematics. Learning this conventional system is a drawn-out process taking several years, and making significant demands on domain-general resources for language and executive function (e.g., Muldoon, Lewis & Freeman, 2009).

Although some researchers still talk in terms of innate concepts of number it is clear that this is a sense of "concept" that is somewhat weaker, but also a good deal more interesting and cognitively plausible than was originally supposed when interpreting the first evidence of infants' success on number tasks. Stephen Butterfill and I have argued that something analogous may turn out to be true for mindreading (Apperly & Butterfill, 2009), and that we should therefore be as attentive to the limits on infants' abilities as we are to their surprising competencies.

Are infants' mindreading abilities in fact limited?

Of course, infants know less than older children or adults, and have fewer processing resources at their disposal. The question is whether infants' mindreading – let us suppose for now that they *are* mindreading – is limited in ways that cannot be explained in terms of infants' limited knowledge or general cognitive abilities. There is currently too little evidence to answer this question clearly. But it is informative to note that the existing findings on infants' abilities on "false belief" tasks could be explained on the basis of simpler mindreading abilities. There is already evidence that infants have simple notions of "perceptual access"[3] including Level-1 visual perspective-taking (Sodian, Thoermer & Metz, 2007). And there is evidence that infants track, to some degree, the information that an agent has accessed (Moll & Tomasello, 2007; O'Neill, 1996). It is possible that the infant's record of what an agent has accessed is sufficient to form an expectation about the agent's behaviour in many "false belief" situations. But notably, there is so far no evidence that infants can pass "Level-2" perspective-taking tasks (e.g., Flavell et al., 1981) that require understanding that the very same situation is seen in different ways by people with different viewing angles. This is significant because, on many analyses, it is this kind of ability that corresponds to the requirements of a normative account of belief understanding, according to which understanding beliefs *as such* requires understanding them as the relation between an agent, the attitude of believing, and a propositional representation of what is believed. And indeed, there is no evidence so far that infants pass a false belief task that requires the ascription of mental states with propositional content (see e.g., Apperly & Butterfill, 2009; Butterfill & Apperly, 2010, for a fuller discussion).

What does this tell us? I think we are led to two conclusions, one negative and one more positive. The current evidence from infants does not support the conclusion that infants have a concept of belief *as such*. But the evidence clearly raises the prospect that a concept of belief *as such* is not necessary for solving a lot of problems that we, as adults, are inclined to gloss as problems that require thinking about beliefs. I think this is an important lesson, and I shall pick up this theme again in chapter 6, once I have reviewed the evidence from other sources.

In sum, based on exciting research from eye movements, looking time and other measures of spontaneous behaviour, the current literature is in danger of jumping to premature conclusions about the conceptual basis of infants' abilities. This is partly in consequence of the "neurotic task-fixation" that led false belief tasks to be viewed as a litmus test for mind-reading. However, whether it turns out that infants are simple mindreaders or sophisticated behaviour readers, these results suggest that infants may be far more sensitive to the minds of others than originally supposed. Together with other research that I shall review in the coming chapters, this demands a re-appraisal of the conclusions reached from research on mindreading in children.

Non-human animals

When Premack and Woodruff (1978) asked whether the chimpanzee has a theory of mind, few commentators would have imagined that 30 years later the same question would be asked, in all seriousness, about a species of bird. The literature on social cognition in non-human animals has developed enormously in that time, both in the refinement of the questions asked, and in the breadth of species that are now being investigated. If there is one clear lesson from this work it is "never say never". Repeatedly, researchers have found evidence of abilities that were once thought to be uniquely human, and, repeatedly, at least some of these abilities have been found in multiple species, some of them very distant evolutionary ancestors of humans. As with research on human infants, the interpretation of these findings is hotly contested (e.g., Penn & Povinelli, 2007; Tomasello, Call & Hare, 2003). However, there is enough stability in the emerging picture for it to be informative about the cognitive basis of mindreading. As in other chapters, I shall focus narrowly on evidence for mindreading of perception, knowledge and belief. Most evidence will come from investigation of chimpanzees (and the closely related species, bonobos), since research in these species has been most extensive, and most intensively discussed. However, I shall cover some of the growing body of evidence from other species towards the end.

Limits on language and executive function

In much the same way as studies of infants, research on non-human animals can inform us about what mindreading may be possible in the absence of the language and executive function that appears necessary for human children to develop adult-like mindreading abilities. Of course, it would be quite wrong to suggest that species such as chimpanzees had no executive function, and were incapable of acquiring any language abilities. But, without entirely ignoring "never say never", there do seem to be good reasons for supposing that these abilities are less than those of a 3-year-old human child. For example, Kanzi is perhaps the best known case of a chimpanzee that has received very extensive language training, with the result that his language abilities, in terms of vocabulary and grammar, compare reasonably well to those of a 2-year-old child (Savage-Rumbaugh et al., 1993).

As an illustration of chimpanzees' relatively limited executive function, consider their performance on "reverse contingency" tasks. Like the "windows" task (e.g., Russell et al., 1991) and the "less-is-more" task (Carlson et al., 2005) used with children, reverse contingency tasks confront participants with a choice between a more desirable option (e.g., a box containing several grapes) and a less desirable option (a box containing fewer grapes). This choice is paired with a counterintuitive rule that the box pointed to or reached for is taken away, leaving the other box with its contents for consumption. Obviously, the optimal strategy is to reach for or point to the less desirable box in order to obtain the more desirable box. Chimpanzees find this extremely difficult to learn, often taking tens or hundreds of trials before they select the less desirable box above chance levels (Vlamings, Uher & Call, 2006), and sometimes flat-lining at below-chance levels for the entire period of study (e.g., Boysen & Berntson, 1995). In this respect, chimpanzees resemble most 3-year-old human children, who also show slow learning or stick to the incorrect strategy for an entire experiment. Many 4-year-old humans, by contrast, quickly grasp the rule, acting on it consistently and with some delight, to obtain maximum reward.

Evidence of mindreading perception, knowledge and belief

"Perceiving"[4]

Povinelli and Eddy (1996) conducted a large study of chimpanzees' understanding of seeing. They made the most of the animals' spontaneous tendency to make a begging gesture requesting food from humans, and examined whether they would gesture preferentially towards a human who could see them (so might give them food) compared with a human who could not see them. When chimpanzees had to choose between a person facing directly towards them and a person facing away, they reliably gestured towards the person facing them, consistent with an understanding of which person could see them. However, chimpanzees failed to discriminate between several other contrasts in which both people were facing the animal, for example where one person covered their ears (so could still see) while the other covered their eyes, or where one person held a bucket next to their head (so could still see) while the other held the bucket over their head. This poor performance contrasted with good performance of 3-year-old human children on similar tests. Povinelli and Eddy (1996) concluded that chimpanzees can use a behavioural cue of facing versus not-facing in order to select a person who might be able to give them food, but that they do not understand seeing as a mental state. Subsequent work suggests that this might be an unduly pessimistic picture, and that chimpanzees may be sensitive both to body orientation and to face orientation (Kaminski, Call & Tomasello, 2004). However, this study still found only limited evidence that chimpanzees were sensitive to whether or not the person's eyes were open.

Hare et al. (2000) tested chimpanzees' understanding of seeing in a completely different paradigm, in which the subject chimpanzee competed for food with a second, dominant, chimpanzee. As can be seen in Figure 3.3, the animals faced each other across an enclosure that contained a barrier. In one condition, a piece of food was placed in common view whereas in another, a piece of food was placed in front of the barrier from the subject chimpanzee's point of view, and therefore out of view of the dominant competitor. Results from this, together with control trials, suggested that subject chimpanzees were sensitive to whether or not the dominant chimpanzee had visual access to the food reward, approaching hidden food more frequently than food that the dominant chimpanzee could see (though see Karin-D'Arcy & Povinelli, 2002).

Consistent with this conclusion is evidence that chimpanzees will actively manipulate a competitor's perceptual access. Hare, Call and Tomasello (2006) had chimpanzees attempt to obtain food placed on either side of a human competitor who would snatch it quickly away if they became aware of the animal's approach. Chimpanzees preferred to approach food from the side that minimized the chances of their approach being seen, either

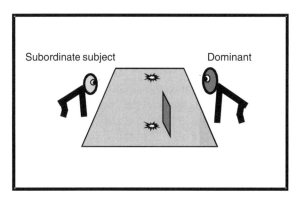

Figure 3.3 Hare et al.'s (2000) Level-1 visual perspective-taking task for chimpanzees. Subordinate subjects were more likely to approach the food that was out of sight of the dominant animal.

because the human competitor was facing the other way or because visibility was restricted on that side by an opaque screen. Melis, Call and Tomasello (2006) extended the same method to "hearing". In this study chimpanzees preferred to reach for food through a tunnel that made no noise (so did not alert the human competitor to the approach) compared with a tunnel that made a loud noise. The same preference was not present in a non-competitive control condition.

In sum, chimpanzees show evidence of understanding "perception" in both the visual and auditory modalities. They may not be sensitive to all of the conditions that are necessary for seeing, such as the need to have one's eyes open. But they do appear to grasp that a competitor who has information access in virtue of facing in a particular direction with an unoccluded line of sight will behave differently from one who does not. These findings are broadly consistent with chimpanzees understanding "Level-1" visual perspective-taking. So far, however, there is no evidence that chimpanzees understand Level-2 perspective-taking, which requires distinguishing how the very same situation is seen by different viewers with different viewing angles (see Figure 2.2b). And there is no evidence of understanding visual attention – for example the possibility that someone may look but not "see" because they are distracted.

"Knowing"

Hare et al.'s (2000) paradigm provides evidence that chimpanzees track what each other see and use this to determine their strategies for food competition. Hare, Call and Tomasello (2001) adapted this paradigm to test whether chimpanzees also track what another *has seen* and thus, in a sense, what the other "knows". As shown in Figure 3.4, a subordinate subject and a dominant competitor faced one another across a space that now had two barriers, and thus two possible locations where food could be hidden out of view of the dominant competitor. In a baseline condition both animals saw food being hidden behind one barrier. In the test condition, only the subject saw the food being hidden. Thus, in both conditions, at the point when the subject chimpanzee had to decide whether to approach the food, the subject chimpanzee could see the food and the dominant competitor could not. What varied was whether or not the dominant chimpanzee *had seen* the food being hidden. The results showed that subject chimpanzees were more likely to approach and obtain the food when the competitor had not seen the food being hidden (so did not "know" it was there), compared to the baseline where both animals saw (see also Bräuer, Call & Tomasello, 2007; Kaminski, Call & Tomasello, 2008).

Of course, "seeing" or "knowing" are relations that obtain between an agent and an object or situation, whereas the results I have described so far could be explained by a simpler strategy of just tracking properties of the food object itself. If, as a result of being seen, the food was tagged in the

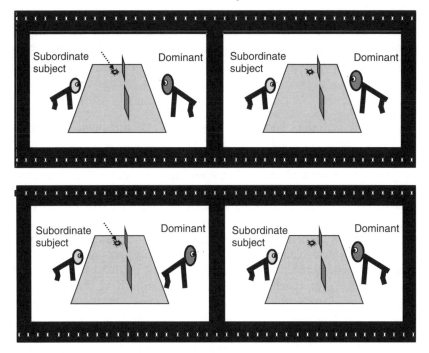

Figure 3.4 Hare, Call and Tomasello's (2001) test of whether chimpanzees track what others "know". Subordinate subjects were less likely to approach the food when the dominant chimpanzee saw where it was hidden (upper two panels) compared with when the dominant did not see (lower two panels).

animal's memory as "seen", or even in entirely non-mentalistic terms as "low quality" or "dangerous", then the animal would behave in the way observed without processing any enduring relation of the dominant chimpanzee "knowing" about the object. It is significant, then, that in a second experiment, Hare et al. (2001) found that subject chimpanzees' reluctance to approach food that had been seen by a dominant competitor was eliminated if the competitor who had seen the food being hidden was replaced by another dominant animal who had not seen. This would not be expected if the subject chimpanzee had encoded the fact that the food had been seen only as a fact about the food. Rather, their strategy involved tracking a relationship between the food and a particular dominant individual.

Interestingly, evidence so far suggests that chimpanzees do not make similar inferences about "knowledge" on the basis of hearing. Bräuer, Call and Tomasello (2008) used an analogous procedure and found that subject chimpanzees did not discriminate between conditions in which food was hidden noisily (so the dominant would be able to hear where it was being hidden) or quietly (so the dominant would not know where it was hidden). If this effect turns out to be the result of a general failure among chimpanzees to appreciate that "hearing leads to knowing" then it is evidence that chimpanzees' abilities may be less coherent than those of human infants, who do show some evidence of understanding that a verbal message changes what people know (Song & Baillargeon, 2008).

"Believing"

In Hare et al.'s (2001) "knowledge" condition, the dominant chimpanzee lacked knowledge of the food's hiding location, and so had to guess where to look. Subordinate chimpanzees exploited this uncertainty, and obtained food more often than when the dominant knew the food's location. However, the authors also included a condition in which subordinate subject chimpanzees saw an event sequence that should have allowed them to compete even more effectively for food. In this case, the dominant chimpanzee saw food hidden behind one barrier, but then did not see it being moved so that it was hidden behind a second barrier (see Figure 3.5). Thus, the dominant chimpanzee had a false belief about the food's location, and so would reliably approach the wrong location to retrieve the food. If the subordinate could predict this reliably wrong search by the dominant, it should be able to approach and obtain the food with a higher degree of success than in the "knowledge" condition, when the dominant's search was merely unpredictable. In fact, subordinates were no more successful at obtaining food in the false belief condition. Similarly, Kaminski, Call and Tomasello (2008) report that chimpanzees discriminated between conditions of a strategic game in which a competitor did or did not know about the location of hidden food. However, they did not discriminate a condition in which their competitor had a false belief from a matched control condition.

What do chimpanzees understand?

The conclusion that chimpanzees think about mental states at all has been strongly contested (e.g., Penn & Povinelli, 2007; Povinelli & Giambrone, 1999). The basic argument was described earlier in this chapter when discussing critiques of research on mindreading in human infants, but in fact it was first made about the interpretation of chimpanzees' abilities. Essentially, the argument is that inferences about mental states as the causes and consequences of behaviour presuppose the ability to reason in a sophisticated way about behaviours. If a chimpanzee (or human infant, or anyone else) reasons in a sophisticated way about behaviours, then for a great many cases it will be perfectly possible to predict that one behaviour (e.g., looking) will lead to another behaviour (e.g., approach) without any need to reason about an intervening mental state (e.g., seeing). So, on this argument, evidence that a chimpanzee expects a competitor who has looked at some food to approach that food does not warrant the conclusion that

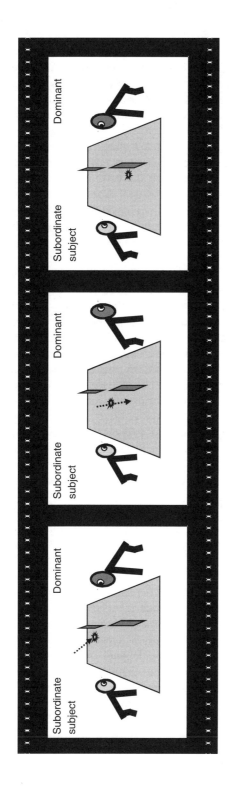

Figure 3.5 Hare, Call and Tomasello's (2001) "false belief" condition. The dominant chimpanzee saw the food hidden in a first location, but did not see it being moved to a second location. In principle, subordinate subjects could be sure that the dominant would search in the food's first location, so could approach the hidden food with confidence. In fact they were no more likely to approach the food in this false belief condition than when the dominant chimpanzee was merely ignorant and so was equally likely to search in either location (Figure 3.4). This suggests that chimpanzees may not understand false beliefs.

the chimpanzee ascribes to the competitor the mental state of "seeing". Against this conclusion, Call and Tomasello (2008; see also Tomasello, Call & Hare, 2003) draw attention to the relatively coherent pattern of chimpanzees' abilities across a variety of test settings, and to the similarities between findings from chimpanzees and from human infants. This debate has resulted in a stalemate, with each side suggesting that their own interpretation is the more parsimonious. I shall return to a discussion of how this stalemate might be overcome in chapter 7, but for now I want to side-step the disagreement and evaluate the proposition that chimpanzees do understand at least some mental states. Call and Tomasello (2008) conclude that chimpanzees understand perception and knowledge, but not belief. If we grant that chimpanzees might understand something about mental states then this initially appears a reasonable gloss of current findings.[5]

Moreover, it would seem to suggest that our folk psychological concepts of perception, knowledge and belief carve neatly at the natural, evolutionary joints, with chimpanzees, one of our closest ancestors, having some, but not all, of these concepts. However, from the perspective of the normative account of mindreading, this conclusion is highly problematic. Firstly, for mental states that they are supposed to understand there is evidence that a chimpanzee's understanding falls qualitatively short of the conditions of the normative account. For example, normatively, an understanding of "seeing" involves understanding the relation between an agent, the attitude of seeing, and a propositional content corresponding to what is seen. But such an understanding would support both Level-1 and Level-2 perspective-taking, whereas evidence so far suggests that chimpanzees are only capable of Level-1.

Secondly, according to the normative account, the meanings of mental state concepts are interdependent (e.g., Davidson, 1989, 1995). From this point of view it is simply incoherent to say that a chimpanzee (or anyone else) understands "perception" and "knowledge" but not "belief". Moreover, whereas the gloss offered by Call and Tomasello (2008) implies that "perception", "knowledge" and "belief" are natural concepts, which may be separately present or absent in different species, a closer consideration of the data suggests that this cannot be correct. Even on the most generous account, chimpanzees do not fully understand "perception" or "knowledge"; rather they might understand some important features of these states and their causes and consequences. Thus, evidence from chimpanzees offers no support to the view that mindreading depends on a clearly-defined set of concepts, and no support for the idea that the normative account cuts at the joints of everyday mindreading. Of course this is unrelated to the question of whether chimpanzees reason about mental states of some kind. It is just that whatever they are doing, it is not well-captured by the normative account.

Parallels with human infants?

Call and Tomasello (2008) draw attention to the similarities between the mindreading abilities of chimpanzees and human infants (though see Herrmann et al., 2007, who emphasize the differences). It is certainly tempting to suppose that the abilities of chimpanzees and infants depend on similar cognitive mechanisms resulting from our shared evolutionary history, and that human children and adults only escape the limitations of these abilities via a uniquely human aptitude for cultural learning and language. I shall discuss this possibility further in chapter 7. However, on the basis of the evidence discussed here, there are two potentially important points on which chimpanzees' abilities fall short of those of infants. Firstly, although chimpanzees show evidence of understanding perception and knowledge across a range of test situations, evidence that they understand something about hearing but do not appreciate that hearing leads to knowing indicates a potential lack of coherence. This is would be significant because a core feature of the concept of "knowledge" is that it provides some unification over the results of a variety of perceptual and inferential processes. If chimpanzees' understanding of "knowledge" is modality-specific then it falls short of providing this conceptual unification. Similar incoherence has not yet been observed in infants' abilities, though this may just reflect the relatively small number of studies conducted so far.

A second discrepancy between evidence from chimpanzees and human infants is the negative findings from false belief tasks used with chimpanzees, compared with the positive findings from human infants. It is important to recall from earlier in the chapter that there is, as yet, no evidence that infants reason about beliefs *as such*. But there is evidence that human infants form specific expectations about the behaviour of an agent (e.g., that she will search in the round box, not the square box) on the basis of what she "thinks". This contrasts with the abilities so far demonstrated in chimpanzees, who do not succeed in making a specific prediction about how a competitor with a false belief will behave.

On both of these points recent history suggests that "never say never" is the safest bet for the time being. It may yet turn out that chimpanzees do show abilities that are highly analogous to those of human infants.

Other non-human species

Although, as our closest genetic relatives, chimpanzees might be the most obvious place to look for evidence of mindreading abilities in non-human species, it is clearly possible that other species will have such abilities, and these may even be better than those of chimpanzees. Moreover, evidence from a wider range of non-human species is of interest for two questions that cannot be addressed by studying chimpanzees alone. On the one hand, if several different ape species, or perhaps other mammals, demonstrate very similar mindreading abilities despite occupying very different ecological niches, this would suggest that shared genes, rather than similar environments, were having a substantial impact on their mindreading abilities. On the other hand, with much greater evolutionary distance from humans it becomes less likely that any mindreading abilities result from common evolutionary ancestry with humans. Therefore, if mindreading is observed in more distant species, this can provide valuable indicators about the kind of evolutionary pressures that might have operated to produce convergent evolution.

Close(ish) relatives

There is currently no evidence that the mindreading abilities of other species exceed those of chimpanzees, though this may be the result of the relatively small number of species that have been tested in any detail. However, there is evidence that several species may be capable of Level-1 visual perspective-taking, including orang-utans (Shillito, Shumaker, Gallup & Beck, 2005), rhesus macaques (Flombaum & Santos, 2005), goats (Kaminski, Call & Tomasello, 2006) and dogs (Kaminski, Bräuer, Call & Tomasello, 2009). Now, the problem is that since chimpanzees, macaques, goats and dogs all live in relatively complex social environments, these species provide little purchase on questions about the contributions of genes and environment to perspective-taking abilities. Orang-utans may be a better test case because they are solitary for large parts of their lives, but even orang-utans none-theless spend several years growing up in close social contact with others. The potential of such studies is only just being tapped, and future research that looks in more detail at the characteristics of perspective-taking in these and other species may yet reveal informative similarities and differences.

Distant relatives

Evidence from species that diverged much earlier from humans comes from studies of birds. Members of the corvid family have shown evidence of quite sophisticated cognitive abilities, including mindreading (e.g., Emery & Clayton, 2004). The most extensive series of investigations has been con-ducted in Western scrub-jays by exploiting their natural behaviour of cach-ing food in hidden locations for later retrieval. Scrub-jays' caching strategies vary according to whether or not they are being observed by a potential competitor. In the presence of a competitor scrub-jays will selectively cache in darker rather than lighter locations (Dally, Emery & Clayton, 2004), in occluded locations rather than locations that are visually accessible, and in locations that are further away from a competitor (Dally, Emery & Clayton, 2005). These results are consistent with scrub-jays taking account of visual perspectives. Moreover, such abilities may extend to taking account of whether or not a competitor can hear (Stulp, Emery, Velhurst & Clayton, 2009).

As for chimpanzees, scrub-jays also appear to keep track of "who has seen". When recovering food in private, scrub-jays prefer to recover caches that were observed by a competitor compared to those cached in private (Emery & Clayton, 2001). Importantly, it seems that these food items are not merely categorized as "vulnerable to pilfering". Scrub-jays selectively recover food that a currently present competitor originally saw being hidden, in comparison with food cached in the presence of another (now absent) competitor (Clayton, Dally & Emery, 2007). That is to say, even when all of the food was vulnerable to pilfering because it was observed at the time of caching, the birds selectively retrieved items that were currently vulnerable because they had been seen by the currently present competitor. This suggests that scrub-jays encoded which competitor had seen which food items being cached, and were able to use this information to guide a flexible strategy for protecting their cached food.

In sum, the evidence for mindreading abilities in scrub-jays is substantial. Evidence in other bird species is more limited, though analogous sensitivity to "what a competitor sees" has also been found in rooks, who adapt their food retrieval strategies on the basis of eye gaze cues of a potential competitor in a way that appears more sophisticated than chimpanzees (von Bayern & Emery, 2009). It is true that all of this evidence remains vulnerable to the same sceptical arguments discussed in relation to findings from chimpanzees and human infants. But, these concerns notwithstanding, the important point for current purposes is that the evidence from scrub-jays appears as strong as any from closer relatives of humans.

This conclusion is important because it seems very unlikely that the last common ancestor of birds and humans (a lizard-like amniote, some 300 million years ago) was capable of perspective-taking. So it is generally assumed that analogous abilities observed in certain birds and certain mammals are the result of convergent evolution in response to analogous ecological pressures. In this case it is notable that scrub-jays and many other corvid species live in complex social groups with a significant degree of both cooperation and competition for resources – that is to say, the problems they encounter are analogous to those of highly social mammals (e.g., Emery & Clayton, 2007). Moreover, although corvid and mammal neuroanatomy is very different, it has been suggested that there are homologous structures associated with "higher cognition" in both groups (e.g., Emery, 2004; Emery & Clayton, 2004). The evidence from scrub-jays and other corvids therefore casts some valuable light on the conditions that might be necessary for the development of perspective-taking in a species.

Summary

There is clear evidence that several non-human species have abilities that are attuned to what other agents perceive and know, and every reason to expect that these abilities extend to more species than have currently been investigated. These species behave in ways that are dependent on another agent's current or past perceptual access, and may act in ways that deny another agent perceptual access. There are interesting parallels with the abilities observed in infants, though on current evidence infants' abilities may be more coherent and more extensive than those of non-human species. However, as for infants, the cognitive basis of these abilities in non-human species remains quite unclear. If these abilities depend on some form of conceptual understanding of mental states (whatever that means), then the concepts at work do not appear to map simply to the concepts of "perception" and "knowledge" that feature in the normative account of mindreading. If these abilities depend on a conceptual understanding of behaviour, but not of mental states, then we must still ask how non-human animals reason in a sophisticated way about behaviour. Neither the "behaviour+mental states" nor the "behaviour only" account explains how non-human animals (or, for that matter, human infants) actually think about agents in a way that does not depend on language and that makes few demands on executive function. And it really is not obvious on a priori grounds which account would be more compatible with reasoning in the absence of such cognitive resources. What the literature from non-human animals does illustrate is that such mindreading is possible, somehow. This conclusion will be important later, in chapter 6, when I discuss how mindreading could be "cognitively efficient".

Notes

1 It is difficult to be sure whether infants treat the message as "correcting" Sally's false belief or as overwriting it with a new, and correct, belief about the object's location. Either way, however, this result suggests that infants' expectations about Sally's behaviour are not based only on what she has or has not seen.
2 I shall use the case of number but analogous findings hold in other conceptual domains such as object-knowledge.
3 Note that a full understanding of perception is far more complex than I am assuming for infants. Being in a perceptual state (e.g., Oedipus seeing his wife arriving for dinner) clearly involves a relation to a propositional mental state that represents its referents only under particular description, and may be inaccurate. I am not supposing here that infants have such a rich understanding of perception, but that they are sensitive to agents' exposure to situations and to some of the consequences of that exposure for what agents "know".
4 It seems felicitous to use the normal terms for these mental states of perception, knowledge and belief, but I place them in scare-quotes in recognition of the fact that – as discussed later – they almost certainly do not correspond fully with adult humans' understanding of these terms. Likewise, although most authors talk about infants' or non-human animals' "understanding" of mental states, it is generally accepted that this does not entail the kind of reflective insight that human adults and older children clearly do have.
5 As was the case in the literature on infants' and children's development, there is also a literature on chimpanzees' abilities with other mental states such as goals

and intentions. To keep things simple I am keeping to the strategy of only discussing epistemic mental states. The wider literature on chimpanzees is full of excellent studies, but does no more to resolve the fundamental problems of interpretation than the literature I summarize here.

4 Evidence from neuroimaging and neuropsychology

The growing accessibility of methods for neuroimaging the intact, functioning, human brain has led to an explosion of research in cognitive neuroscience in the last 15 years. Combined with the theoretical proposition that parts of the brain may be specifically devoted to social perception and cognition (e.g., Brothers, 1990), this has given rise to the new field of social cognitive neuroscience (e.g., Blakemore, Winston & Frith, 2004; Lieberman, 2007), including within it research on mindreading. Curiously, this work has drawn sceptical responses about whether the brain can tell us anything at all about the psychology of mindreading (e.g., Carpendale & Lewis, 2006). I hope to show that this is unduly pessimistic, but I also believe there are good reasons for caution. From a cognitive perspective, most of the informativeness of a functional neuroimaging study depends on having clear hypotheses and good paradigms for testing the cognitive basis of the functions we wish to study. With such tools, patterns of neural activation can be a useful additional dependent variable, which might vary across different conditions even when behavioural measures such as response time and error rate do not. However, since one of my key points in this book is that we are only just developing clear hypotheses and good paradigms for testing the cognitive basis of mindreading, especially in adults, it should not be surprising that I think we have only just begun to see what might be learned from neuroimaging studies.

The recent surge of interest in neuroimaging has somewhat eclipsed neuropsychological research with brain-injured patients. This is unfortunate for at least two reasons. Firstly, patterns of spared and impaired function following brain injury afford stronger inferences than neuroimaging data about the causal dependence of one cognitive process on another, or of the causal dependence of a cognitive process on a particular neural region. This is because neuroimaging methods such as fMRI and PET tell us about the neural correlates of a cognitive function, but do not demonstrate that a particular pattern of neural activity is causally necessary for the cognitive function. Secondly, for the hardened sceptic who is concerned that cognitive neuroimaging might be little more than neo-phrenology (Uttal, 2003), it is possible to be agnostic about the precise relationship between neurological and psychological functions, and still accept studies of the effects of brain injury as natural experiments in the causal interdependence of psychological functions. For example, from a cognitive point of view it is informative that there are three reports of patients who pass false belief tasks despite severely impaired grammatical abilities (Apperly, Samson et al., 2006; Varley & Siegal, 2000; Varley, Siegal & Want, 2001), and this informativeness is largely independent of the further informative fact that all three patients had overlapping lesions to left fronto-temporal cortex.

In fact, just as much information about the cognitive basis of mindreading comes from studies of patients with brain injury as from functional neuroimaging, and I will summarize the evidence from each source in separate sections of this chapter. The overall picture that emerges is surprisingly consistent. Mindreading recruits a complex network of functional and neural processes. Included among these are neural regions that appear highly selective for mindreading, but it seems clear that mindreading per se is a function of the network rather than of specific, specialized brain regions. Understanding the network, and the functions it supports, provides valuable evidence for understanding mindreading.

Functional neuroimaging

By far the most common way of measuring neural activity in research on mindreading is functional Magnetic Resonance Imaging (fMRI).[1] This method divides the brain into a large number of small cubic volumes and monitors oxygen in the blood in each of these voxels over time. This gives a spatial resolution of 3–6 millimetres. The level of oxygen in the blood is physiologically yoked to the local level of neural activity, but with a significant time lag. Thus, whereas a single neuron may fire up to 200 times per second, the temporal resolution of fMRI is in the order of a few seconds. This trade-off between spatial and temporal resolution means that fMRI studies tend to focus on differences in the spatial location of activation across experimental conditions, rather than on the fine-grained timing of functional processes. Furthermore, the constraint of having to keep very still in a noisy scanner environment also means that most studies to date have been with adults rather than children.

Identifying activity of interest

The neural activity recorded while a participant undertakes a mindreading task may or may not include activity specifically associated with mindreading, but it will certainly include activity resulting from general perceptual and cognitive processing of the cartoon, video or verbal stimulus that is used to present the task. The typical approach to this problem is to have participants complete a second task that makes the same general perceptual and cognitive demands as the mindreading task, but does not involve mindreading. If the tasks are well-matched, then subtracting the neural activity recorded in this control task from the activity recorded during the mindreading task should leave the pattern of activity uniquely associated with mindreading. Of course, the success of this approach depends on how well-matched the tasks really are, and what can be learned from any activity uniquely associated with mindreading depends on having a good account of what mindreading actually involves. Initial studies took a fairly broad-brush approach to both of these issues, but subsequent studies have begun asking more precise questions.

The "Mindreading Network"

The first neuroimaging study of mindreading was conducted by Fletcher et al. (1995; see also Goel et al., 1995), and used PET rather than fMRI (see note 1). Their mindreading stimuli were verbal stories that invited inferences about the mental states of story characters. In one story a robber was running away from the scene of a robbery and dropped his glove in the street. A policeman saw him drop the glove and told him to stop, whereupon the robber gave himself up. Participants read the story and were requested to think about why the story unfolded that way, which presumably required them to reason that the robber incorrectly presumed that the policeman knew he was a robber. One set of control stimuli were "physical" stories of similar general complexity that did not invite mindreading. For example, a burglar was carefully stealing jewels from a shop, but startled a cat, which triggered the alarm as it ran away. A further set of control stimuli were a series of unconnected sentences that took a similar time to read as the mindreading and physical stories. Subtraction of the neural activity recorded during these control stories from that observed during the mindreading stories left significant activation in four neural regions: medial prefrontal cortex (mPFC), Temporo-Parietal Junction[2] (TPJ), temporal poles (TP) and Precuneus/Posterior cingulate cortex (PC) (see Figure 4.1).[3]

This pattern has proved remarkably robust over a large number of subsequent studies that have used a variety of different stimuli and methods, including humorous cartoons as well as mindreading stories (e.g., Brunet et al., 2000; Gallagher et al., 2000), animations of apparently intentional squares and triangles (e.g., Castelli et al., 2000), and simple strategic games that involve anticipating the strategy of a competitor (e.g., Gallagher et al., 2002). Moreover, these studies include reasoning about a variety of mental states, including beliefs, knowledge, desires and intentions (see e.g., Carrington & Bailey, 2009, for a review of a very large number of studies). This raises confidence in the view that activity in this network of regions is involved in mindreading independent of whether the task is visual or verbal, and is involved in thinking about mental states in general, not just some particular tasks, such as false belief tasks. In further support of the view that this network supports rather complex cognitive processes that might be

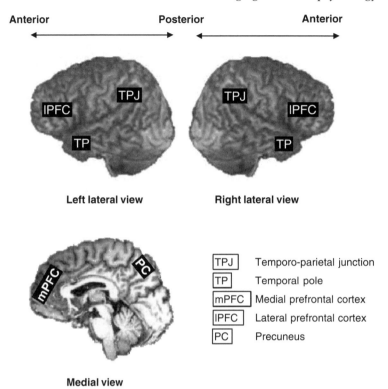

Figure 4.1 Lateral and medial views of a human brain, identifying five regions frequently implicated in neuroimaging and neuropsychological studies of mindreading. Note, although all of these regions occur in both left and right hemispheres, only the more lateral structures show strong evidence of left/right differences for mindreading. For example, in the text I distinguish between L- and R-TPJ, but not between L- and R-mPFC.

unique to humans or our closest ancestors,[4] there is evidence that components of it (especially mPFC) have changed very recently in our evolutionary history (e.g., Gallagher & Frith, 2003), and areas such as mPFC and TPJ are among the last to mature in human development (e.g., Blakemore, 2008). The consistency over studies has led some researchers to christen this combination of brain regions as the "theory of mind network" (e.g., Carrington & Bailey, 2009; Gallagher & Frith, 2003) or "mentalizing network" (Frith & Frith, 2003), and, more dramatically, to suggest that such neural specialization is evidence in favour of a cognitively specialized module for mindreading (e.g., Gallagher & Frith, 2003; Leslie, 2005).

However, if this conclusion were accepted in its strongest sense it would mean that neuroimaging evidence was largely uninformative for understanding the cognitive basis of mindreading. That is to say, if this large network of brain regions was concerned with mindreading and nothing else, and if components of the network were equally likely to be recruited irrespective of the kind of mindreading involved in a task, then simply knowing that the network exists tells us nothing about how mindreading is achieved, or how it interfaces with other cognitive processes such as social interaction and communication. Fortunately, neither of these general points appears to be correct.

Is the mindreading network specialized for mindreading?

The short answer is "no". The full answer, doing justice to the range of functions that have been associated with mPFC, TPJ, TP and PC, could fill a book on its own. I will aim to give a flavour of the similarities and differences across competing views by summarizing two ends of the spectrum. On the one hand, Legrand and Ruby (2009) review neuroimaging studies implicating these regions of the "mindreading network" in mindreading, but also introspection, recalling information from memory, reasoning in general, and particularly inductive reasoning and reasoning under conditions of vagueness or uncertainty. This is clearly consistent with the general observation that these brain regions are strongly connected both with each other and with a wide variety of other regions, suggesting that their function is more likely to be with integration and abstract information processing. On this view, mindreading would be just one among many entirely domain-general functions of such a system.

On the other hand, Frith (2007) suggests that different neural regions in the network serve distinct functions, but ones that are nonetheless domain-general and rather abstract in character. For example, mPFC and adjacent regions seems to be involved in high-level executive processes such as orientation of attention towards incoming stimuli versus internally generated information (e.g., Burgess et al., 2005; Gilbert, Frith & Burgess, 2005), with self-reflection (Gusnard et al., 2001), with episodic memory (e.g., Rugg et al., 1999) and perhaps with forming temporary, integrated representations of event scripts, including social events (e.g., Krueger, Barbey & Grafman, 2009). Intriguingly, Frith (2007) speculates that the area of mPFC most strongly implicated in mindreading may be most specifically involved in "second-order" representations, involved not only in mindreading but potentially in conscious experience. Likewise, TPJ may be involved in processing different perspectives whether they are mental or spatial, and which may or may not be related to a more general role in reorienting of attention (e.g., Corbetta & Shulman, 2002; Decety & Lamm, 2007; see below for more discussion). The temporal poles may be involved in representing high-level semantic knowledge in the form of scripts (e.g., Funnell, 2001), which is equally important for more general reasoning as it is for social reasoning.

Importantly, while Frith's view involves significantly more specialization of function in different neural regions than that of Legrand and Ruby (2009), the different functions assigned by Frith could easily amount to a network with the overall functions envisaged by Legrand and Ruby. In either case, the conclusion is that these regions of the social network do not constitute a domain-specific mindreading module. In fact, the possible roles that have been suggested for these different neural regions – in representing or integrating script-based knowledge, in forming complex, secondary representations, in processing complex patterns of movement, and in processing different perspectives – gives valuable hints about potential component processes of mindreading. The next question is whether there is, in fact, evidence from research on mindreading that different regions of the mindreading network perform different tasks.

Is there functional differentiation within the mindreading network?

Here, the short answer is "yes". However, most neuroimaging studies are not well-designed to address this question, creating a misleading impression of undifferentiated function. Summarizing this pessimistic picture, Carrington and Bailey (2009) reviewed a large number of neuroimaging studies of mindreading, and found little evidence of systematic differences in neural activation according to the mental state targeted (e.g., beliefs or intentions), whether stimuli were verbal or non-verbal, whether the paradigm involved the classification of single words, comprehension of stories, cartoons, animations or a competitive game, or whether mindreading was explicitly instructed rather than implicit in the demands of the task. This lack of systematic variability is clearly consistent with the view that the mindreading network is functionally undifferentiated, with all of the relevant regions equally likely to be involved in a given mindreading task.

However, there are several reasons why this view may be unduly pessimistic. Very few of the studies reviewed involved within-study (and within-participant) comparison of different mindreading tasks, so the conclusion that there is no systematic variability across tasks rests on statistically weak between-study comparisons. It is also the case that many of the mindreading tasks used in these studies are highly opaque with regard to the underlying cognitive processes. For example, in the Fletcher et al. (1995) study described above, the most obvious mindreading demand on the participant may be to judge that the robber falsely believes that the policeman knows he is a robber. But the task probably also involves reasoning about the intentions of the robber (to escape the scene, but not to resist arrest) and the policeman (to alert the robber that he has dropped his glove), as well as their emotions. Thus, even such simple scenarios can invite surprisingly rich mindreading, making it very difficult to generate clear comparisons between the neural activity associated with different types of mindreading. Moreover, because it is not clear what participants are doing in the mindreading task it is difficult to be sure that control tasks are well-matched. For example, although the "physical" control stories used by Fletcher et al. (1995) did require participants to make inferences beyond what was directly stated in the sentences (e.g., that it was a cat that the burglar scared, and that it was the cat that tripped the burglar alarm) it is not clear that these matched the cascade of mindreading inferences afforded by the mindreading stories. In research that followed from these original studies, significant progress has been made by using more simple stimuli and more closely-controlled comparisons, which has led to much clearer evidence of functional differentiation.

False beliefs versus "false" photographs

In a series of studies, Saxe and colleagues have followed the developmental literature in using "false" photograph tasks as a closely-matched control condition in studies of false belief reasoning. In Saxe and Kanwisher (2003, Experiment 2) participants read five types of short story describing false beliefs, "false" photographs, desires, physical characteristics of people (e.g., height and weight) and physical scenes not involving people (e.g., the arrangement of planets in a solar system). An example of a false belief and a "false" photograph story are given in Figure 4.2. Participants were instructed to read the stories and, in response to the test stimulus, press a left or right button to indicate the correct word to complete the sentence.

The authors examined which brain regions were more active during the false belief stories than during the "false" photo stories, and identified activity in three regions of the mindreading network – bilateral TPJ, PC and mPFC.[5] Here, and in several subsequent studies, Saxe and colleagues used this False Belief-"False" Photo contrast as a "functional localiser", enabling them to narrow their further enquiries to a subset of brain regions that are selectively activated for thinking about false beliefs and not for the similar problem of thinking about "false" photographs.[6] In Saxe and Kanwisher (2003) the criteria for the functional localiser meant that only areas in left and right TPJ[7] were singled out for further analysis. In these regions there was a significant neural response during the desire stories, but not the stories describing physical situations, or those describing physical characteristics of people. That is to say, regions activated more for false belief trials than for "false" photo trials were selectively activated when participants thought about mental states, not merely when they thought about people.

This interpretation was refined in a series of further studies showing dissociations in the function of these neural regions. Saxe and Powell (2006) used the same False Belief-"False" Photo localiser, and identified (among other regions) mPFC, bilateral TPJ, and PC as showing more activation on false belief trials than "false" photo trials. In the main experiment, participants read stories about people's physical appearance, their bodily sensations and their thoughts. PC and particularly left and right TPJ showed significant activity to stories about a character's thoughts, but not to the other stories, suggesting that TPJ was involved in processing

False belief story stimulus

John told Emily that he had a Porsche. Actually, his car is a Ford. Emily doesn't know anything about cars though, so she believed John.

Response stimulus:

When Emily sees John's car she thinks it is a: Porsche   Ford

False photograph story stimulus

A photograph was taken of an apple hanging on a tree branch. The film took half an hour to develop. In the meantime, a strong wind blew the apple to the ground.

Response stimulus:

The developed photograph shows the apple on the: Ground   Branch

False sign story stimulus

The sign to the monastery points to the path through the woods. While playing, the children make the sign point to the golf course.

Response stimulus:

According to the sign, the monastery is now in the direction of the: Golf course   Woods

Figure 4.2 Example stimuli from the false belief, false photograph conditions of Saxe and Kanwisher (2003), and the false sign condition of Perner et al. (2006). Participants read the text of the short stories, and registered their response by indicating either the left word or the right word in the response stimulus.

intentional mental states (like beliefs and desires) and not just subjective body states (such as hunger or sickness). In contrast, mPFC showed little activity to any story type. Saxe, Moran, Scholz and Gabrieli (2006) identified the same four neural regions using the False Belief-"False" Photo localiser, and found that a self-reflection task (participants judged whether adjectives applied accurately to themselves) showed activation in the mPFC and PC, but not in either TPJ. Saxe and Wexler (2005, and Young & Saxe, 2008) found that during a story sequence, right TPJ (R-TPJ) was particularly sensitive to precisely when information about a character's mental state was presented, and was sensitive to the re-use of this information to reconcile it with background information about the character or to make a moral judgement about the character's actions. Left TPJ (L-TPJ) and PC showed a similar though less neat pattern of activity, whereas mPFC showed much less activation overall.

Altogether, this series of studies suggests that regions of R-TPJ, and to a lesser extent, L-TPJ and PC, respond in a selective way to written stimuli involving mental states, and much less to stimuli describing physical situations, or people's physical appearance or their subjective body states. It is noteworthy that these regions respond to beliefs that are known to be true or false, irrespective of whether these states need to be inferred or whether they are merely described. This is analogous to the finding that 3- to 4-year-olds have difficulty on both standard false belief tasks, which require a belief to be inferred, and tasks where they must simply remember what they are told about someone's false belief. By contrast, in the above studies, mPFC either shows relatively indiscriminate responses to all kinds of social stories, or no response at all. This has led to claims that R-TPJ may be the location of a domain-specific module for mindreading (e.g., Leslie, 2005).

Further division: false signs and visual perspectives

Saxe and colleagues identified regions of the brain that had a relatively specific role in thinking about mental states, but recall from chapter 2 that there are legitimate reasons for caution about the comparison of false belief and "false" photograph tasks. "False" photograph tasks are clearly a good match for the general demands that false belief tasks make on memory and on thinking about abstract representations. But, they are not a minimally different control task because they differ in two ways from false beliefs: "false" photographs are not only physical rather than mental representations, but they are also not false. Perner et al. (2006; see also Aichhorn et al., 2009) adapted Saxe et al.'s stimuli, creating new versions in German and adding a false sign condition. The advantage of false signs is that they are genuinely false, and so, like false beliefs, generate a perspective difference with respect to the participant. A translation of a false sign trial appears in Figure 4.2.

For the contrast between false belief and "false" photo trials, Perner et al.'s new stimuli replicated the results obtained by Saxe and colleagues, with activation observed in TPJ bilaterally, mPFC, PC as well as in middle and superior temporal gyri. Importantly, the regions of R-TPJ identified by the False Belief-"False" Photo contrast showed little activity on false sign trials, consistent with Saxe and colleagues' claim that R-TPJ really is specific to thinking about *mental* states, rather than perspective problems in general. However, this study led to different conclusions about regions of L-TPJ (and a small region of mPFC) identified by the False Belief-"False" Photo contrast, because these regions were also activated significantly more during false sign trials than during "false" photo trials. This suggests that these regions were not selective for thinking about mental states, but were nonetheless selective for thinking about perspectives. This conclusion is consistent with the results from an independent study that examined neural activity during Level-2 visual perspective-taking (Aichhorn et al., 2006) and found strongest evidence for activity in L-TPJ rather than R-TPJ.

In summary, studies using "false" photo and false sign control tasks that are closely matched to false belief tasks have made it possible to break down the mindreading network, and provide evidence relating to questions about the cognitive basis of mindreading. First, these studies provide strong evidence for neural regions (especially R-TPJ[8]) that respond selectively when participants reason about mental states, compared to very closely matched reasoning tasks without mental content. Second, they suggest that R-TPJ is responsive to the content rather than the form of mindreading problems. That is to say, R-TPJ seems selectively sensitive to content-bearing mind-reading concepts (like a belief that the car is a Porsche) rather than to the form of the processing required. In contrast, other neural areas (notably L-TPJ) seem more selectively sensitive to the form of processing, and so to the fact that mindreading is just one among several kinds of perspective-taking problem. This apparent division of labour has an interesting correspondence with behavioural findings from young children, who at 3-years-old may talk about mental states and make simple judgements about their causes and consequences (e.g., Bartsch & Wellman, 1995), but may not pass false belief tasks, which test their appreciation that beliefs are perspectives (e.g., Wellman, Cross & Watson, 2001; Wimmer & Perner, 1983). It also clearly suggests that mindreading (or even just reasoning about beliefs) may be the product of interactions between multiple systems with distinct functions, rather than the task of a single homogenous module. Indeed, I shall argue below that even in combination, R-TPJ and L-TPJ are likely to underwrite just some of the demands of mindreading.

Limitations of subtractive methods and functional localisers: telling what is baby and what is bathwater

The method of subtracting activation observed during a control condition (such as a false sign task) from that observed in a condition of interest (such as a false belief task) is an essential tool in neuroimaging. As just described, this approach can be further extended by using a neat subtraction to localise functional regions of interest, which can then be examined more carefully for their responses to other kinds of stimuli. However, while this approach has clearly advanced neuroimaging studies of mindreading, it is vital not to lose sight of the effect of assumptions made along the way. Put simply, the False Belief-"False" Photo (or False Belief-False Sign) subtraction may be a very precise instrument, but it might be too precise for answering some questions. By using such a well-matched control task there is a danger of subtracting out processes (and thereby neural activations) that are critical for a proper understanding of our ability to reason about beliefs.

There are good reasons for supposing that this may be so from both a functional and a neuroanatomical point of view. Functionally, the literature on children and adults suggests that there is more to belief reasoning than having belief concepts. Reasoning about beliefs often requires abductive and deductive inferences and may well make a variety of demands on executive function. However, the whole purpose of the "false" photo or false sign tasks is to match false belief tasks in terms of the form of thinking that is required, and therefore most, if not all, of the demands that are likely to be made on reasoning and executive processes. So studying the neural activation surviving the False Belief-"False" Photo subtraction is not the obvious method for determining what cognitive functions have a role in mindreading. From a neuroanatomical perspective, it is striking that studies using the False Belief-"False" Photo localiser typically find a minor role for mPFC, and no role at all for Temporal Poles, despite the fact that both areas are heavily implicated in other neuroimaging studies of mindreading. It could be that this is just because the less specific control conditions used in other studies failed to exclude neural activation that was irrelevant for mindreading. But another possibility is that the False Belief-"False" Photo localiser is only identifying a subset of the functional and neural systems genuinely involved in mindreading.

Other investigations of the role of mPFC

One approach to this problem is to manipulate the presence or absence of a mindreading demand alongside another task of interest. Gilbert et al. (2007) had participants complete tasks that either required them to direct their attention towards a perceptually available object (e.g., pressing buttons for left/right turns as they mentally navigated around a simple, visually presented maze) or to direct their attention towards an internally-generated object (the same task but with an imagined version of the maze). Previous studies had shown greater activation in mPFC when participants directed their attention towards the visually presented stimulus than towards the same stimulus "in their head" (e.g., Gilbert, Frith & Burgess, 2005). The intervals between different phases of the task were either short or long, and in half of the experimental blocks Gilbert et al. (2007) additionally required participants to judge the timing of the intervals. This was the non-mindreading condition. For the other half of the experimental blocks, which made the mindreading condition, participants were told that an experimenter would be controlling the timing of intervals, and were required to judge at the end of the block whether the experimenter was being helpful or unhelpful (in fact the inter-phase intervals were fixed in exactly the same way in both the mindreading and non-mindreading conditions).

The study yielded two findings of particular relevance here. Firstly, the main effect of mindreading was associated with significant activations in mPFC and in right temporal pole but not in either TPJ. It may be significant that the mindreading judgement just required a general, somewhat emotive, evaluation of the helpfulness of the experimenter and did not require judgements about beliefs or desires (associated with R-TPJ), or about perspectives (associated with L-TPJ). Secondly, regions of activation in mPFC associated with mindreading showed no overlap with those activated during orientation of attention towards external stimuli in the main task.[9] One interpretation of this finding is that mPFC has a role in mindreading that is independent of its role in orienting attention. However, the authors also offer an alternative interpretation, that the role of mPFC is with orientation of attention in both cases, but that more caudal regions are specialized for performing this operation for social purposes. There is an interesting similarity here with debate about the function of R-TPJ, where close or even overlapping brain regions are implicated in mindreading and in switching attention away from features or locations that are irrelevant to the task at hand (e.g., Decety & Lamm, 2007; Mitchell, 2008).[10] In both cases it is unclear whether nearby regions of cortex are serving unrelated functions (for attention and mindreading), or whether they are serving related functions, with the content (social or non-social) over which the function operates causing variability in the precise neural regions activated.

Another alternative to functional localisers is to use a less restrictive subtraction method to identify areas associated with mindreading, and then examine what activation is conditional on an independent dimension of interest. For example, Mitchell, Banaji and Macrae (2005) measured neural activation while participants rated how pleased the subject of photographs were to have their photographs taken. From this they subtracted activation recorded while participants made non-social judgements about the same photographs (they rated the photographs for the symmetricality of the subject's face). The authors found activation in a region of mPFC (ventral mPFC) – an area activated in independent studies of self-reflection (e.g., Gusnard, Akbudak, Shulman & Raichle, 2001; Vogeley et al., 2004) – that was selective for social rather than non-social judgements. In a post-test, participants rated perceived similarity between themselves and the person in each photograph. Combining this with the neuroimaging results showed that ventral mPFC was proportionately more active for social judgements about individuals rated similar rather than dissimilar to self. Mitchell, Macrae and Banaji (2006) replicated this effect, and additionally found the inverse pattern for a different area of mPFC (dorsal mPFC), which was more active for social judgements about dissimilar others.[11] This study highlights the role of the mPFC in introspection on our own mental states as a potential source of information about the mental states of others, and the application of that information contingent on how similar a particular other person is to ourselves.

To test whether this reflects a fundamental property of mindreading, it would clearly be informative to know whether similarity-to-self has a similar effect on how we make judgements where self-other similarity has little or no relevance. This is the case in most of the simple false belief or visual perspective-taking tasks that have been discussed in earlier chapters, where any sentient agent with intact senses – however similar or dissimilar s/he was to self – would see, know or think the same thing. Although similarity-to-self has not been manipulated in such mindreading studies where the agent's similarity-to-self is irrelevant, it is noteworthy that several neuroimaging studies of visual perspective-taking (where similarity-to-self is irrelevant) have failed to find activation in mPFC (e.g., Aichhorn et al., 2006; Vogeley et al., 2004; Zacks et al., 2003), despite finding activation in some other areas in the mindreading network.

This raises the possibility that judgements about similarity-to-self may not be a fundamental process in all mindreading judgements. Instead, such judgements may be particularly important under conditions of uncertainty, where they help to narrow the set of all possible things that people might be thinking about to a manageable subset that are plausible (Jenkins & Mitchell, 2009). I shall return to this later, in chapter 6.

Is there life beyond the mindreading network?

The studies just described suggest that functional localisers may sometimes lead to the exclusion of important regions of the mindreading network. There is, of course, also a danger of excluding a yet broader set of neural regions that also serve important mindreading functions. The idea of a mindreading network that is distinct from other functions taking place in nearby brain regions is consistent with the observation that peak activations reported in studies of mindreading do not overlap with peak activations reported in other studies of language or executive function (e.g., Frith & Frith, 2003; Saxe, Carey & Kanwisher, 2004; but see Decety & Lamm, 2007; Legrand & Ruby, 2009). However, this conclusion should be treated cautiously in view of concerns that some mindreading-control comparisons are too restrictive, and eliminate activations corresponding to processes that are important for mindreading.

One way of tackling this issue is to run additional localiser experiments for other potentially relevant cognitive processes. Saxe, Schulz and Jiang (2006) used the False Belief-"False" Photo localiser to identify neural regions involved in mindreading and an executive function task to identify brain regions involved in response selection and inhibitory control.[12] There was almost no overlap between the brain regions identified by these tasks, which is consistent with the hypothesis that mindreading does not require executive function, but also with the hypothesis that the subtraction of "False" Photo from False Belief succeeded in removing any activation due to executive function in the false belief task. Importantly, the authors also ran a further, very simple, mindreading task, and examined whether activation was observed in any of the neural regions responsive to the executive function task. Compared to a simple baseline condition using the same visual stimuli, the mindreading task showed significant activation in every neural region involved in the inhibitory control task. This finding suggests that, in addition to neural regions that are strongly selective for mind-reading, performance of a mindreading task also recruits neural regions that are selective for executive function. This important conclusion would have been missed if the researchers had only paid attention to regions activated by the False Belief-"False" Photo localiser, suggesting once again that such localisers may be too restrictive for some purposes.

Vogeley et al. (2001) provide evidence that indicates one role that these executive processes might serve. This study adapted the mindreading and control stories employed by Fletcher et al. (1995) so that they described the experimental participant as an agent in the stories (for example, as the owner of the shop that the robber stole from). Patterns of neural activation during these stories, which raised the salience of the participant's own perspective, was compared with the patterns during the original stories, in which the participant's own perspective was less salient. Only one brain region was selectively activated in the condition where participants had to make mindreading judgements (e.g., about the robber) when their self-perspective was made salient by their own presence in the story; this was an area of right, lateral prefrontal cortex. This is not part of the "mindreading network", but is regularly implicated in studies of executive function and is one of the areas identified by the executive function localiser and recruited by mindreading in Saxe, Schulz and Jiang (2006). Thus, Vogeley et al.'s findings indicate that mindreading may require inhibition of self-perspective, and this need is met by generic executive processes.

Time-course and automaticity of mindreading

The poor temporal resolution of fMRI does not lend itself to the study of the time-course of mindreading, and, in chapter 7, I shall discuss the potential for new methods to cast light on this question. However, with fMRI it is, nonetheless, possible to test hypotheses about automaticity by examining whether stimuli that afford mindreading necessarily lead to activation of the mindreading network. This question was addressed in the study described above (Saxe, Schulz & Jiang, 2006), who presented participants with the same sequence of visual stimuli in a mindreading and a non-mindreading condition. The visual sequence showed an object initially moving into one box and then switching to another box. A cartoon character faced the boxes during the initial movement of the object. Half of the time the character saw the subsequent switch (so she had a true belief) but half of the time she turned away before the switch (so had a false belief about the object's location). In the mindreading condition, participants judged which box the cartoon character thought the object was in. These judgements yielded activations in regions of interest in the mindreading network. In the non-mindreading condition, participants viewed exactly the same stimuli, and judged according to the simple rule that if the character was facing the boxes at the end of the trial (i.e., the "true belief" condition) they should indicate the first box that the object went into, and if the character was facing away from the boxes at the end of the trial (i.e., the "false belief" condition) they should indicate the second box that the object went into. These latter judgements were logically equivalent to those made in the mindreading condition, and were made in response to stimuli that clearly afforded inferences about the character's beliefs. If mindreading inferences were driven automatically by such stimuli then one might have expected to observe neural activation corresponding to mindreading, even though mindreading was not necessary. In fact, none was observed.

Conclusions from neuroimaging studies

Neuroimaging studies provide evidence for a network of brain regions that are consistently involved in mindreading in adults, and whose maturation may be associated with successful mindreading in children (Sabbagh, Bowman, Evaire & Ito, 2009). There is strong evidence that regions of right temporo-parietal junction (R-TPJ) are activated in a highly domain-specific way by tasks with mindreading content. However, it remains unclear whether this corresponds to discrete representations or processes that are unique to mindreading, or to the execution of an entirely domain-general process (such as reorientation of attention) for the particular case of mindreading. But whatever the correct interpretation of activity in R-TPJ, the neuroimaging data provide clear reasons for thinking that other brain regions are also important. These regions are associated with functional processes that are definitely not unique to mindreading, and their regular recruitment in mindreading tasks contributes to the view that mindreading is a complex problem involving multiple processes.

For example, there is evidence that other neural regions – L-TPJ in particular – are sensitive to the perspectival nature of mental states such as beliefs, and are involved with processing other non-mental perspectives such as signs. It is also the case that brain regions involved in executive processes – right lateral prefrontal cortex in particular – appear to be recruited in the service of mindreading, with likely involvement in inhibiting, or resisting interference from self-perspective. Regular recruitment of mPFC and the temporal poles hint at a yet broader set of processes that may be involved in mindreading. mPFC may be involved in introspection, but is also regularly implicated strategically attending to externally available information, episodic memory and the on-line generation of event scripts. Temporal poles are often implicated in representation of personal and semantic memory, including rather abstract, schematic representations, as well as the integration of such information with more emotional information. These roles for mPFC and TP fit with a point I shall develop in chapter 6 where I discuss the dependence of mindreading on general abilities to parse situations for information that is relevant for mindreading.

Neuropsychological studies

Studies of adults with brain injury provide important evidence on two kinds of question about mindreading. Regarding anatomy, they can overcome the essentially correlational nature of neuroimaging methods, and test whether a particular brain region is actually necessary for mindreading. This, in turn, has implications for accounts of the cognitive basis of mindreading, though only to the degree that we are confident in associating particular neural regions with particular functions.

Regarding function, it is not necessary to assume neat mappings between cognitive functions and neural structures to recognize that different instances of brain injury can lead to dramatically different patterns of spared and impaired abilities. This makes it possible to test whether severe impairment to functional processes, such as executive function or language, necessarily leads to impaired mindreading. In practice, most neuropsychological studies use information both from direct tests of function and from neuroanatomy to reach their conclusions.

Can brain injury impair mindreading?

One story emerging from the survey of the developmental, comparative and neuroimaging literatures is that at least some aspects of mindreading are rather complicated, and probably depend on multiple functional processes and multiple regions of the brain. Moreover, it seems that mindreading tasks often make substantial demands on language, memory and executive processing that are unrelated to mindreading. It should be no great surprise, then, that brain injury often leads to social impairment, and that patients with brain injury often perform poorly on mindreading tasks. The challenge is to distinguish between the many possible reasons for error.

Brain injury can often lead to difficulty with language, either because of direct impairment to language, or because of the indirect effects of impaired memory or executive processes. Since many mindreading tasks depend heavily on language processing, several initial neuropsychological investigations tested patients with relatively mild levels of general impairment, who would be able to meet these general demands, but therefore used mindreading tasks that were relatively complex and subtle. For example, Stone, Baron-Cohen and Knight (1998) found that patients with frontal lesions made few errors on 1st order false belief tasks or 2nd order false belief tasks (testing comprehension of beliefs about beliefs), but that patients with orbito-frontal lesions performed less well than control participants on stories that required an understanding of social faux-pas. Several other studies have used stories involving comprehension of lies or ironic jokes (Winner et al., 1998), double-bluff, mistakes, white lies and persuasion (Happe, Brownell & Winner, 1999; Happe, Malhi & Checkley, 2001) and social misunderstandings (Channon & Crawford, 2000). Another used non-verbal cartoons, but required participants to give a verbal explanation of the humour, which, in the critical condition, involved describing a character's mental states (Happe et al., 1999).

Each of these studies demonstrated mindreading impairment in patients with brain injury compared with matched control participants, leading to claims about the importance of the right hemisphere (Happe et al., 1999; Winner et al., 1998), bilateral orbito-frontal regions (Stone et al., 1998), left anterior regions (Channon & Crawford, 2000), the amygdalae (Fine et al., 2001; Shaw et al., 2004; Stone et al., 2003) and temporal poles (Olson, Plotzker & Ezzyat, 2007). However, viewed together these studies do not lead to any consistent picture about which specific brain regions might be most important. One impediment to progress is that the demands these tasks made on mindreading may have been confounded with other demands on language comprehension (e.g., Surian & Siegal, 2001; Siegal, Carrington & Radel, 1996), executive function (Channon & Crawford, 2000) and memory (Stone et al., 1998), with the result that participants with different brain injuries might be making errors on these tasks for different reasons. Another difficulty with interpreting these findings is that the tasks used in these studies – like those used in early neuroimaging studies of mindreading – are rather opaque with regard to underlying cognitive processes. Thus, although these tasks might give a useful general index of mindreading abilities, they make it very difficult to test more finely grained hypotheses about subcomponents of mindreading, or about the role of language or executive function in mindreading.

In a series of studies we[13] set out to address these problems by devising simpler tasks that allowed us much better control over factors that are important for investigating the cognitive basis of mindreading. Of course, we are not the only researchers to have adopted this approach, and I will review other relevant studies along the way.

A task analysis of false belief tasks

Our research began with a task analysis of false belief tasks, which drew heavily on insights from developmental studies reviewed in chapter 2. Firstly, false belief tasks make a range of *incidental performance demands*. They are almost invariably verbal, and although this may be actively beneficial for children, it can pose an unnecessary burden on an adult with brain injury. They also necessarily involve following a sequence of events, and maintaining and updating relevant information, such as the location or identity of a hidden object, and whether or not characters in the story (e.g., Sally and Andrew) witnessed critical events. In our work with brain-injured patients we have tried to reduce or entirely eliminate language demands, and simplify the event sequences to reduce unnecessary difficulty. Of course, some incidental demands remained in the tasks. And so, where possible, we created closely matched control trials that made the same incidental processing demands but did not require mindreading.

Secondly, false belief tasks typically make specific performance demands. In particular, in most false belief tasks the participant knows the true state of reality (the true location or identity of the object) and must resist any interference from this knowledge in order to judge what Sally thinks or what she will do. This corresponds to the need to *resist interference from self-perspective* discussed above, and to "executive expression" accounts discussed in chapter 2. Although this demand is almost ubiquitous in false belief tasks, it is not necessary, and we manipulated its presence or absence in two different tasks.

Thirdly, false belief tasks necessarily require that the participant *take Sally's perspective* in order to judge what she thinks or what she will do. This was a constant across our tasks, and our interest was in whether we would observe impairment to this ability that was not due to a patient having difficulty with the incidental performance demands of the tasks or with resisting interference from self-perspective.

Manipulating self-perspective inhibition in false belief tasks

On the basis of this task analysis, we formed short video clips of false belief tasks adapted from those used in studies of 3- to 4-year-old children.

The *high-inhibition* false belief task was a standard unexpected transfer false belief task (e.g., Wimmer & Perner, 1983; Figure 2.1a). This required participants to infer Sally's false belief *and* also inhibit their own knowledge of the object's true location. In false belief trials, and in several types of control and filler trial, participants always made the same judgement: at the end of the sequence, which box would Sally open to retrieve the object? This principle was established in warm-up trials, after which, test trials could be administered entirely without language. A large number of test trials made it possible to assess an individual participant's performance against chance for false belief and control trials.

The *low-inhibition* false belief task was adapted from the task Call and Tomasello (1999) had used with children and chimpanzees (described in chapter 2; Figure 2.5a). On each trial the participant's job was to work out which of two boxes contained a hidden object, and this required them to interpret a clue from Sally who may have a true or a false belief about the object's location. On false belief trials, participants needed to infer that Sally had a false belief, but they did not need to inhibit knowledge of the object's true location, since at this point they did not know where the object was. We expected this to reduce the demands for self-perspective inhibition in comparison with the high-inhibition false belief task.

Executive function and self-perspective inhibition

An initial study using the reality-unknown false belief task (Apperly et al., 2004) found four (out of 12) patients who were not above chance either on false belief trials or on control trials that made similar demands on memory and inhibitory control. Thus, even though the task was non-verbal, and even though it was designed to reduce demands on self-perspective inhibition, it remained too difficult for some patients. It is noteworthy that all four patients had frontal brain lesions, and all four showed at least some impairment on standard neuropsychological tests of memory and executive function. This supports the general conclusion that at least one role of executive function and frontal lobe structures is in meeting the entirely incidental cognitive demands of false belief tasks.

More surprising were the results from one of the patients in this study, WBA, who was significantly above chance (11/12 correct) on low-inhibition false belief trials. WBA's success on the low-inhibition task was striking because he was impaired on many tests of working memory and executive function, including inhibitory control, and had a large right frontal lesion. This included regions of right lateral prefrontal cortex implicated in imaging studies of the contribution of executive function to mindreading (Saxe et al., 2006) and to self-perspective inhibition in particular (e.g., Vogeley et al., 2001). We were therefore very interested to know how he would perform on tasks that made greater demands on self-perspective inhibition.

Further investigation (Samson et al., 2005, 2007) revealed that WBA did, in fact, suffer severe interference from his own perspective when it was more salient. He performed below chance (1/12 correct) on the high-inhibition false belief task (i.e., a "standard" false belief task), despite performing at ceiling on control trials. That is to say, just like many 3-year-old children, WBA showed a strongly egocentric pattern of judging from his own point of view, rather than Sally's. This systematic bias towards egocentric responses was also apparent on a 3-option false belief task (described below), on a task that required the attribution of desires or emotions to the supporter of an opposing team in a football match, and on a Level-2 visual perspective-taking task (Figure 2.2b). Importantly, his success on the low-inhibition false belief task suggests that this egocentric pattern did not stem from an absolute inability to take someone else's perspective. Rather his difficulty was with resisting interference from his own perspective when it was salient to him.[14] WBA's case therefore provides strong converging evidence with the neuroimaging findings reviewed above, suggesting that executive function, and regions of right prefrontal cortex, are implicated in a specific aspect of mindreading performance: inhibiting self-perspective.

There was one intriguing exception to this general pattern, which was that WBA showed no sign of egocentric error on a test of Level-1 visual perspective-taking (see Figure 2.2a) (Samson et al., 2007). This is surprising, because in a Level-1 task, there is no a priori reason for thinking that self-perspective should be less salient than on a Level-2 task, on which WBA did make egocentric errors. This finding raises the interesting possibility that Level-1 perspective-taking is distinct from more sophisticated perspective-taking in terms of its cognitive demands. I shall return to this with evidence from neurologically intact adults in the next chapter.

Domain-specificity and the role of L-TPJ

Our initial study of 12 patients (Apperly et al., 2004; Samson et al., 2004) identified three with the same functional profile of impaired belief reasoning despite ceiling performance on closely-matched control trials. Inspection of these patients' structural brain scans showed that all three had overlapping lesions to left temporo-parietal junction, providing converging evidence with the results of neuroimaging studies that this region has a specific role in mindreading. In a further study we investigated just how specific that role might be by devising a false photograph task that was directly matched to the low-inhibition false belief task insofar as it was non-verbal, used very similar event sequences and made low demands on the need for self-perspective inhibition. As depicted in Figure 2.5b, on false photograph trials, a photograph is taken showing the object in its original location. Next the boxes are swapped. Then the photo is presented as a clue to help the participant find the object. Importantly, this task addressed the problem that the photographs in more conventional "false" photograph tasks are not in fact false. In our task, the photograph is genuinely false, and behaves more like a false sign, because it is presented as a clue to the object's true, current location. Thus, this task allows a strong test of whether a participant's errors on the false belief task are specific to the mindreading domain.

Findings from this false photograph task were very clear. All three patients with L-TPJ lesions showed exactly the same pattern of impairment as they had on the false belief task, with impaired performance on false photo trials, but above-chance performance on control trials (Apperly et al., 2007).[15] Thus, while these patients' errors could not be explained away in terms of general difficulty with the demands of the tasks (because they passed control trials) their difficulties did generalize outside of the very narrow domain of mindreading, to structurally similar reasoning tasks. This pattern is strikingly consistent with findings from neuroimaging studies, which show neural activation in L-TPJ on false belief, false sign, and, to a lesser extent, "false" photo tasks. It is clearly consistent with the conclusion that mindreading requires a domain-general ability to perspective-take, which is associated with L-TPJ.

There is more to perspective-taking than representing a perspective

It would be very nice if we could conclude that L-TPJ was the neural seat of perspective-taking (e.g., Perner et al., 2006) or meta-representation (Stone & Gerrans, 2006), and move on to other questions. However, there is a danger of creating an illusion of progress by substituting one thing we don't really understand with another. Although it would be interesting if there were domain-general abilities for perspective-taking, this would not tell us how perspective-taking was achieved or what the role of the L-TPJ might be in achieving it. In fact, data from a more detailed study of one of the patients with a lesion to L-TPJ works against this conclusion that the role of L-TPJ is simply with representing perspectives, and casts further light on the complexity of the problem of mindreading.

Of the three patients with lesions to L-TPJ, PF showed the lowest levels of general cognitive impairment, making it possible to test her on a variety of other tasks (Samson et al., 2007). To our considerable surprise, PF performed above chance when she was tested on the non-verbal high-inhibition false belief task.[16] This clearly indicates that her difficulties are not with the representation of perspectives per se, and certainly not with resisting interference from self-perspective.

To examine the origin of PF's errors in more detail we used a 3-choice false belief task[17] (Samson, Apperly & Humphreys, 2007). This involved a container with expected contents (e.g., a pizza box) that turned out to have an unexpected content (e.g., a passport) that was then swapped for a second unexpected content (e.g., scissors). Each trial followed the same principle, but had different boxes and contents. In trials where the target character saw the first unexpected content (passport) but not the second (scissors), there were two plausible ways in which PH might mistakenly identify the character's belief: by judging egocentrically (character thinks there are scissors in the box); or by judging that the character's false belief will be determined by what the character currently sees (character thinks there is pizza in the box). Interestingly, PF's errors were almost never egocentric. Instead, she often judged that a character would think the box's contents corresponded to the appearance of the box, not reality, and not the item that the character had seen in the box. This pattern contrasted markedly with the performance of WBA, who did show a strong tendency for ego-centric errors on the same task (Samson et al., 2007), as do young children on a similar task (Saltmarsh, Mitchell & Robinson, 1995).

A second notable feature of PF's performance on this task was that she made all of her errors in the first block of trials. After a short break she performed without error on the second block. This reinforces the conclusion that PF's difficulty is not with representing alternative perspectives per se, because she clearly was capable of a run of consistent, accurate performance on the second block of trials. But it makes her significant difficulties in the first block of trials and on the low-inhibition false belief task even more mysterious. Our speculation is that this offers an insight into the broader problems involved in perspective-taking and mindreading. While much of the literature on mindreading has focused on the representational problems posed by holding in mind someone else's perspective, researchers have tended to overlook the problem of how we work out what the other person's perspective actually is, or even how we decide to take their perspective in the first place. The low-inhibition false belief and false photograph tasks both require a decision about *when* to use the strategy of monitoring perspectives, because nothing in the task instructions actually directs participants to do so. The 3-choice false belief task requires participants to work out precisely *what* information is relevant for calculating someone's belief (is it the agent's past perceptual access or the currently misleading appearance of the box?). PF's performance suggests that both when and what judgements pose some difficulty for her. Her success on the 2nd block of trials in the 3-choice false belief task suggests that with time she could identify what information was relevant for the task.

I suggest that we might think of the 3-choice false belief tasks as a laboratory model of two circumstances for everyday mindreading. In very novel situations it may require effort to identify when we need to take account of other people's perspectives and what information is relevant. For PF this is modelled by the first block of the simple, but unfamiliar 3-choice task. In contrast, mindreading in highly familiar situations is less likely to require effort – everyday experience suggests that it is "just obvious" what others will think and why. For PF this is modelled by the second block of the task, once she has gained experience with its repetitive structure.

If PF's difficulty is with working out when to mindread, and what information is relevant when she does so, it still remains unclear whether these difficulties arise because of direct impairment to some high-level executive function, because of inaccessibility of relevant social knowledge, or for some other reason. What *is* clear is that PF's case does not provide support for the conclusion that perspective per se is represented in L-TPJ (e.g., Perner et al., 2006; Stone & Gerrans, 2006).

The role of syntax in mindreading

Our first study (Apperly et al., 2004) provided some validation of our strategy of using video-based rather than verbal stimuli. Alongside the video-based false belief task we also included a set of simple, six-line false belief stories, which included questions to check memory for facts about the story. Five of the patients who managed to perform above chance on control trials for the non-verbal false belief task (meaning that their performance on false belief trials could be interpreted with confidence) failed to perform above chance on control trials for the verbal task (meaning that their performance on the associated false belief questions could not be interpreted). For patients (though, as I said earlier, perhaps not for children), the presence of language in a false belief task could provide a significant additional burden on general comprehension of each trial.

As with executive function, we tested more specific hypotheses about the relation between language and mindreading by conducting a detailed case study of one patient who had a particularly striking language impairment. Two previous studies had tested two patients who showed disproportionately impaired syntax on standard neuropsychological test batteries, but appeared to perform well on false belief tasks (Varley & Siegal, 2000; Varley, Siegal & Want, 2001). We identified a further patient, PH, from the panel of participants visiting the lab in Birmingham, who, like those studied by Varley and colleagues, had a left-sided lesion that resulted in a similarly specific profile of impaired syntax, but left other aspects of language relatively spared. We extended previous work by devising new tasks that enabled us to test PH on specific aspects of language that appear to be most important in the development of mindreading, and by testing him on fully non-verbal 1st order and 2nd order false belief tasks (Apperly, Samson et al., 2006).

The relatively precise nature of PH's difficulties (and the sophistication of his coping strategies) are illustrated starkly by the contrast between two tasks. We had carefully designed a set of six-line false belief stories so that they followed a simple unfolding event sequence and did not involve complex syntax. In particular, they did not require comprehension of embedded complement syntax, associated with reports of mental states. What they did require was the ability to follow a verbally-described event sequence described over six lines, and to answer a verbal question about where the character with a false belief thought an object was located. Consistent with his relatively spared general language abilities and his ability to piece together the meaning of a story from what comprehension he could manage, PH scored without error on control trials and above chance on false belief questions, showing no sign of impaired mindreading.

This excellent performance contrasted markedly with PH's performance on a task that was a great deal simpler, but did require comprehension of embedded complement syntax. In this task he was read a single sentence, such as "He thinks there's a red ball in the box but really there's a blue ball in the box". He then had to accept or reject pictures that depicted what the man thought or what was really the case. PH made consistently correct judgements about the real colour of the object, but was not above chance at judging what colour the man thought it was. That is to say, when someone's false belief was represented within an embedded complement clause, PH was unable to understand what he had been told.

Several further tests confirmed this general picture. On a test of mindreading semantics that required much more subtle distinctions than those employed in Moore, Pure and Furrow's (1990) task, described in chapter 2, PH had no difficulty choosing to believe a speaker who offered him advice using mental verbs that implied more certainty (e.g., "I assert it's in here") compared with less certainty (e.g., "I suppose it's in here"). However, on tests of syntax he was unable to comprehend relative clause sentences (e.g., "The woman pushed the man that opened the box") or adverbial clause sentences (e.g., "Before the woman pushed the man, the man opened the box"). In all, PH was unable to pass tests of syntax that are passed by 3- to 4-year-old children, and this included just those aspects of syntax that have been specifically implicated in the development of mindreading.

PH's performance on non-verbal mindreading tasks confirmed his successful performance on the simple false belief stories. On our two tests of 1st order belief reasoning (the low- and high-inhibition false belief tasks) PH made just one error. To test the extent of his abilities we devised a rather complicated (but non-verbal) 2nd order false belief task. This is illustrated in Figure 4.3. The task resembles the low-inhibition false belief task, but an additional character (Granny in this illustration) takes the role of a participant whose job is to work out which box contains a hidden object on the basis of Sally's clue. On the critical trials, Granny thinks that Sally fails to see the boxes being swapped, so Granny thinks (falsely) that Sally has a false belief. PH's job was to predict which box Granny would open on each trial. (Just in case you haven't followed, on this trial, Granny will search in the box that Sally doesn't indicate, because Granny falsely believes that Sally has a false belief!) Despite the inelegance of this task, PH performed without error.

In all, PH's case is fully consistent with the earlier studies by Varley and colleagues, but makes the same point even more strongly. Adults' abilities to reason about beliefs can remain fundamentally intact despite severe impairment to syntax. The contrast with studies of children appears stark, and will be returned to in chapter 7. Here it is important to stress that this conclusion only follows for syntax. PH's case provides no evidence on the role of semantics in mindreading. It is also important to recognize that, although PH's ability to reason about beliefs may be fundamentally intact, his grammatical impairment deprives him of access to a great deal of everyday talk about what people think, as evidenced by his difficulty with

Figure 4.3 The non-verbal 2nd order false belief task used by Apperly, Samson et al. (2006). Granny must work out which box contains a hidden object on the basis of the clue from Sally. The participant must predict which box Granny will think contains the object. Critically, Sally sees Andrew swap the boxes (centre panel) but Granny doesn't see this. So Granny thinks (falsely) that Sally thinks (falsely) that the object is in its original location. So Granny will look in the box on the right.

simply comprehending and recalling verbally presented statements about what someone thinks. Thus, his case does nothing to undermine the fact that much of what we know of other people's mental states comes from what we are told. It does undermine claims that reasoning about false beliefs is fundamentally dependent upon syntax (e.g., Carruthers, 2002; de Villiers & de Villiers, 2000).

Is mPFC necessary for mindreading?

Recall from earlier in the chapter that medial prefrontal cortex (mPFC) is a brain region that has been consistently identified in neuroimaging studies of mindreading, and has often been singled out as the most important area (e.g., Frith & Frith, 2003, 2006). It is striking, then, that a patient with a very extensive bilateral lesion to mPFC showed no sign of impairment on mindreading tasks (Bird, Castelli, Malik, Frith & Husain, 2004). Patient GT passed 1st order false belief tasks, comprehended stories involving double-bluffs, persuasion, white lies, violations of social norms and detection of social faux-pas. She also performed at the same level as control participants when attributing mental states to simple animations involving geometric shapes. Note that these are among the very tasks that have demonstrated neural activation in mPFC in neuroimaging studies. Importantly, GT did show non-social impairments consistent with damage to mPFC, including impaired auditory working memory, autobiographical memory and planning abilities. On tests of executive function she showed inflexibility; for example, when she was read sentences that strongly cued one particular word she found it very difficult to generate an unrelated word. However, she was within the normal range on a variety of other executive measures, including tests of inhibitory control.

GT is a very interesting complement to the case of WBA, who did show impaired mindreading. At a functional level, both patients appear to retain at least the basic ability to reason about beliefs though GT is clearly also capable of more sophisticated judgements than WBA. WBA's distinctive mindreading difficulty is with inhibiting his own perspective, and this co-occurs with a general deficit in inhibition on non-social tasks. GT shows no such deficit in inhibition and no such deficit in mindreading. Moreover, at a neural level, although both patients have frontal lesions, GT's is largely restricted to bilateral medial PFC, whereas WBA's lesion extends to right lateral regions of cortex implicated in self-perspective inhibition and inhibition on non-social tasks. Thus, although both patients have frontal lesions there is no contradiction between their cases.

What does GT's case tell us about the functional and neural basis of mindreading? At a neural level, this depends critically on the extent of GT's mPFC damage. It is very difficult to be certain about this on the basis of structural scans, and Bird et al. do caution that GT's lesion may not overlap with every one of the various peak activations observed in mPFC in functional neuroimaging studies. But nonetheless it is clear that a large portion of mPFC is affected, and this must lead us to question claims that mPFC is necessary for mindreading. There are at least two possible solutions to this conundrum. As Bird et al., note, it might be that mPFC is necessary for the development of mindreading, but although in adults mPFC may show activity during mindreading tasks, its function (whatever it is) is no longer necessary.[18] Another related possibility is that mPFC does retain a necessary role in adults' mindreading, but not on the tasks used by Bird et al. (2004).

Recall from earlier that mPFC has been implicated in a variety of functions, including introspection, on-line formulation of event representations and controlled re-direction of attention. It seems highly plausible that such processes might be involved in mindreading, but they might be most important when thinking about particularly novel or complex problems, where background knowledge of social scripts does not yield a straight-forward answer. Although the mindreading tasks on which GT succeeded were relatively complex by the standards of laboratory tasks, we might speculate that it is possible to make such judgements – about simple faux-pas, white lies, double bluffs, etc. – on the basis of intact social scripts for interpreting the stories and an intact ability to represent other people's mental states as distinct from one's own. Based on the studies reviewed earlier, it seems possible that GT's lesion to mPFC would not have affected these abilities. This is, of course, rather speculative. But I think some speculation is warranted in the face of these surprising findings, and parti-cularly if speculating about GT's surprising success on mindreading tasks sheds light on when it is that very high-level planning and control processes might be necessary for inferring what others are thinking, and when accu-mulated knowledge of social scripts might suffice. Interestingly, this specu-lation receives some support from a recent neuroimaging study suggesting that neural activity in mPFC during a mindreading task was significantly higher when the belief or desire to be inferred was poorly specified by the context than when it was well-specified (Jenkins & Mitchell, 2009).

Conclusions from neuropsychological studies

Neuropsychological studies have the potential to show whether a function or neural structure is necessary for mindreading. Some findings converge strikingly with the evidence from neuroimaging studies. For example, the case of WBA suggests that executive processes of inhibitory control, involving right fronto-lateral cortex, are critically involved in resisting interference from one's own perspective but may not be necessary for simply representing someone else's perspective. Also consistent with neuro-imaging studies, there is evidence that L-TPJ is necessary for perspective-taking of all kinds, and is not domain-specific for mindreading. However, the detailed case study of PF indicates that it may be an over-simplification to suppose that the role of L-TPJ is to represent perspective, and hints at the hidden complexity of identifying what people will be thinking and when it is useful to do so.

The case of GT seems strongly at odds with the conclusion from neuro-imaging studies that mPFC is centrally involved in simple mindreading, but is consistent with mPFC being important for problems that are complex and ill-structured. In light of this case, it is noteworthy that no study has examined mindreading in patients with lesions restricted to R-TPJ, which neuroimaging studies implicate very selectively in mindreading. The clear expectation must be that lesions to this region should disrupt mindreading in a highly specific way. Indeed, this expectation is consistent with evidence suggesting that moral decision-making that requires taking account of a protagonist's mental beliefs and intentions is disrupted when neural activity in R-TPJ is disrupted with transcranial magnetic stimulation (Young et al., 2010). Nonetheless it would be reassuring to check the specificity of this disruption on a direct test of mindreading.

Finally, the results from three patients with selectively impaired syntax converge on the conclusion that grammatically structured representations are not necessary for thinking about beliefs, or even beliefs about beliefs. It would be very interesting to know whether an analogous pattern would be observed in patients with selectively impaired semantics.

Notes

1 A small number have used Positron Emission Tomography (PET). Like fMRI, PET depends on the haemodynamic response to neural activity, but PET measures the concentration of radioactively labelled oxygen, whereas fMRI measures the ratio of oxy- to deoxy-haemoglobin. Both methods have relatively good spatial resolution, but relatively low temporal resolution.
2 Some studies report Temporo-parietal junction, others posterior Superior Temporal Sulcus (pSTS). There is some controversy over whether these constitute separate effects, or whether they are different anatomical labels for the same observed pattern of neural activity.
3 Note that because the brain consists of two hemispheres, each of these areas appears on both the left and the right side of the brain. For the more lateral regions, such as TPJ and TP, left and right regions may show rather different patterns of activity and are often discussed separately (e.g., as L-TPJ and R-TPJ). In contrast, left and right regions of midline structures, such as mPFC and PC, are rarely distinguished in studies of mindreading.
4 This is not to rule out the possibility of convergent evolution of mindreading abilities in more distantly related species, as discussed in the last chapter.
5 Activity was also identified in right anterior STS and the frontal pole.
6 This is one way of reducing the level of correction that needs to be made for multiple comparisons across a very large number of voxels, thereby increasing the statistical power of fMRI investigations (see Friston et al., 2006; Friston & Henson, 2006; Saxe, Brett & Kanwisher, 2006 for a discussion of the merits of this method).
7 And right anterior STS.

8 It has been questioned whether such activations are really specific to mind-reading, or whether they reflect more general demands on selective attention (e.g., Mitchell, 2008). I think the fact that R-TPJ activation for False Belief survives the subtraction of activation for False Sign makes it very difficult to explain away this finding in terms of a confounding factor such as selective attention. However, it is possible that what is being identified in R-TPJ is selective attention to *mental content*. This is a point I return to below in discussion of the findings of Gilbert et al. (2007).

9 The mPFC regions associated with mindreading were more caudal in location whereas those associated with orientation of attention to external stimuli were more rostral.

10 It is noteworthy that L-TPJ has also been implicated in attention orientation in a role that complements that of R-TPJ by enabling participants to orient away from salient stimuli (Meverach, Humphreys & Shalev, 2006). The relationship between the role of L-TPJ in attention orientation and in perspective-taking has not yet been investigated.

11 The authors interpret this pattern as supporting simulation theories of mind-reading. I have argued elsewhere that these findings do not in fact discriminate between simulation- and theory-theories (Apperly, 2008), but the pattern of findings reported in these studies is certainly interesting, for the reasons discussed here.

12 The behavioural task was a stimulus-response incompatibility task where participants had to press buttons in response to objects on the screen that were either spatially compatible with the required button press, or spatially incompatible. The contrast between incompatible versus compatible trials yielded activation in bilateral intraparietal sulcus, frontal eye fields, frontal operculum, middle frontal gyrus, and additionally, right middle temporal gyrus and pre-supplementary motor area/anterior cingulate.

13 It will be clear from the authorship of papers reviewed that this was a thoroughly collaborative effort, involving a number of people, but most centrally, Dana Samson and Glyn Humphreys.

14 This pattern on laboratory tasks was also consistent with general observations of egocentric bias during everyday life.

15 In fact, all 11 out of the original 12 patients we were able to test showed similar patterns on the false photograph task to the one they had shown on the false belief task.

16 This was very reassuring for our interpretation of WBA's performance, described above, because it demonstrated a double-dissociation between the low-inhibition false belief task (PF failed, WBA passed) and the high-inhibition false belief task (PF passed, WBA failed). On the basis of this evidence it is difficult to argue that WBA's success on the low-inhibition false belief task was just a consequence of this task being generally easier than the high-inhibition task.

17 In Apperly et al. (2009) I described this as a novel task. Of course, I should have known better. It is particularly shameful that the authors of an analogous developmental study included a former colleague and my PhD supervisor! (Saltmarsh, Mitchell & Robinson, 1995).

18 Similar claims have been made for the amygdale (Fine et al., 2001; Shaw et al., 2004; but see Stone et al., 2003).

5　Evidence from adults

Research on mindreading in adults occupies a rather strange position in the literature. Developmental and comparative psychologists typically ignore adults because adults "pass" most tests of mindreading. Researchers of human language and communication typically assume that mindreading is a problem that other researchers have already solved. And social psychologists get cross because they have been studying many forms of mindreading for decades but have often been overlooked by other psychologists and by linguists interested in mindreading. Therefore I need to start this chapter with a brief discussion of work in human communication and social psychology, partly in order to glean important lessons from these well-established literatures, and partly to clear some space for the studies I shall discuss in more detail. Along the way I shall point out the potential relevance of work on adults for developmental and comparative psychology, and will return to this again in chapter 7.

Language and communication

Grice (1957, 1989) was very influential in pointing out that communication not only requires the encoding and decoding of verbal messages, but also the ability to make pragmatic inferences based on what speakers and listeners know and intend. Interpreting someone's offer to buy you a drink in a bar requires that you speak their language, but also depends on assessments of mutual knowledge ("doesn't she know I'm married?", "do I look desperate?") and assessments of intentions (is she inviting a conversation or making a proposition?). Grice's motivation was to provide a philosophical account of meaning, but his insights have greatly influenced psychological accounts of communication.

Imagine we arrive at the same staff meeting and I say "the cat's been sick this week". If you only attend to syntax and semantics then my utterance means nothing more than "there is a cat, and there is some period of time (of duration 7 days), and a cat has been sick in the period of time". In almost any circumstance this will fail to correspond with the communicated meaning. Clark and colleagues (e.g., Brennan & Clark, 1996; Clark & Marshall, 1981) have long argued that successful communication depends on speakers and listeners working within a "common ground" of mutually known information. On this basis you are entitled to assume that "the cat" refers to a cat that we both know about (and not just one I'm thinking of), and the deictic expression "this week" refers to our shared time-frame. Still, there are likely to be multiple cats in our mutual knowledge, so how do you know which cat I mean? Sperber and Wilson (1995) argue that listeners are entitled to expect speakers to be relevant, and speakers are entitled to expect listeners to recognize that they are trying to be relevant. Thus, given that we are in a staff meeting, you are entitled to assume I am referring to the head of department, who we jokingly refer to as "the cat", not my pet cat or any other cat we both know because these cats are not relevant in the current context.

This may offer a solution to the problem that utterances radically underspecify their meanings. But it appears to do so at the expense of a significant burden on mindreading, which seems necessary to generate, maintain and update representations of what is mutually known, and to calculate what is relevant in the current context. Moreover, all of this mindreading needs to be achieved quickly enough to keep up with an on-going conversation and efficiently enough that the primary objective of communication is not deprived of cognitive resources.

Sperber and Wilson (1995, 2002) propose that these needs are met by having a mindreading module, which operates quickly and efficiently. However, although they are surely right in identifying a need for mindreading in communication, their solution begs the psychologically interesting questions about how mindreading could be fast and efficient. A "mindreading module" is not an *explanation* for speed and efficiency. Rather, it *presupposes* that the task of mindreading (or at least some aspects of it) can be rendered in a way that makes it tractable to fast, efficient computation. Nobody has yet shown how this is possible. In fact, as I discuss in chapter 6, the "problem of relevance" looms just as large for mindreading as it does for communication.

Social psychology

There is a long tradition within social psychology of studying social cognition in adult participants. This includes topics that seem closely related to those discussed here, such as adults' ability to make inferences about the beliefs, desires and intentions of others (see e.g., Gilbert, 1998 for a broad overview). The lack of interaction between this literature and the research on mindreading that I have described so far is truly surprising. I have sometimes been told by social psychologists that research on mindreading is doing little more than reinventing the wheel (and worse, reinventing it with no regard for socially important issues, such as stereotyping or prejudice). Actually, I think there are some genuine differences.

Social psychologists have typically studied adult participants' inferences about traits and beliefs that are enduring characteristics of people (whether

Bob is an anxious person; whether he believes in capital punishment). Researchers' interest is often in how participants make such inferences on the basis of scant behavioural evidence or brief descriptions, the contribution that information about the target's characteristics (e.g., race, class, age or gender) makes to these inferences, and participants' ability to take account of the mitigating effects of context. For example, social psychologists have examined participants' ability to interpret behaviour (e.g., target person fidgets) on the basis of underlying traits (e.g., target is an anxious person). Participants are less likely to attribute a general trait such as anxiety if they know that the person fidgeting was being asked embarrassing questions, but taking account of such "situational constraints" appears to require executive resources (e.g., Gilbert, Pelham & Krull, 1988). In contrast, research on mindreading has typically studied beliefs and desires that are short-term characteristics of an agent and are normatively warranted. For example, in a false belief task, it does not matter who Sally is: provided she is a sentient, rational agent, she will necessarily arrive at the false belief that the object is in its original box. And this is not an enduring characteristic of Sally, but can change with further perceptual access.

It is not clear that the relatively simple judgements most often studied in the mindreading literature will have the same cognitive basis as the judgements studied in social psychology. This, of course, cuts both ways. On the one hand, there may be concepts and processes that are studied in the mindreading literature that add to the phenomena studied by social psychologists. On the other, I suspect that when researchers in the mindreading tradition extend their reach beyond relatively simple cases they might do well to examine the concepts and processes studied in social psychology. As already indicated, one particular lesson is that when participants make social judgements quickly, while busy with another task, or with little attention, their judgements are more likely to be based on fast-and-frugal heuristics, such as social scripts or stereotypes (e.g., Bargh, 1994; Gilbert, 1998). Taking account of contextual factors, or conforming to socially acceptable norms is time-consuming and cognitively effortful (e.g., Macrae, Bodenhausen, Schloerscheidt and Milne, 1999). I shall return to this in chapter 6. Another lesson is that there is substantial evidence suggesting that when making judgements about what others might feel (e.g., Van Boven & Loewenstein, 2003) or believe or know (e.g., Nickerson, 1999), participants often begin with their own feelings, beliefs or knowledge and adjust effortfully towards those of the target person they are supposed to be judging. This is thought to result in egocentric reasoning biases, which I discuss next.

Biases in adults' mindreading

Without time pressure, adults tend not to make errors on simple mindreading tasks, meaning that they cannot be tested on the tasks most typically used with children, non-human animals and patients with brain injury. One solution is to modify the tasks so that judgements are prob-abilistic or uncertain, and then examine whether adults' judgements are subject to systematic bias.

In an early study of this kind, Mitchell, Robinson, Isaacs and Nye (1996) presented adult participants with videos where Sally heard a message that contradicted her belief about the contents of a container (e.g., she thought the jug contained milk, but she was then told it contained orange juice). Participants were required to judge whether she would change her mind about what she thought was in the container on the basis of the message. This study found that when participants knew that Sally's original belief was true they judged it less likely that she would change her mind than when they knew that her belief was false. Note that this is illogical because the information known to Sally is the same in either case. What this study suggests is that adult participants allowed their own knowledge to contaminate their mindreading judgement about Sally's decision-making. A very similar study was conducted by Birch and Bloom (2007), who adapted the unexpected transfer false belief task so that, rather than judging where Sally would look, adult participants rated the probability that she would look in different search locations. In the critical conditions, Sally always had a false belief that the object was in one location, but on some trials participants knew precisely where the object really was but on other trials only knew that it was somewhere else. When adults knew precisely where the object really was they judged it less likely that Sally would search incorrectly compared to the condition where they did not know for sure. Once again, the adults' knowledge was irrelevant, but nonetheless resulted in biased mindreading. This effect was called a "reality bias" by Mitchell et al. (1996) and a "curse of knowledge" by Birch and Bloom (2007).

In fact these effects fit with a more general tendency for egocentric errors in adults' mindreading (e.g., Nickerson, 1999; Royzman, Cassidy & Baron, 2003). For example, Epley, Keysar et al. (2004) found evidence that privil-eged knowledge influenced how adults thought people would interpret ambiguous verbal messages or make difficult perceptual discriminations. Moreover adults were more biased by privileged knowledge when they had to make quick judgements, and less biased when they were given a financial incentive for accuracy. These findings led Epley, Keysar et al. (2004) to propose that adults make judgements about others by adjusting away from an egocentric starting point, and this adjustment is cognitively effortful.

Altogether these studies paint a consistent picture of egocentric bias in adults' mindreading judgements. They indicate that, when mindreading under conditions of uncertainty, adults often use the heuristic that other people will be like them, and then make corrections from this starting point, with varying degrees of success. Of course, this does not tell us on what basis those adjustments are made, but at least it gives a starting point for thinking about what processes might be involved. The pattern of egocentric bias also resembles the egocentric errors observed in young children's performance on mindreading tasks such as the false belief task. This has led to claims that the main difference between infants and adults is the ability to muster the cognitive effort necessary to overcome an egocentric bias (e.g., Birch & Bloom, 2007; Fodor, 1992; Mitchell, Currie & Ziegler, 2009). I think this is indeed likely to be one important development. However, as I suggested in chapter 3, I think it is very unlikely to be the whole story, not least because it offers no clear way of explaining how infants appear to perform better than older children on false belief tasks (and other mindreading tests) despite a distinct lack of executive resources (e.g., Apperly, 2009).

Speed and accuracy of mindreading

Although adults typically "pass" simple mindreading tasks, it would be very surprising if there was not residual variation in their speed and accuracy when making different mindreading judgements. Of course such variability is the stock-in-trade of much work in mainstream cognitive psychology, meaning that with the right kinds of task it should be possible to pose specific questions about the cognitive basis of mindreading in adults. In recent years some progress has been made in this direction. I will frame this section in terms of the approach that I have taken in my own work[1], and identify other relevant studies as I go along.

Our work has had three general motivations. Firstly, we have aimed to keep our tasks relatively simple. This makes it easier to devise well-matched control conditions, and reduces the likelihood of confounding mindreading with incidental demands on language and executive function. Secondly, our tasks tend to be closely related to those used in developmental research. This helps make the findings informative about development, as well as about mindreading in adults (e.g., Apperly, Samson & Humphreys, 2009). Thirdly, we have tried to decompose mindreading into component processes, including those involved in holding in mind information about mental states, in inferring such information from behaviour, and in using such information to make further judgements.

Holding in mind what people think: A non-inferential false belief task

One basic component of mindreading is to keep in mind what someone else thinks. People often tell us what they think, or report what other people think, and it is important to be able to retain this information and not get it confused with one's own knowledge or opinion. However, it is rare for this to be studied in isolation because many mindreading tasks confound the need to hold in mind what someone thinks with the need to infer the mental state in the first place, and often also with the need to use it to predict an agent's behaviour. Interestingly, the few studies of children that have isolated this demand – by simply telling children about someone's false belief – have found that children often mis-remember what someone thinks, and are biased to report instead what they know to be truly the case (de Villiers & Pyers, 2002; Flavell et al., 1990; Wellman & Bartsch, 1988). However, in children it is unclear whether this reflects difficulty with holding in mind what someone thinks (Flavell et al., 1990; Wellman & Bartsch, 1988) or with understanding the syntax (the embedded complement clause) of the reported false belief (de Villiers & Pyers, 2002). This ambiguity would be resolved in a study of adults, who would not have any difficulty understanding embedded complement syntax.

In our non-inferential false belief task (Apperly, Back, Samson & France, 2008) participants read two briefly-presented sentences. In false belief trials, one sentence described a male character's belief (e.g., "He thinks the object on the table is red") and the other described the conflicting reality (e.g., "Really, the object on the table is blue"). These sentences were followed by a picture probe either depicting the character's belief or "reality", and we measured participants' speed and accuracy to judge whether the picture corresponded accurately to the information presented in the sentences (see Figure 5.1 for a schematic of the event sequences for this task). False belief trials were compared with a minimally different baseline condition in which the sentences described unrelated aspects of belief and reality (e.g., "He thinks the object on the table is red / Really the object on the chair is blue"). The sentences and amount of information to be held in mind were very similar in the false belief and baseline conditions; the only clear difference was that in the false belief condition information about belief and reality was in conflict. We found that this conflict had a significant effect on performance. Participants were slower and/or more error prone in the false belief condition than in the baseline condition, and this

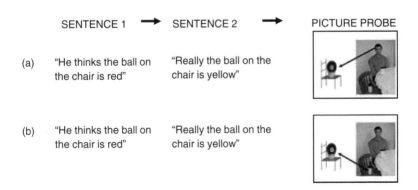

Figure 5.1 Non-inferential false belief task (figure adapted from Apperly, Back, Samson and France [2008]). On each trial we measured participants' speed and accuracy to judge whether the picture probe accurately corresponded to the situation described in the sentences. The figure depicts the event sequence from a False belief experimental trial, followed by (a) a Belief probe (ball in the box is coloured red), or (b) a Reality probe (ball in the box is coloured yellow).

effect was apparent on *both* belief and reality probes. That is to say, participants did not merely suffer interference from knowledge of reality when judging what the male character thought, they also suffered interference from knowledge of his false belief when judging reality. A second experiment found that this was not affected by the time available for reading the sentences, suggesting that participants' difficulty was with holding in mind the conflicting information about belief and reality, not with encoding this information in the first place.

These findings suggest that the very business of holding in mind what someone thinks carries a detectable processing cost when this conflicts with what we know. Given that participants only held this information in mind for a matter of seconds it seems likely that this interference arises in working memory. It would be interesting to know whether similar effects were obtained for longer retention intervals that required commitment of the information to long-term storage. This evidence from adults also provides indirect support for the view that children's errors on analogous tasks are due to difficulties with holding false beliefs in mind, rather than with understanding the syntax of belief reports.

Mindreading inferences

One of the central tasks in mindreading is to make inferences about unobservable mental states that are the causes and consequences of observable behaviour. If you see me walking out of my house into the rain you may predict that I will see that it is raining, that I would probably prefer not to get wet, and that I will therefore return inside to retrieve an umbrella. We have conducted two series of experiments targeted specifically at mindreading inferences, with results that appear to reflect the conflict in the literature from children, infants and non-human animals on the role of cognitive control in mindreading.

Evidence that belief inferences are not automatic

Although it is often stated as a matter of fact that belief inferences are automatic (e.g., Friedman & Leslie, 2004; Sperber & Wilson, 2002; Stone, Baron-Cohen & Knight, 1998) these assertions are not based on any direct evidence. Interestingly, indirect evidence from people's ability to make other kinds of everyday inference as they comprehend text or speech provides reasons for expecting quite the opposite. Although readers frequently make inferences to form a coherent "situation model" of a text they are reading, these inferences are spontaneous, not automatic. For example, McKoon and Ratcliff (1986) had participants read sentences such as "The woman, desperate to get away, ran to the car and jumped in". On a subsequent test participants were prone to judge that the word "drive" appeared in the sentence, when in fact it did not, suggesting that they had spontaneously inferred "driving" as part of their mental model of the event described. However, such inferences are not always made. Readers are less likely to make such inferences if they have low motivation for comprehension (e.g., if they don't think they will be asked detailed questions about what they have read) or if the inference requires the incorporation of information over larger tracts of text (e.g., McKoon & Ratcliff, 1998; Sanford & Garrod, 1998; Zwaan & Radvansky, 1998). Many mindreading tasks – such as false belief tasks – are based on short verbal stories, and there is no reason to suppose that inferences about Sally's belief should be exceptions to the general rule of non-automaticity. In an unpublished pilot study using false belief stories we indeed found some evidence consistent with this conclusion (Simpson, Riggs & Apperly, 2000). This motivated a series of further experiments focused on belief inferences, but using videos and pictures, which proved more easy to manipulate and control in experimental tasks than our original text-based stimuli.

Our rationale was that if we automatically infer an agent's beliefs when we see an agent behave, then such inferences will be made even when they are not necessary (Apperly, Riggs, Simpson, Chiavarino & Samson, 2006). We therefore presented participants with an "incidental false belief task" consisting of video event sequences in which they needed to monitor the location of a hidden object, but did not need to monitor where Sally thought the object was located (see Figure 5.2). To test what information participants were inferring and encoding we probed with unpredictable probe questions about what was happening in the videos, including questions about where Sally thought the object was located. We found that participants were significantly slower to answer probes concerning Sally's false belief about the object's location (which they could have monitored but did not need to) compared with probes concerning the object's location (which they needed to monitor on every trial). In a second condition we additionally instructed participants to keep track of Sally's belief about the object's location, thereby ensuring that they were encoding both the object's location *and* Sally's belief. This time participants responded as quickly to probes about Sally's belief as to probes about the object's location. Clearly then, there was no intrinsic difference in the time required to respond to probes about Sally's belief. Rather, the fact that responses were slower to probes about Sally's belief in the first condition suggests that participants were not automatically inferring and encoding Sally's belief.

Back and Apperly (2010) replicated this finding with false beliefs and found that the same pattern obtained when Sally had a true belief. This is significant because some authors have proposed that true beliefs are a "default setting" for belief ascription (e.g., Fodor, 1992; Leslie & Thaiss, 1992). Our findings suggested that this may not be so.

Back and Apperly's study also uncovered an unexpected phenomenon, which complicates the story a little, but ultimately produces further evidence suggesting that belief reasoning may occur spontaneously but is not

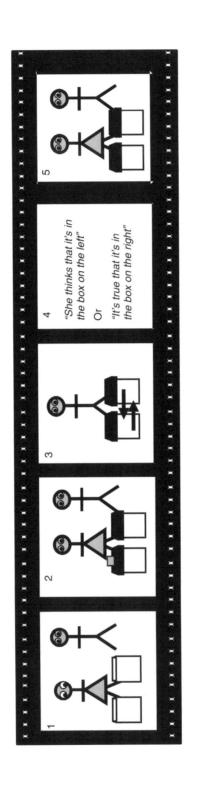

Figure 5.2 Schematic event sequence for experimental trials of the "incidental false belief task" (figure adapted from Apperly, Riggs et al., 2006). The participant's task is to locate the object hidden in one of the two boxes, and to respond "yes" or "no," to probe sentences (only experimental probes are depicted). 1. Sally looks in open boxes (so gains true belief about object's location). 2. Sally places marker to indicate location of object, then leaves room. 3. Andrew swaps boxes (so Sally has false belief). 4. Probe sentence (examples of a **Belief** probe and a **Reality** probe are shown, though only one was presented on any given trial). 5. Sally returns and participants are prompted to indicate location of hidden object.

automatic. We found that participants took significantly longer to respond to belief probes than to reality probes (about the object's location), whether Sally's belief was true or false. But we also found that responses to either type of probe were significantly slower when Sally's belief was false than when it was true. I must emphasize that this effect held for *either type of probe*: participants were slower to respond to belief probes *and* to reality probes when Sally's belief was false. We were struck by the similarity between this effect and what we had observed in Apperly et al. (2008) when we asked participants to hold in mind information about what someone thinks: in both cases there is a processing cost on false belief trials that affects judgements about belief *and* judgements about reality. The difficulty was that, for this explanation to apply to the current experiment, it would have to be that participants *were* in fact inferring Sally's belief spontaneously, at least on some trials, even when it was not necessary to do so. We reasoned that because participants were repeatedly probed for information about Sally's belief during the experiment they might have been more likely to make belief inferences, even though they did not need to. If so, then if we stopped probing for information about Sally's belief, participants should no longer make these spontaneous belief inferences, which should, in turn, eliminate any difference in response times to reality probes presented in false belief trials compared with true belief trials. This was indeed the pattern that we observed.

In summary, we find that when participants attend to a stimulus that affords an inference about a character's belief, they do not necessarily make the inference, and this is reflected in a processing cost (higher response time and error rate) when they are explicitly asked about the character's belief. Participants may spontaneously infer the character's belief, and if they do, then holding this information in mind results in interference when making judgements about related aspects of reality. However, spontaneous belief inferences require some motivation. In an experiment this might be the frequency of judgements about belief. In real life, I am sure that people are frequently motivated to infer what others are thinking. But in the absence of such motivation there is no evidence at all that beliefs are inferred. This pattern is wholly consistent with what would be expected from all of the other kinds of everyday inference studied in the literature on discourse processing and text comprehension. And it fits with the general view of mindreading as a domain-general inferential process that requires cognitive effort and that is unlikely to be undertaken without good reason.

Evidence that Level-1 visual perspective-taking is automatic

Of course, although claims that mindreading is automatic have been made without direct empirical evidence, they are well motivated. If infants and non-human animals have mindreading abilities, and if mindreading is to serve a role in on-line social interaction and communication, then we should not expect mindreading to be heavily dependent on strategic use of executive control processes. It would just be too hard and too slow. This leads to the expectation that we should be able to find cognitively efficient mindreading if we look in the right places. One obvious place to look is in simple visual perspective-taking, because there is good evidence of this ability in human infants and non-human animals, and it is the ability that has the closest link between observable cues (body orientation and eye gaze) and an epistemic mental state ("seeing"). If any of the mindreading processes I have been considering is a candidate for specialized, efficient processing based on domain-specific perceptual cues, it is Level-1 perspective-taking.

Our rationale (Samson, Apperly, Braithwaite, Andrews & Bodley Scott, in press) was essentially the same as for the series of experiments just described but with opposite predictions. If participants infer a simple visual perspective automatically then they should do so even when they do not need to, and perhaps even when doing so incurs a cognitive cost. In the basic paradigm, participants viewed a visual scene in which an avatar was standing in a room with dots on the wall (see Figure 5.3). Sometimes the avatar could see the same number of dots as the participant, but sometimes

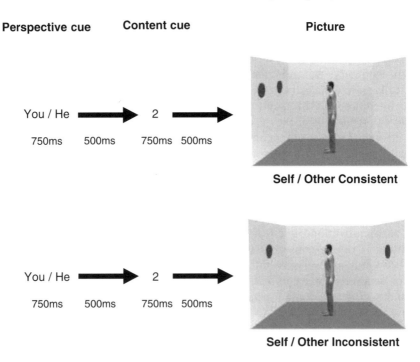

Figure 5.3 The Level-1 perspective task (figure adapted from Samson et al., in press). On each trial a perspective cue told participants whether to evaluate their own perspective or that of the avatar. Participants then judged whether the Content cue accurately described what could be seen from that perspective in the picture.

he saw fewer. On each trial participants were cued either to judge how many dots the avatar could see or how many they could see themselves.

We found that when participants judged what the avatar could see, responses were slower and more error prone when the participant saw more dots than the avatar, compared with when they saw the same number. This phenomenon of egocentrism had not been observed before in adults' Level-1 visual perspective-taking, but it clearly fits with observations of egocentrism in many other studies of mindreading. More striking for us was the existence of an analogous "altercentric" effect when participants judged how many dots they themselves could see: participants responded more slowly and with more errors when the avatar saw a different number of dots than when he saw the same number as them. It appeared that when judging their own perspective participants might also be working out the avatar's perspective, which then interfered with their judgements.

We checked some alternative explanations of this effect. It would not have been interesting if participants were slower to respond on perspective-incongruent trials merely because the dots on the wall were further apart on these trials. A second experiment kept the spacing of the dots constant across perspective-congruent and perspective-incongruent trials, but still found both egocentric and altercentric effects. Likewise, it would not have been interesting if slow responses on perspective-incongruent trials were merely due to participants finding it difficult to enumerate the full set of dots when the avatar was standing in the middle of the set. Fortunately, on a sub-set of perspective-incongruent trials the avatar saw no dots, so the entire set of visible dots was in a single group behind the avatar. Results on these trials were the same as for the entire data set. Thus, it seemed that the effects could not easily be explained away.

It is noteworthy that the event sequence for test trials began with a cue telling participants whose perspective they should judge. Thus, on trials where they were cued to judge their own perspective they had the opportunity to ignore the avatar's perspective entirely. The fact that they still suffered interference from the avatar's perspective suggests that they were not able to stop themselves from inferring what he saw. However, this was only relatively weak evidence that the process of inferring the avatar's perspective is automatic. Another possibility was that this "automaticity" was an artefact of trial-to-trial switching between perspectives. Thus, in a further experiment we conducted a much stronger test in which participants judged the same stimuli, but were only ever required to judge their own perspective throughout the entire experiment. In this case there is simply no way that interference from the avatar's perspective could be a carry-over effect from the requirement to judge the avatar's perspective on other trials. In fact, although the effect was now smaller, we still observed interference from the avatar's incongruent perspective when participants judged their own perspective. A similar effect was not observed on trials where the avatar was replaced with a featureless grey bar of similar dimensions, confirming the conclusion described above, that the effect of the avatar was not merely due to its disruption of the array of dots on perspective-incongruent trials.

In summary, we found evidence that participants calculated the avatar's perspective even when they did not need to, even when they were never told to, and even though calculating his perspective made it more difficult for them to judge their own perspective. These "altercentric" effects were apparent when participants' explicit task was to judge their own perspective, suggesting that altercentric interference may be an indirect or implicit test of perspective-taking. These effects are compatible with evidence suggesting that people automatically process gaze direction (e.g., Driver et al., 1999) and evaluate the objects of gaze dependent upon the expression on the face that is gazing at the objects (Bayliss, Paul, Cannon & Tipper, 2006). But altercentric effects go beyond such findings by suggesting that we actually calculate "what is seen" when someone gazes. It is notoriously difficult to demonstrate that a cognitive process is automatic (e.g., Moors & De Houwter, 2006), and it is far from clear that these effects would meet the most stringent tests of automaticity. However, what matters for my current purposes is that the cognitive characteristics of these effects appear very different from those we found in our studies of belief reasoning.

Comparison with studies of infants and non-human animals

Both human infants and non-human animals show evidence of tracking what an agent sees (Level-1 perspective-taking). The findings just described suggest that analogous processes are "cognitively efficient" in human adults, in the sense they are made quickly enough to cause interference with on-line judgements about self-perspective, and they are relatively independent of cognitive control processes (this latter point is reinforced by findings from a dual-tasking study, described later in this chapter). Thus, there appears to be some convergence between what infants and non-human animals can do, and what human adults can do efficiently. However, the findings from adults appear to show something that has not yet been demonstrated in studies of infants or non-human animals: the efficient calculation of *mental content* for the avatar, which results in interference when judging self-perspective. This is important because, as described in chapter 3, the ascription of mental content is a critical criterion for deciding whether someone is engaged in mindreading or whether they are just reasoning about behaviour. I shall return to this in chapter 7.

Can mindreading inferences be both automatic and non-automatic?

I think they can. Indeed, I shall argue in chapter 6 there are good reasons why adult humans *should* have different ways of making mindreading inferences, which make different trade-offs between flexibility and efficiency. If this is correct then Apperly, Riggs et al.'s (2006) "incidental belief task" summarized earlier could be seen as a laboratory model for studying mindreading inferences about belief, knowledge and perceptions *as such*. These inferences would conform (at least approximately) to the normative model, whereby mindreading involves the ascription to an agent of a mental attitude with propositional content. But the flexibility entailed by this must come with some requirements for cognitive effort. In contrast, the alter-centric interference effect observed in the Level-1 perspective tasks (Samson et al., in press), could be seen as a laboratory model for studying relatively effort-less mindreading inferences. If this is correct then we should predict that such inferences will not meet the requirements of the normative model, and might only be made on the basis of certain perceptual cues, for certain kinds of agent and with certain limited kinds of content. This is clearly fertile ground for further research, and will be discussed further in chapter 7.

Mindreading use

Inferring mental states and being able to hold this in mind is all very well. But this would all be rather pointless if information about people's mental states was not put to use in explaining, predicting and interpreting their behaviour.

Deductive inferences about beliefs and desires

In the standard unexpected transfer false belief task it is easy to overlook the fact that Sally's false belief is not the only determinant of her behaviour. In fact it is only in combination with Sally's desire to find her object that we can use knowledge of her false belief to predict where she will look. Of course, people do not always have positive desires for objects, and may therefore wish to avoid them rather than find them. Recall from chapter 2 that this problem is not entirely trivial for children, who find it significantly harder to predict Sally's behaviour when she has a false belief and a desire to avoid an object than when her desire is to find it (e.g., Cassidy, 1998; Friedman & Leslie, 2004; Leslie & Polizzi, 1998; Leslie, German & Polizzi, 2005).

We tested adults on a similar task (Apperly, Warren, Andrews, Grant & Todd, in press). Participants predicted which of two boxes would be opened by Andrew (see Figure 5.4). On every trial there was food hidden in one of the two boxes. Sometimes Andrew liked the food, in which case he would try to obtain it. Sometimes he disliked the food, in which case he would try to avoid it. On each trial, participants read three sentences telling them where the food was, where Andrew thought it was (this could be true or false) and whether or not he liked the food. This generated four possible combinations of true versus false belief crossed with positive versus negative desire. After reading the sentences a picture appeared with Andrew seated

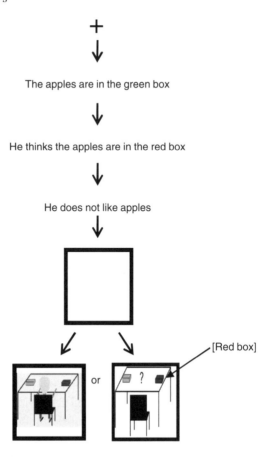

Figure 5.4 The belief-desire reasoning task (figure adapted from Apperly, Warren et al. (in press). On each trial participants saw a fixation cross followed by three sentences describing which box contained the hidden food, where the character in the chair thought the food was located, and whether or not he liked the food. A black square warned of the following response cue. Experimental response cues (left-most response cue in diagram) required participants to judge which box Andrew would open. Catch trials (right-most response cue) required participants to judge where the food was located.

in front of the two boxes, and we measured participants' speed and accuracy to judge which box he would open. We found that adults responded more slowly and with more errors when Andrew had a false belief rather than a true belief, and were also slower when he had a negative desire than when he had a positive desire. This pattern is directly analogous to that observed in the age at which children first pass these different combinations of belief-desire reasoning.

In terms of the demands made on mindreading, this design obviated any need for participants to make abductive inferences about Andrew's belief or desire.[2] Of course, participants did need to hold all of this information briefly in mind. Importantly, in addition, participants needed to deduce from the given information what Andrew would do. It is not possible to say whether the origin of participants' difficulty on false belief trials was with holding this information in mind (consistent with our non-inferential false belief task, described above), or whether it was with reasoning how Andrew would behave on the basis of his belief. However, the effect of desire is easier to interpret. There is no particular reason to expect that Andrew's negative desires were any more difficult to hold in mind than his positive desires. Therefore, we may suppose that at least the effect of desire was due to differences in how easily participants were able to deduce Andrew's search behaviour.

Using mindreading inferences in referential communication

As described in the first section of this chapter, communication seems to require mindreading inferences to monitor what information is mutually available in the "common ground" of speaker and listener. However, direct studies of the use of mindreading inferences during communication provide a mixed picture of adults' abilities.

Keysar, Barr, Balin and Brauner (2000) devised a communication game during which experimental participants followed the instructions of a "director" to move items around a grid. Figure 5.5 depicts participants' view, with the director positioned on the opposite side of the grid. All items in the grid were visible to participants, but covers on some slots in the grid meant that the director could not see items in these slots. This created a perspective difference between the participant and the director. However, this itself was not expected to pose any conceptual difficulty for adult participants, since even 2-year-old children can solve visual perspective problems of this "Level-1" type. Keysar et al.'s question was whether adults could *use* such information about the director's perspective to interpret his instructions. For example, for the grid in Figure 5.5, the director might instruct the participant to "move the small ball down one slot". Because the director does not know about object y, the smallest ball in the grid, he must be referring to object x, which is the smallest ball in his view. Keysar et al. found that adults frequently failed to take the director's perspective into account, and moved the object that was the best fit for the director's instruction from their own point of view (i.e., object y) on a significant proportion of trials. Moreover, the record of where participants looked prior to moving an object revealed that they frequently considered the object that the director did not know about, even when they went on to move the correct object. Keysar, Lin and Barr (2003) found that the same pattern extended to cases where the director was not merely ignorant about objects in the closed slots but had a false belief about their identity.

Figure 5.5 Illustrative stimulus from Apperly, Carroll et al. (in press), with added x and y labels for this figure. Participants were instructed by the director to move items around the grid. Critical instructions, such as "Move the small ball down one slot" required participants to select ball x, which could be seen by the director, and ignore object y, which could not be seen by the director.

These findings suggest that adults, who are fully capable of making the necessary mindreading inferences about the director, and who are given ample time in the experiment to make these inferences, nevertheless do not use this information reliably for communication. However, they give little indication about why adults have such difficulty. In Apperly, Carroll et al. (in press) we found that adults' difficulty did not seem to be with the need to switch from their own perspective to the perspective of the director. Using a computer-based task that simulated Keysar's original "live" communication task, we found that participants were error-prone when they had to take the perspective of the director, consistent with Keysar et al. (2000, 2003). However, they were no worse when we explicitly required participants repeatedly to switch perspectives, by introducing a second director who shared the participant's own perspective, and then posing instructions from this informed director immediately before instructions from the original, ignorant director.

In a further experiment, we tested whether adults' difficulty was with general demands of the task, such as processing which objects in the grid were available referents or inhibiting accidental selection of the incorrect object (object y). We created a non-mindreading condition in which the director was removed from the screen and participants were instructed to follow the simple rule that they should avoid objects in the closed slots of the grid as they followed the instructions played on the computer. This meant that they faced the same grids of objects, needed to avoid the same sub-set of objects, and followed the very same instructions, but critically, they were not having to consider anyone's perspective. Participants in this non-mindreading condition made significantly fewer errors than participants in the mindreading condition. This suggests that holding in mind and using information about the speaker's perspective makes demands over and above the general demands of the task.

Taken on their own these studies would suggest that adults are rather poor at using information about a speaker's knowledge or belief to constrain interpretations of what they say. In all studies adults showed the ability to use such information, but they clearly struggled to use it reliably. However, several other studies suggest that children and adults may use such information more effectively in at least some circumstances. Nadig and Sedivy (2003) tested 5- and 6-year-olds on a similar referential communication task using a smaller 2×2 grid with just one hidden object, and found that children were much more likely to look at potential referent objects for the speaker's message that the speaker could see, compared to objects that he could not see. Using a similar task, Nilsen and Graham (2009) found that even 4-year-olds often selected the correct referent object in such circumstances. Again, using a simpler communication task, Hanna, Tannenhaus and Trueswell (2003) found that adult communicators were more likely to look at items that both they and the speaker could see, though they nevertheless did look at objects that only they could see, suggesting that such objects were not entirely excluded as potential referents (see also Barr, 2008). Notably, the studies using eye tracking methods not only showed sensitivity to the speaker's perspective but showed this to be apparent very quickly, within no more than 500ms of the onset of the critical word referring to the object (Nadig & Sedivy, 2001) or even before onset (Barr, 2008).[3]

So why is it that children and adults are better at using information about a speaker's mental states in some circumstances compared with others? An obvious clue comes from the fact that studies showing the best performance have used systematically smaller arrays of objects, with a single hidden item. So it seems plausible that taking account of a speaker's ignorance of a single item falls easily within the general executive or attentional capacity of children and adults, but errors become increasingly apparent as the task becomes more complex and makes greater demands on these resources. It is important that such hypotheses about a role for executive function in mindreading are tested directly, and it is to such studies that I turn next.

Individual differences in executive function and mindreading

One way of testing whether executive functions are involved in mindreading in neurologically intact adults is to test whether there is a relationship between performance on tests of executive function and performance on mindreading tasks. Only a very few existing studies have used this approach. Maylor et al. (2002) found that a relative deficit in mindreading performance in elderly participants could not be explained by participants' performance on two measures of executive function. However, the mind-reading task used in this study involved the comprehension of stories involving white lies, double-bluffs and other relatively varied mindreading problems. As discussed in the last chapter, although comprehending these stories undoubtedly involves mindreading in some way, it is very difficult to identify specific processes that might be common across stories. This makes it difficult to interpret the absence of a clear relationship with executive function.

German and Hehman (2006) overcame this problem by using stories that made systematically different demands on participants' reasoning about beliefs (that could be true or false) and desires (that could be positive or negative).[4] Performance on this task was correlated with measures of working memory, processing speed and inhibitory control, but in regression analyses, processing speed and inhibitory control were the more important factors. This study provides support for the idea that general processing factors, including executive function, contribute to an individual's performance on a mindreading task. However, because German and Hehman's task required participants to infer a character's beliefs from given information, hold this information in mind along with information about the character's desires, and use these pieces of information to predict the character's action, it is not possible to say precisely where executive function has a role in mindreading: it could be with just one of these sub-processes, some combination of them, or all three.

In recent work we have addressed this issue to some degree by testing the contribution of executive function to performance on the communication game used by Apperly, Carroll et al. (in press; Keysar, Lin & Barr, 2003). Qureshi (2009) found that adults' egocentric errors – reflecting a failure to use information about a speaker's visual perspective – were correlated with executive tasks that required participants to hold in mind and select between alternative responses, but were not correlated with a variety of other tests of inhibition and working memory.

Using a secondary task to interfere with mindreading

In the last chapter I described evidence that patients whose brain injury has affected their executive function sometimes show distinctive impairments in mindreading. It would be neat if we could induce a similar effect in healthy participants by having them perform a task that taxes their executive function at the same time as they undertake a mindreading task. In practice, this approach poses significant methodological challenges. Nonetheless it has been adopted in some recent studies.

McKinnon and Moscovitch (2007) found that concurrent performance of a working memory task disproportionately impaired performance on a story-based mindreading task that required inferences about white lies and double-bluff (Happe, 1994b) compared with a non-mindreading control condition that did not require such inferences. Using similar materials, Bull, Phillips and Conway (2008) found impaired performance of both mindreading and non-mindreading trials when participants concurrently performed tasks that required inhibition, switching and updating. Although these studies clearly break new ground in studying mindreading with dual-task methods, they illustrate three difficulties that need to be overcome in further work. First, the most obvious difficulty is that a secondary task may well disrupt participants' ability to handle components of the mindreading task that have nothing specifically to do with mindreading. This seems to be the case in the Bull et al. study, where the secondary tasks disrupted performance on both mind-reading and non-mindreading trials. Second, it is not entirely clear whether the pattern of selective mindreading disruption reported by McKinnon and Moscovitch (2007) is actually inconsistent with the non-selective pattern of disruption (on both mindreading and non-mindreading tasks) reported by Bull et al. (2008). This is because executive function is multi-faceted, and any given executive task typically makes multiple executive demands. This means it is difficult to tell whether the secondary "working memory" task used by McKinnon and Moscovitch makes highly similar or rather different demands to the three different executive tasks used by Bull et al. Third, as already discussed, complex mindreading tasks, such as Happe's "stories" task, are useful for generating variable performance in typical adults, but are rather opaque with regard to what mindreading processes are actually being assessed. Therefore, although these studies provide general support for the view that performance of mindreading tasks requires executive function, it is difficult to make more specific conclusions.[5]

One recent study that does allow more specific conclusions was conducted by Qureshi, Apperly and Samson (2010). In this study participants undertook the Level-1 visual perspective-taking task described earlier (Samson et al., in press), either on its own or at the same time as a task that taxed executive function.[6] The results suggested that the secondary task exaggerated the egocentric effect observed on trials where participants explicitly judged the avatar's perspective. Critically, the secondary task also exaggerated the altercentric effects observed on trials where participants judged what they themselves could see. Recall that altercentric interference arises when participants "automatically" calculate the perspective of the avatar even though they do not need to. If this irrelevant processing of the avatar's perspective was demanding of general executive resources, then the secondary task should have disrupted this processing, and the altercentric effect should have been reduced or eliminated. The fact that the altercentric effect was actually exaggerated suggests that calculation of the avatar's perspective is not only relatively automatic, but also relatively independent of general executive resources. Instead, the pattern of exaggerated egocentric *and* alter-centric interference when performing a secondary executive task suggests that executive resources are required for resolving the interference between self and other perspectives, which are both available automatically.

Summary

Unlike young children, most adult participants are clearly capable of mindreading, but they can still be very informative subjects for investigation. Just as psycholinguists find adults' competence with language no barrier to testing the cognitive basis of their linguistic abilities, so research on mindreading can benefit from studying adults. Indeed, testing adults who are largely co-operative, able to follow task instructions, and willing to sit through tens or hundreds of experimental trials opens up a range of methods that cannot be used with other participants. The potential of these approaches is only just being explored.

The studies conducted so far provide clear evidence that many aspects of mindreading in adults remain subject to systematic egocentric biases, and are relatively effortful and demanding of cognitive resources for executive function. This is reflected in slower response times when adults perform accurately, but equally, adults do continue to make mindreading errors, even on conceptually simple tasks. The data from adults show clearly that having the conceptual capacity to understand a particular task is no guarantee that this capacity will be used when appropriate.

Contrasting with this is evidence that at least some mindreading, for simple cases such as Level-1 perspective-taking, is actually performed in a way that is cognitively efficient and relatively automatic. There are many reasons to think that mindreading must have these properties, at least some of the time, and the way in which this might be achieved will be discussed further in chapter 6.

Finally, the research summarized in the current chapter brings together a set of distinctions that have cropped up in earlier chapters, between processes involved in inferring mental states, those used in holding such information in mind, and those necessary for putting this information to use in explaining or predicting behaviour. I do not suppose that these are definitive categories, but I do think they can function as a starting taxonomy of mindreading processes. Such a taxonomy enables us to ask more precise questions about the demands of particular tasks, and the way in which those demands might be met by different aspects of memory and executive function and by more specialized mindreading processes.

Notes

1 Once again, all of this work has been conducted with collaborators, especially Dana Samson.

2 This was significant because the most common interpretation of the combinatorial effect of belief and desire on children's reasoning traces the origin of children's difficulties to the need to infer a belief as part of the task (e.g., Leslie, German & Polizzi, 2005). This account cannot easily explain our findings.

3 Interestingly, however, Barr (2008) goes on to show that although from very early in processing adults pay less attention to objects in privileged ground compared with those in common ground, they are much slower to integrate this information with the Director's instructions in order to resolve referential ambiguities.

4 This, of course, was the inspiration for the study by Apperly, Warren et al. (in press) described above. The important difference between these studies, and the reason why I described our study in the earlier section, is that German and Hehman's task required beliefs to be inferred from the story, whereas Apperly et al.'s task eliminated this inferential demand.

5 Newton and de Villiers (2007) employed a dual-task method to examine whether false belief reasoning required language. However, it is difficult to tell whether this study succeeded in isolating demands on language from demands on executive function (Apperly, Samson & Humphreys, 2009). My own experience is that these are tough problems to solve. We have tried repeatedly to use similar dual-task methods with the non-verbal high-inhibition and low-inhibition false belief tasks used successfully in our studies of adults with brain injury. We found similar interference on both false belief and matched control trials, but it was impossible to tell whether this was due to an entirely non-selective pattern of interference, or whether the effects of interference with belief reasoning were being washed out by general interference, or whether there was actually no interference with belief reasoning.

6 The task required participants to tap once when they heard two beeps and twice when they heard one beep, continuously during their performance of the perspective-taking task. This makes some demands on working memory – to remember the task rule and the number of beeps in the stimulus – and also on inhibitory control, which is required to avoid a prepotent tendency to tap the same number of beeps heard in the stimulus.

6 The cognitive basis of mindreading: A "two-systems" account

Overview

The current chapter starts by drawing together some general lessons from the empirical literature reviewed in chapters 2–5. One important but rather worrying lesson will be that we seem to have good reasons for reaching contradictory conclusions on several key questions about the processing characteristics of mindreading, and the relationship between mindreading, language and executive function. This justifies some careful thinking about how mindreading is possible at all, which I first mentioned briefly in chapter 1. The final section will bring these strands together to sketch a model of how mindreading is achieved.

My basic proposition is that adult humans have "two-systems" for mindreading. Simple ascriptions of perception, knowledge and belief are achieved via cognitively efficient "low-level" processing modules, at least some of which develop early and may be shared by humans and non-human animals. In contrast, more complex and flexible, "high-level", mindreading makes use of the same general knowledge and inferential processes available for any other reasoning; it is more cognitively effortful and slower to develop than modular processing, and may be unique to humans. The implications of this model for further research in children, non-human animals, cognitive neuroscience and cognitive psychology will be explored in the final chapter.

Checking off the cognitive psychologist's wish-list

What are the representational characteristics of mindreading?

Mindreading concepts

The dominant question in the literature on mindreading has been when children acquire particular mindreading concepts, and whether any such concepts are present in non-human animals. The dominance of this question seems to rest on two premises: Firstly, that we can agree upon clear criteria for possessing such concepts; and secondly that if we do agree that such concepts are present in an individual, then we have gone a long way to explaining their ability to mindread. The previous four chapters give reasons for doubting both.

Doubts about the first premise come from studies of children and non-human animals. In children, there is widespread use of benchmark tasks, such as the false belief task, and success on these tasks is often taken as a proxy measure of concept possession. Yet there is clear evidence that children are thinking and talking about beliefs before they pass false belief tasks, and clear evidence that children who do pass false belief tasks do not fully understand beliefs as characterized by the normative account.

It would be wrong to identify this problem only with the over-use of false belief tasks as the "one true measure" of mindreading. Moves towards assessing children's mindreading with a more diverse range of tasks are surely a good thing, but one thing this will not do is settle questions about when children *really* have a concept such as "belief". The same problem arises in the comparative literature, where there is good evidence that some non-human species "understand something about" seeing or knowing, but do not understand these mental states completely and have no under-standing of other mental states, such as believing. This evidence may very well be an accurate reflection of the abilities and limits of these species. The problem is that this undermines the utility of discussing mindreading concepts, as understood by the normative account of mindreading, because it is just not clear what it means to have half a concept of seeing or knowing, or half a "theory of mind" that includes some such mental states and not others.

Doubts about the second premise come from studies of adults, or rather, from the practical business of trying to study adults. Any theory that places concepts centre-stage in accounts of mindreading would hold that adults have mindreading concepts. The problem is that granting these concepts tells us very little about how adults actually read minds. Trying to study adults shifts the kind of questions we want to ask away from *whether* an individual is a mindreader (and therefore whether she has mindreading concepts) to *how* she solves the cognitive challenges of mindreading. My contention is that this shift in perspective is not only necessary for studying adults, but is equally important for thinking about children and non-human animals.

Domain-specificity

Although it is often claimed that mindreading poses unique representational problems, and should therefore rely on specialized (domain-specific) cog-nitive processes, the theoretical case for this is far from clear. As reviewed in chapter 2, there are principled reasons for supposing that reasoning about beliefs, for example, does pose quite specific representational problems. But these problems are similar in important ways to the problems posed by reasoning about non-mental representations (e.g., false signs or photographs) and about counterfactuals. The empirical literature largely reflects this sense that mindreading is special, but not *that* special.

Developmental disorders, such as autism, suggest that mindreading can be severely impaired in comparison with an individual's level of general intelligence. However, disproportionate impairment is also observed in reasoning about false signs and counterfactuals, and perhaps in executive function. Likewise, studies of patients with brain injury suggest that performance on mindreading tasks can be impaired despite success on control trials that check participants' ability to follow the task. However, very similar patterns of impairment are observed on well-matched false belief and false photograph tasks. These findings accord with data from typically developing children, whose performance on false belief tasks correlates with performance on false sign and counterfactual reasoning tasks, even when verbal intelligence is taken into account.

Neuroimaging studies suggest that there is a "social brain" or "mindreading network", consisting of a set of brain regions that show different patterns of activation during mindreading tasks compared with comparison conditions. One interpretation of this consistent finding is that these brain areas are specialized for mindreading. However, at a general level, this conclusion is undermined by the fact that every region of the "social brain" is also implicated in a variety of functions that are clearly not specifically social. Much more promising evidence for domain-specificity comes from studies that have contrasted neural activity observed during false belief tasks compared with closely-matched "false" photograph and false sign tasks. These studies have identified small sub-sets of the social brain that are selectively responsive when participants think about beliefs and desires (right Temporo-Parietal Junction) and when they think about perspectives (left Temporo-Parietal Junction in particular). What remains unclear, however, is the nature of the cognitive processes involved. It is tempting to conclude that these studies have uncovered the respective domain-specific neural seats of representing others' perspectives and mental contents. However, a broader consideration of the many functional requirements of mindreading and the many other neural regions that are regularly implicated suggests that the story is unlikely to be this simple.

Language

There is compelling evidence to suggest that language is involved in the development of mindreading in human children. In typically developing children, language abilities are strongly correlated with performance on mindreading tests such as false belief tasks, and language delay in atypical development causes a corresponding delay in the age at which children first pass such mindreading tests. There is some evidence to suggest that syntax may be particularly important in development, though perhaps *only* in development. In adults who have had the chance for language to serve its role in development, subsequent impairment of grammar as a result of brain injury does not lead to impairment on 1st order or 2nd order false belief tasks.

Importantly, there is equally compelling evidence that at least some mindreading abilities are wholly independent of language from the start. Non-human animals and human infants have little or no access to language, but nonetheless show mindreading abilities in natural behaviour and on laboratory tests. Many researchers interpret these abilities as essentially similar to those of older children and adults, involving concepts of perception, knowledge, and perhaps belief. Any account of the cognitive basis of mindreading will need to reconcile such apparent contradictions about the role of language.

What are the processing characteristics of mindreading?

Executive function

As with language there is a large body of evidence suggesting that executive function is important in children's developing ability to mindread. There are significant correlations between children's performance on tests of executive function and tests of mindreading, and evidence that earlier executive function predicts later mindreading whereas the reverse relationship is less strong. Unlike the case of language there is equally clear evidence that executive function continues to have a significant role in the mindreading abilities of adults. Adults' performance on mindreading tasks is correlated with their performance on independent tests of executive function, and adults' mindreading may be impaired if their executive function is taxed by the demands of a second task, or impaired by the effects of brain injury. Moreover, one interpretation of the close relationship between performance on mindreading tasks and other tasks matched for their reasoning complexity (e.g., false sign or counterfactual reasoning) is that all of these tasks make similar demands on domain-general executive processes. All of this evidence fits with the view that mindreading is cognitively effortful, and demanding of scarce cognitive resources for attention, memory and inhibition.

However, there is also good evidence that some mindreading processes are much less effortful and resource demanding. Infants and non-human animals have limited executive function, suggesting that any mindreading of which they are capable cannot be heavily dependent on such cognitive resources. And there is evidence that adults can implicitly and automatically calculate what someone else sees (Level-1 visual perspective-taking) using processes that are not greatly affected by simultaneous performance of another task that taxes executive function.

Speed and automaticity

Evidence about automaticity largely mirrors the evidence concerning the role of executive function. To the degree that mindreading depends on limited cognitive resources for executive control, we should expect mindreading to occur when needed, rather than automatically whenever we encounter one of the many environmental stimuli that afford mindreading inferences. There is indeed evidence that adults do not automatically calculate a character's false belief in conditions where it is neither necessary nor particularly relevant to do so. And there is evidence that a speaker's knowledge or belief is not automatically taken into account when interpreting what they say.

Of course, the flip-side of this line of reasoning also holds: mindreading processes that do not make heavy demands on executive resources are more likely candidates for being fast and automatic in their operation. And this appears to be the case with adults' ability to calculate what someone else sees or has seen. When asked to judge how many objects they themselves see in a scene, adults suffer interference from the perspective of another person appearing in the scene if that person can only see some of the objects. This processes appears automatic insofar as adults suffer interference from the other person's perspective even when they are given every opportunity to ignore the avatar's perspective.

There is little direct evidence regarding the speed of mindreading. Cohen and German (2010) conducted the only study that has compared the absolute speed of mindreading judgements against a meaningful baseline, and found that adult participants made faster judgements about false beliefs compared with misleading pictures and misleading arrows. This is an important step, but for now it remains unclear whether this corresponds to faster mindreading inferences, faster retrieval of mindreading information, or whether information about belief was more likely to be encoded spontaneously than information about pictures or arrows.

More generally, we might predict that mindreading processes that are not automatic and involve effortful executive control processes will tend to be "slow" in comparison with ones that are automatic. But care is needed here. At one extreme, mindreading processes that include careful deliberation, as one might undertake in judging the guilt or innocence of the accused in a court of law, really are likely to be "slow". In contrast, as I go on to discuss in this chapter, it is clear that everyday reasoning, reading and discourse processing require a large number of diverse inferences to be made on the fly. These inferences are spontaneous (rather than automatic) and require executive and memory resources, but they must be made quickly enough to keep up with fast-moving activities, such as conversation. There is every reason to think that many "non-automatic" and "effortful" mindreading inferences will nevertheless be made equally quickly.

What are the architectural characteristics of mindreading?

Surprisingly little empirical evidence bears directly on the questions raised under this heading. I will summarize some key findings here, and reserve a more complete discussion for later.

Does mindreading depend on a single, dedicated faculty?

Although the literature often supposes that mindreading is one kind of cognitive process, the empirical findings suggest two quite different senses in which it is not. Firstly, contrasting evidence about the speed and automaticity of mindreading, and the dependence of mindreading on executive function point to the possibility of there being multiple processes involved in mindreading, that make different cognitive demands. Secondly, there is evidence that multiple processes contribute to a given instance of mindreading. Behavioural evidence suggests that language and executive function – both of which serve a wide range of cognitive roles – are both closely involved in mindreading. Moreover, the "social brain", regularly implicated in mindreading, consists of a network of neural regions with diverse functions. Some of these functions may be highly specific to mindreading; others are certainly not. Importantly, studies of patients with brain injury indicate that both specific and non-specific functions may be *necessary* for mindreading.

The flow of mindreading information

The most commonly used mindreading tasks combine a range of potentially distinct processing steps. Frequently, participants must infer what someone perceives, knows or thinks, hold this information in mind and then use it to generate a prediction about what the person will do or say. Researchers have only just begun developing tasks that separate out these processing steps. So far the evidence points to the involvement of executive control processes at every step.

Although it must be possible for mindreading processes to influence other cognitive processes, existing evidence suggests limits on this exchange. For example, in a communication task, adults pay more attention to objects that the speaker knows about than objects that he does not, but this information is not immediately available when interpreting what the speaker says. Moreover there is evidence that different mindreading processes may not share information with each other. The very same child may look to the correct location on a false belief task, but answer with the wrong location in response to an explicit question. Such evidence is currently limited, but is potentially very informative about the organization of mindreading processes in relation to each other and with other cognitive functions.

In summary, the existing literature provides a rich evidence base of empirical phenomena with which to evaluate the cognitive basis of mindreading, but this evidence remains limited. Existing evidence tells us little about the architecture of mindreading, and the way in which it is integrated with other cognitive processes. And on other questions, such as who has mindreading concepts, the role of language or executive function in mindreading, and the degree to which mindreading is automatic versus controlled, the existing evidence is often strikingly contradictory. One possibility is that evidence on one side of each contradiction will turn out to be wrong, or to have been misinterpreted. Another possibility is that these contradictions, and the explanatory limits of the current literature, are the result of an overly narrow view of what mindreading entails. To develop a broader view I want to take a step back, to consider mindreading from a more theoretical perspective.

Is mindreading actually necessary for social cognition?

It may seem odd to say this in a book on mindreading, but I think that we researchers often hugely overestimate the role that inferences about the mental states of others actually play in everyday social interaction and communication. If we start out with an interest in mindreading there is a tendency to see a need for it in almost any social activity. How else could we explain an infant's ability to engage in a teasing interaction with its carer, a child's ability to understand everyday social interactions, or adults' remarkable ability to work out what one another are talking about? Surely in all of these cases it is necessary to think about what other people know, think, want or intend? Actually there are many reasons for thinking that this is often unnecessary, and the tendency for imperialism about the importance and ubiquity of mindreading explanations has resulted in a backlash from several quarters, each seeking to downplay the importance of mental state ascription in everyday activities (e.g., Andrews, 2008; Breheny, 2006; Costall & Leudar, 2007; Hutto, 2009; Leudar & Costall, 2009). Doing full justice to the arguments and evidence on this question would require another book. Here, I shall just highlight some illustrative examples of processes that perform work that might be glossed as "mindreading" but may not require mental state ascription.

Behavioural cues

If someone tells you to "pick up the red block" but there is more than one red block in the set of items in front of you, then you will not know from the instruction alone which one you should pick up. One option would be to ask for clarification. However, if you can clearly see that the speaker is looking at one of the two red blocks then suddenly it seems obvious that this is the one she means. And indeed, listeners can do this almost immediately (e.g., Hanna & Brennan, 2007). How do we do this? One possibility is that we use eye gaze to make a mindreading inference about the speaker's referential intent and use this to disambiguate the message. Another is that we skip the mindreading inference, and use the speaker's eye gaze directly as a reliable statistical cue that this is the object she means. The fact that listeners use eye gaze extremely quickly points to the latter, non-inferential route.

Alternatively, imagine that you see someone picking up a box. I suspect that you share my intuition that you would notice if the box turned out to be rather heavier than the lifter was expecting. And indeed, experimental participants are reliable at making such judgements (e.g., Runeson & Frykholm, 1983). The question is whether these judgements actually require us to infer explicitly that the agent has a false belief about the box. As ecological psychologists, Runeson and Frykholm clearly did not think so: ". . . .there is no warrant for postulating that extraction of this information [about the lifter's surprise] must occur through inferential processes . . . We must instead entertain the likely possibility that natural systems are solving the problem in a much more elegant and direct way than we would do intellectually" (p. 613). Recent research suggests that an important part of this "elegant solution" is the processing of information about actions we observe using the same functional and neural systems involved in formulating our own actions.[1] Such "common coding" for self and other is widely believed to support our ability to process and co-ordinate with the actions of others without any need to make inferences about mental states (e.g., Knoblich & Sebanz, 2006).[2]

Alignment between communicators

As already described, normative accounts of communication hold that speakers and listeners must make complex inferences about one another's mental states (e.g., Grice, 1957). Inferences about what the speaker knows or intends seem to be necessary for identifying the speaker's intended meaning from among the many possible interpretations afforded by a given utterance or signal. Sperber and Wilson (1995) develop a cognitive account of communication, in which a "theory of mind module" underwrites the need for fast, on-line mindreading inferences to guide listeners towards the most "relevant" interpretation of the speaker's words. However, in a later account, Sperber and Wilson (2002) envisage a different way of achieving many of the same effects. They note that listener and speaker are in complementary predicaments: Of course the listener needs to identify the most likely interpretation of the speaker's message, but it is also strongly in the speaker's interest to produce the message that is most likely to communicate their intended meaning. Sperber and Wilson (2002) argue that because of this, it is a good bet for speakers and listeners to follow their own individual cognitive paths of least resistance. In the simplest case this might amount to speakers saying the first utterance formulation that comes to mind for conveying their meaning, and for listeners to take the first interpretation that comes to their mind as the most likely interpretation intended by the speaker. If this does not make sufficient sense then speakers and listeners can work down the gradient of "what comes to mind", stopping at the first formulation or interpretation that does make sufficient sense. The authors retain their original terminology, and describe this comprehension procedure as ". . . a metacommunicative module [that] might have evolved as a specialisation of a more general mind-reading module . . .". But in fact it might be more appropriate to say that such a comprehension procedure allows each communicator to do without mindreading completely: it manages to approximate to a normative account of pragmatic inferences without actually having to compute other people's mental states at all, and without having to represent one's own perspective as such.

There are many reasons for believing that speakers and listeners may just be equipped to pull off the trick that Sperber and Wilson propose. From a rather different research tradition in psycholinguistics, Pickering and Garrod (2004) highlight evidence that partners in communication actually align themselves on multiple linguistic levels, tending to converge on similar phonology, words, syntactic constructions, and mental models of the discourse. Such alignment can only help the chances that speaker and listener converge on the "first thing that comes to mind" when formulating and comprehending an utterance. Interestingly, Pickering and Garrod (2004) explicitly argue that their account does not depend upon speaker and listener actually going to the trouble of making mindreading inferences about one another.

Of course, this does not mean that mindreading inferences can have no role at all. Dealing with situations where alignment is difficult to achieve (e.g., when talking to someone from a very different culture) or where the implicit assumptions behind alignment break down (e.g., if you doubt the sincerity of the speaker) may well require effortful thought about what your interlocutor is thinking or trying to do. But it suggests that the role for mindreading inferences is much less than might have been imagined.

Social scripts, narratives and normative rules

How do you know to say "thank you" when the shopkeeper hands you the receipt for your shopping? We might readily gloss this in mindreading terms: you say "thank you" because you judge that doing so will help keep your local shopkeeper happy, and that not doing so might lead him to think that you were rude or dismissive. But although we may be capable of making these judgements, is this really what we do each time we say "thank you" to our local shopkeeper? Might not you do it just because this is what you *should* do (as drilled into you by your parents), or just because saying "thank you" is *what you usually do* at that point in the social exchange?

It is a standard view in cognitive psychology that our representations of events and situations are organized into scripts and schemas (e.g., Schank, 1982; Schank & Abelson, 1977). These contain information about the regular sequences in which events unfold (e.g., when shopping you first select your items before taking them to the till and then paying) and the different objects and roles involved (e.g., there must be a shopper and a shopkeeper or checkout assistant; there may be shopping baskets and carrier bags). And of course they may involve social information about what usually happens and normatively should happen (such as saying "thank you"). The idea that our understanding of the social world follows similar organizing principles has been extensively developed by social psychologists (e.g., Cantor, Mischel & Schwartz, 1982; Fiske & Taylor, 1984; Gilbert, 1998). Social categories, scripts and schemas are regarded as indispensable tools for managing the complexity and ambiguity that is typical of social information, keeping the need for cognitively controlled reasoning and decision-making within manageable limits (e.g., Gilbert, 1998).

As mentioned briefly in chapter 2, some developmental psychologists and philosophers have proposed that researchers in the mindreading tradition have been looking in the wrong place for the drivers of children's developing social understanding, and should instead pay attention to children's developing representations of structured events, social interactions and narratives (e.g., Hutto, 2008, 2009; Nelson, 1996, 2005). We might add to this list children's understanding of social normativity, which is early-developing, and may do some of the work often attributed to mindreading (e.g., Andrews, 2009; Rakoczy, Warneken & Tomasello, 2008). I am sure that this is right to a significant degree, and can do a good deal to explain the basis of everyday social competence.

Nonetheless, it seems equally clear that we cannot do away with the need for mindreading. Social scripts, narratives and normative rules deal in *generalizations* about how the social world tends to work or should work. Mindreading allows us to think about someone's mental states on a wholly ad hoc basis: What can she see right now? Doesn't he know he'll be late for his meeting? Why has John – who is usually such a nice chap – just been rude to the shopkeeper? In answering such questions we may receive help from social scripts, narratives and normative rules. Indeed, I shall argue that they are indispensable. But we must clearly also go beyond them.

In summary, recognizing that the role of mindreading in everyday cognition is perhaps more limited than is often claimed is important for two reasons. First of all, a more modest role for mindreading reduces the need for a cognitive miracle that enables unbounded inferences about mental states to be performed with great speed and precision. Secondly, recognizing the existence of other processes, such as interactive alignment, social scripts, and knowledge of normative conditions for everyday interaction, provides important clues about how mindreading *as such* is actually achieved. These points are critical to the next section.

Why mindreading should be impossible

Let us go back to the false belief task, as a relatively simple and well-understood instance of mindreading. In the unexpected transfer version of the task, Sally puts her object in the round box, leaves the scene, and in her absence, Andrew moves the object to the square box (see Figure 2.1). The critical question concerns where Sally thinks her object is located. For most people the answer seems glaringly obvious: she'll think it's in the round box. But why should she? If you were to ask a philosopher she would likely say that it is not obvious at all, and that the only appropriate answer is "I don't know". For isn't it possible that Sally knows Andrew, and his deceptive ways? Maybe she'll guess that he moved it to the square box. Or maybe that he hid it under the table. Didn't I mention the table? But surely you didn't think the room was empty? Actually there are lots of possible hiding places. Maybe he hid it up his sleeve, or in the next door room, or at the school. Or maybe Sally and Andrew had an agreement that she would leave the object for him in the square box, and he would move it to the round box. Or maybe Sally has some unusual beliefs about the object's ability to spontaneously appear and disappear in different places. I didn't tell you she was rational, did I? Maybe she thinks it's on the moon! I could go on . . .

Of course, this is the kind of behaviour that can make philosophers unpopular at dinner parties. But they have a point. Reaching the "obvious" conclusion that Sally will think her object is in the round box actually requires us to make a great many assumptions about what is and is not relevant, which are not spelled out in the story. Now, the practically-minded may grudgingly concede the philosopher's point, but feel that this is all rather contrived and unrealistic. But consider other everyday instances of mindreading, such as deciding the guilt of a defendant in court, or the motives behind a lover's ambiguous text message. In these cases it is surely clear that the amount of potentially relevant information is arbitrarily large, and we might suppose that this is reflected in the care and attention that is devoted to such decisions. A reasonable response from the philosopher might be to say that it is the apparent simplicity of the standard false belief task that has a rather unrealistic correspondence with many important instances of everyday mindreading.

The reason for these problems is that inferring beliefs (including Sally's) requires an *abductive* "inference to the best explanation". That's to say, other beliefs will always be possible, but on the balance of the evidence, we should identify the one that seems most plausible. This is not a peculiar property of mindreading: "best guess" inferences are a general feature of many more or less formal decisions. For example, we make abductive inferences when we formulate hypotheses about experimental observations, or when we suppose that the reason we haven't been able to concentrate all day is because we have a cold coming on. Critically, a notorious feature of abductive inferences that there is no way of being certain what information may or may not be relevant (Fodor, 1983). So, I might not have been able to concentrate for any number of reasons: because I am tired, because I am worried about any number of possible things, because I have any number of other undiagnosed ailments . . . etc. And there are any number of things that might point towards a cold: perhaps I already know someone who had a cold recently, or perhaps I have other symptoms that resemble a cold I had once (though perhaps not the last one I had) and, of course, the weather at this time of year lends itself to colds . . . etc. On balance, it may seem pretty clear that I have a cold coming on. But there seems no principled way of working out what knowledge (hypochondriac and otherwise) I should bring to bear on this "best guess", and what I can safely ignore.

The open-endedness of abductive inferences, and the closely related "frame problem" and "problem of relevance" has been discussed extensively in the cognitive science literature (e.g., Fodor, 1983, 2000; Pylyshyn, 1987, 1996). The reason is that if it is really impossible to limit what information might be relevant for a particular inference or decision, then for anything other than the simplest system there is essentially no limit on the processing that is necessary to search exhaustively through the information that is available. Unlimited search is a computationally intractable problem, with the unpleasant result that reaching a decision or making the inference is impossible. Viewed this way, we should never manage to mindread, not even for the simple case of Sally's false belief.

How can mindreading be turned into a tractable problem?

There is a fair consensus that the frame problem and the difficulties of abductive inference are real, and that no direct solution exists. Researchers have instead sought different ways in which this central problem can be worked around, delivering different levels of approximation to the impossible goal of unbounded information processing. Short of a miracle, mindreading cannot be an exception to this rule, so in the following sections I explore different potential solutions for mindreading. These solutions all involve constraining the amount of information that is a candidate for processing. Severe constraints will greatly reduce the potential burden on information processing, but this improved efficiency always comes at the expense of flexibility. My suggestion will be that we actually implement multiple solutions that impose different levels of constraint and so make different trade-offs between efficiency and flexibility. The discussion that follows is summarized in Figure 6.1.

Hard constraints on information processing

Fodor (e.g., 1983, 2000) led the way in suggesting "modularity" as one way in which cognitive processes can be made computationally tractable.

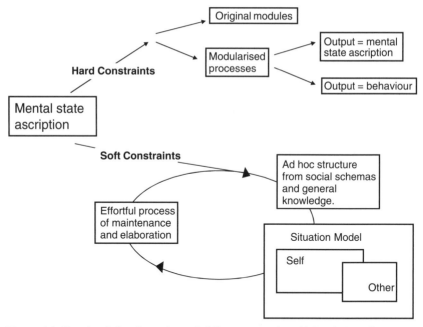

Figure 6.1 Sketch of the discussion of different ways in which mindreading can be made tractable (not a sketch of the cognitive processes themselves!). I first describe the possibility of placing hard constraints on information processing. Original modules develop from scratch to solve narrowly circumscribed mindreading problems. Modularized processes start out as effortful processes under soft processing constraints, but become modularized with repeated use. I then describe the possibility of soft constraints on information processing derived from schemas, episodic memory and other general knowledge. Such information processing yields a situation model that requires cognitive resources to maintain and elaborate.

The essential idea is to carve up larger cognitive tasks into smaller, simpler, sub-processes. For example, "visual perception" might be carved into sub-processes including "edge detection" and "motion detection". Each sub-process performs a narrowly-defined function, so does not need access to most of the information available in the cognitive system as a whole. (My ability to detect edges does not require information about the English cricket team's latest performance, or most other things I know.) These limited requirements can be built into the cognitive architecture by having processing "modules" that perform specific operations using their own small set of knowledge and representational resources, and are receptive to only a small set of external inputs. By limiting the information it can ever represent or respond to, a cognitive module avoids the problem of never knowing when to stop processing.

In the jargon of modularity, the above property of modules is referred to as "informational encapsulation". Fodor (1983) lists a variety of other characteristics that are associated with modularity: domain specificity, fast and automatic operation, fixed neural architecture, and innateness. When modularity is discussed in relation to mindreading, it is typically in relation to some or all of these other characteristics (e.g., Fodor, 1992; Leslie, 2005; Leslie & Thaiss, 1992; Sperber & Wilson, 2002). However, none of these other features is essential to modularity (e.g., Coltheart, 1999), and more importantly, none of them is directly involved in solving the problem of making a cognitive process computationally tractable. In fact, domain specificity may merely be one consequence of limiting the kind of information that goes into a module. Speed and automaticity can be seen as valuable consequences of the computational efficiency that a module makes possible. And whether there is a strong innate basis or a fixed neural architecture should be viewed as empirical questions about the origins and the implementation of a module.

I have no interest in arguing about the appropriate definition of modularity, but I shall follow Coltheart (1999) in emphasizing informational encapsulation because of its direct relevance to my questions about how mindreading is possible at all. In what follows I shall briefly describe some different ways in which at least some mindreading could be achieved via modular processing. Only later will I evaluate the other properties commonly associated with modules against the empirical evidence.

Original modularity[3]

Original modularity supposes that constraints from genes and environment mean that we are pre-destined to develop a modular architecture with a certain structure. Fodor's original conception emphasized genetic constraints, and this has influenced much of the discussion of modularity in relation to the development of mindreading (e.g., Baron-Cohen, 1995; Leslie, 1994a, 2005). Other authors emphasise the environment, arguing that enough regularity and structure exists in an organism's interactions with the world to be a significant source of constraint on the kind of modules that develop[4] (see e.g., Elman et al., 1996; Karmiloff-Smith, 1992). Ways of distinguishing between these possibilities will be discussed in chapter 7. The essential proposition for now is that genes and environment might combine to channel development reliably towards the emergence of one or more modules for mindreading[5].

I think there are very good reasons for taking this proposition seriously, and, indeed, I think there are viable candidates for mindreading processes that are modular in this sense. For example, I have already identified the processing of Level-1 visual perspectives as a process that is, in fact, early-developing in children and cognitively efficient, even in adults. Most critical of all in the current context, it seems plausible that the processing of such relatively simple perspectives may be simple enough to be modular. I suspect that such modules will have a place in a two-systems account of mindreading, such as the one that I shall propose. But the requirement that modules only process "simple", clearly circumscribed problems also means that they can only ever provide part of the explanation.

The problem for a wholly modular account is that the arguments for modularity are distinctly double-edged. Recall that modules avoid impossible processing burdens by placing hard constraints on the kinds of information that they represent or respond to. Necessarily, then, modules are unable to represent or respond to any other information, even if that information might be relevant. For Fodor, the clear consequence of this limitation is that modules can never account for *all* cognitive processes. He distinguishes modular processes from "central" processes, which seem, in principle, to require unlimited access to information available from the whole cognitive system. Most notable among the function of these central processes are abductive inferences to the best explanation, such as those required by full-blown mindreading. Thus, Fodor both articulates powerful arguments in favour of modularity for some cognitive processes, and provides powerful reasons for supposing that our everyday ability to understand perceptions, knowledge and beliefs cannot possibly be the task of a module[6]. Curiously, Fodor (2000) does not make this link himself, and actually cites the "theory of mind module" proposed by Leslie and colleagues as evidence in favour of his general account of modularity. But since Fodor argues that our ability to form our own beliefs cannot be a modular process, it would be truly surprising if our ability to ascribe beliefs to other people could be achieved in this way.

In reaching this conclusion it is informative to consider how mindreading compares with language processing. Sometimes people argue that an ability as complex and flexible as mindreading could be the function of a module by making an analogy with the case of language (e.g., Stich & Nichols, 1992). Language is as complex and flexible as any human cognitive ability, and yet many people suppose that our faculty for language is modular: so why should mindreading be any different? There are two stages to the explanation. Firstly, the aspects of language for which there is good (though still highly contested) evidence for modularity are those that are codifiable in terms of a limited set of rules, such as phonology or grammar. In contrast, more open-ended aspects of language, such as those involved in the "higher-level" processes of discourse comprehension, show much less evidence of modularity, and this is unsurprising, since the kinds of process that they are likely to entail are exactly those that are not readily codifiable in a system of rules. So the next question, crudely put, is whether mindreading is more like grammar or more like discourse processing? Answering this question requires care, because the popular view that mindreading involves having a "theory" about mental states at first appears to resemble the role proposed for grammar in language. But closer inspection suggests that this analogy is wrong. Nobody, not even the strongest proponents of the "theory-theory" of mindreading, has actually articulated a system of formal rules that attempts to capture the underlying structure of our mindreading abilities. The reason, I think, is that mindreading is not codifiable in this way, but is in fact as open-ended as linguistic discourse processing. Thus, if we pursue an analogy with language, we really should be led to the view that mindreading per se – as described by the normative account – is most unlikely to be modular. Of course, this still means that modules can perform some of the work of mindreading, and this, together with the potential attendant benefits of fast and cognitively efficient processing, will be discussed in the coming pages.

Downward modularization

Importantly, original modularity is not the only way in which we might arrive at mindreading processes with hard constraints on their information processing. It is well-known that demanding cognitive tasks can become much easier with repeated practice. Just recall learning to drive, playing a musical instrument, or any similar task. At first it seems impossible, with every aspect of the task requiring effortful attention and memory: Look around; keep the steering wheel straight; monitor the engine so you know when to change gear; find the gear stick; remember the next gear position; don't forget the clutch; check your mirrors! However, with practice all of these components become more fluent and much less effortful. It is generally supposed that practice leads to the formulation of cognitive schemas representing the relationship between particular kinds of input (such as hearing the revs of the engine reach a certain level) and particular kinds of output (the action schema for changing gear) (e.g., Norman & Shallice, 1986; Shallice & Burgess, 1996). Once in place, these schemas can co-ordinate activity in well-practised situations without the need for effortful memory, attention or decision-making. As with original modules, this efficiency is achieved by limiting the inputs that can be processed and the outputs that can be produced. And as with original modules, this efficiency comes at the cost of flexibility: even an experienced driver has to concentrate whenever the input-output relationships are less predictable or well-practised, as when driving a new car, or approaching roundabouts, or when the car in front behaves erratically. Critically, in contrast with original modules, which develop from scratch, downward modularization requires a pre-existing ability. The pre-existing ability may be highly flexible, but cognitively effortful. Downward modularization extracts regularly-occurring aspects of this ability into a schema of input-output relations that can operate efficiently but inflexibly.

In relation to mindreading, we can imagine downward modularization operating in two rather different ways. Consider, first of all, the difference between an amateur and an expert poker player. An amateur player may have to think carefully and effortfully in order to interpret their opponent's sequence of card playing and pattern of betting and to reach the conclusion that "he thinks I'm bluffing". In contrast, it seems plausible that years of practice could lead an expert player to form schemas that link observed patterns of playing and betting directly with an inference about what the opponent thinks. This would free up valuable resources for effortful thought, allowing the expert player to build more sophisticated counter-strategies than the amateur player.

Now consider the difference between an amateur and an expert at fencing. An amateur at fencing will learn a repertoire of basic actions that can be performed. Basic success against an opponent depends on being able to execute these actions efficiently, on being able to recognize what move an opponent is making, and on making an appropriate counter-move. However, a more sophisticated fencer will also bluff or feint a move in order to dupe the opponent into a predictable counter-move, which can then be exploited. And of course, this can spiral further: an expert fencer might even double-bluff being duped by an opponent's bluff, and so on. The point here is that, while the process of learning will often entail careful, effortful consideration of the beliefs and intentions of self and other in this competitive spiral, the purpose of training and practice is to ensure that these moves and counter-moves can be made very quickly, without care and effort. As Perner (2010) suggests, in this case it seems plausible that expertise consists in having trained into the player a reliable set of schemas that efficiently parse sincere and faked moves and link them directly with appropriate counter-measures. Learning entails reasoning about the thoughts of an opponent, but practice takes this out of the equation, enabling very fast performance exclusively on the basis of parsing behaviour in an expert manner.[7]

These examples of modularization differ in that, in the first case, the output of the modularized process is actually an inference about the target's mental state, whereas in the second case the output is a motor response. But in both cases, modularization has led to the formation of a specialized process that is only responsive to a limited set of possible inputs, only processes those inputs with respect to limited information encoded in the schema, and is only capable of producing a limited set of outputs. These limits are what make the module's information processing tractable and efficient. Of course they mean that such modules will only operate in highly specific domains for which they are specialized. Thus, when it comes to mindreading in the many and varied circumstances of everyday life, which would not normally fit with the domain of their expert modules, we would not expect an expert poker player or fencer to be any better than the rest of us. And of course, there would be no point in trying to broaden the domain of modules ever outwards until they *could* respond to the inputs and produce the outputs required for everyday mindreading. Doing so would undermine the economy achieved by limiting what the module could do, leading it to become ever less efficient, and its processing to be ever more open ended and difficult to achieve.

So what is the difference between original modules and downward modularized processes?

First and foremost, you must already be a mindreader before you can generate a downward modularized routine for mindreading. Across individuals, there will be considerable variation in the kinds of task that will be of sufficient importance or interest for downward modularization to occur through repeated practice. But in any case, the mindreading that becomes modularized is initially an effortful product of general mindreading abilities.

Original modules, by contrast, do not require a pre-existing general mindreading ability. Instead, the combined constraints of genes and environment would reliably generate cognitive processes that solve relatively simple mindreading problems. Of course, this does not mean that the developmental story for these abilities will necessarily be simple! But one should expect a relatively consistent set of such original modules to emerge under "typical" genetic and environmental conditions. And, critically, their emergence would not depend on pre-existing resources for mindreading or other potentially demanding cognitive processes such as executive function or language.

Summary

The kinds of module described above provide one solution to the problem of keeping information processing within manageable limits. Insofar as modular processing is regularly associated with other cognitive characteristics, this would also help explain the observation that at least some aspects of mindreading appear to be fast, efficient, automatic, and in the case of original modules, early developing. However, it is equally true that such modules could not explain how mindreading manages to be flexible (recall that the normative account entails that mindreading must be enormously flexible), and modules do not fit well with the empirical evidence that mindreading is often cognitively effortful. In short, modules can only be part of the solution, because they cannot explain why mindreading often seems less like perception and more like reasoning.

Soft constraints on information processing

So how might mindreading sometimes manage to be more flexible without posing an impossible information-processing burden? Stich and Nichols (2003) offer the most detailed model of mindreading in the literature, which allies mindreading very closely with general reasoning processes. At the heart of their model is the idea that thinking about someone else's beliefs, and working out the consequences for their behaviour, depends upon an entirely generic capacity to reason about counterfactual or hypothetical states of affairs. When we mindread we build a hypothetical model that initially inherits all of our own beliefs by default. We then adjust specific beliefs on the basis of what we know about the target person (for example, that Sally didn't see Andrew swap the object's location) and update our record of any of the target's beliefs that are affected by this change.[8] I think this offers a useful starting point for thinking about how a more flexible capacity for mindreading might work, but Stich and Nichols' model runs into at least two severe problems.

Firstly, it is far from clear how to implement the proposition that my initial model of Sally's beliefs starts out by inheriting every single one of my own beliefs. If we think in terms of a spatial metaphor, however much space in my own mind is taken up by my own beliefs, Stich and Nichols' account seems to imply that I must have just the same amount of space standing empty for the occasion when I want to think about Sally's beliefs, let alone when I want to think about what Sally thinks Granny thinks. Stich and Nichols acknowledge that this can't really be right, but say little about how I make things manageable by deciding what relevant subset of Sally's beliefs I ought to import, or how this information is then held in mind.

Secondly, Stich and Nichols assume that it is straightforward to work out that Sally thinks the object remains in the round box from the fact that I know she did not see it being moved to the square box. But as we have already seen, we cannot assume that this is straightforward, even for this simple case, and especially not for more complicated but perfectly normal cases that we want to fall within our capacity for mindreading. Thus, on both points, Stich and Nichols' account comes up hard against the problem of identifying relevant information, as well as running the risk of making impossible demands on the capacity to keep in mind a very large, hypothetical model of someone else's beliefs.

These are tricky problems. But they are also problems confronted in the literatures on reasoning and language processing, and there is some convergence on the kind of solution that might be possible.

Incomplete models

It is widely held that everyday thinking, reasoning and language comprehension involves the on-line construction of some kind of "mental model" (Byrne, 2005; Fauconnier, 1985; Garnham, 1987; Johnson-Laird, 1983). Although the details of these models vary in important ways, which need not concern us here, it is typically assumed that in order to be psychologically plausible, the information actually represented in the models must be a tiny subset of the information available in the rest of the cognitive system.

For example, in Johnson-Laird's mental models theory, representing the conditional "if p then q" involves building a mental model that explicitly represents *p* and *q*, and a second "implicit" model representing the possibility of an alternative situation, without representing its specifics. Of course, there are many possible alternative situations, and modelling all possible alternatives exhaustively would be demanding or even impossible. The purpose of keeping this initial model "implicit" is to represent the possibility of alternatives economically, leaving the reasoner the option of elaborating these models only according to need.

In language comprehension it is commonly supposed that readers or listeners generate a "situation model" that represents the gist of what has been said or read (e.g., Zwaan & Radvansky, 1998). This model includes information explicitly mentioned plus further information inferred on the basis of background knowledge from semantic and episodic memory. In a well-known example, someone who reads "The cleaner swept up the mess on the floor" will be likely to form a situation model that includes a broom, even though "broom" was not explicitly mentioned (Corbett & Dosher, 1978). But they will not make all of the possible inferences that their background knowledge affords. For example, a reader might not include "low paid" as a property of the cleaner in their situation model, unless the foregoing context makes this especially relevant. The literature suggests that the inferences that are in fact made depend heavily upon context, upon motivation, and on the availability of cognitive resources, such as working memory (e.g., Graesser, Singer & Trabasso, 1994; Just & Carpenter, 1992; Narvaez, van den Broek & Ruiz, 1999). Moreover, parts of the situation model may remain underspecified or indeterminate between alternative interpretations of the linguistic input, though the comprehender remains able to commit to one or other interpretation if required to do so (e.g., Ferreira & Patson, 2007).

It seems reasonable to suppose that the same kinds of modelling process might be used for mindreading. Indeed, looking from a perspective outside of the specific literature on mindreading, it would be rather surprising if inferences about a person's mental states were somehow a special case. If mental models are a general account of reasoning then surely they should account for reasoning about mental states. And surely inferences about people's mental states are regular features of verbal discourse processing, which involves the construction of situation models? If so, then to the extent that mindreading is achieved with some such processes, we should expect that thinking about Sally's false belief about her object's location involves the construction of a relatively sparse, on-line model, as envisaged by such researchers. At a minimum it would seem necessary to represent the object being in the round box, and the relationship between those items in Sally's model and the same items in one's own record of "reality", where in fact the object is in the square box. Whether the model also included other known features of the object or box, or any other aspects of the situation would depend on context, motivation and the availability of the necessary cognitive resources.

In sum, no empirical work has actually examined the scope of belief inferences – that is to say, we do not actually know "how much stuff you put in the head" of someone to whom you ascribe a belief. However, indirect evidence from related research suggests a) whether or not you even make a belief inference[9] will be highly dependent upon context b) if you do make a belief inference, its scope will most likely start out quite narrow c) the initial inference can be elaborated if the need arises. This would explain how mindreaders keep the storage demands of thinking about someone else's mental states within realistic limits. It would fit well with evidence that mindreading is not automatic, but is dependent on executive function. And it would fit with the notion that mindreading is often more like reasoning than perception – because from this perspective, mindreading just *is* reasoning, with particular structure and content.

What has yet to be explained, however, is how on earth we actually manage to identify the information necessary for even a simple belief inference.

Using schemas, narratives and norms to identify relevant information

Earlier I drew attention to the open-endedness of mindreading inferences. Even for a very simple inference about Sally's false belief there are in fact endless considerations that we might take into account when deciding what belief should be ascribed. But it certainly doesn't feel this way: it really feels perfectly obvious where Sally will think the object is located, and indeed it may require some effort to see that there are actually many alternative scenarios. Why is this, and what does it tell us about how people might solve the everyday problem of making mindreading inferences?

Let's start with Sally. It is important to recognize that the question about what Sally will think follows a particular sequence of events in a carefully constrained narrative. Part of the skill of writing any narrative is to guide the reader towards constructing the intended situation model of the situation described[10] (e.g., Fauconnier, 1985; Gernsbacher, 1990; Graesser, Millis & Zwaan, 1997; Zwaan & Radvansky, 1998), and this clearly applies just as forcefully to the construction of experimental materials for studies of reasoning. (Indeed, as discussed in chapter 2, false belief tasks have been subjected to endless tweaks and modifications designed to guide children away from unintended interpretations of the narratives.) Obviously this includes information that is explicitly mentioned (false belief tasks usually emphasize Sally's absence when Andrew swaps the object's location), but also information that is omitted (false belief tasks do not hint at any past history of Andrew playing tricks on Sally, so there's no reason to think this may be the case). And, unless the narrative indicates otherwise, it can be presumed safe to make inferences on the basis of normal assumptions about the world (Sally is rational and does not have X-ray vision; the world described in the narrative obeys normal physical laws about objects staying where they are put). Thus, the simple, carefully constructed narrative of this false belief task helpfully limits the degrees of freedom about likely beliefs that Sally might have. It is logically possible that she might think Andrew played a trick, or that the object has spontaneously moved, or any number of other things, but the constraints of the narrative and background knowledge make these possibilities improbable and seemingly irrelevant. And we are so good at making inferences on this probabilistic basis that we often do not notice that probabilities are not logical necessities. This is why the philosopher's doubts about what Sally might think seem strange.

This may be all very well for experimental tasks, and we might reasonably hope that the same principles would scale up to account for our ability to make reliable mindreading inferences in response to other, more sophisticated, narratives. But of course, everyday events do not come carefully packaged by a narrator whose objective is to constrain the degrees of interpretive freedom and guide us towards an intended mental state ascription. So how do we make mindreading inferences in these common situations? Very simply, I suggest that we provide our own constraints via our own structured representations, consisting of social scripts and schemas, narrative structures and normative principles.

As discussed in an earlier section of this chapter, it is well established that we routinely interpret events via structured representations that draw upon both semantic and episodic memory, and in which social information may feature heavily. These structured representations may do some of the work that is often misattributed to mindreading, by assisting with the "alignment" of communicators and co-actors, and so helping people to interact appropriately in social situations. And structured representations of events and situations may of course encode information about what people typically think, know, want and intend in particular situations. But here I am suggesting that they play an additional, critical role in everyday mindreading. Because scripts, schemas, narratives and norms provide structures through which everyday situations are understood, they serve as strong biases on what information is perceived to be important or relevant in a given context.

To illustrate, consider the example of a shopping script described earlier. Imagine the checkout assistant asks whether I want some help carrying my heavy shopping to my car. Since I actually walked to the shop, I might interpret this as an offer to accompany me on the 15-minute walk back to my house, where my car is parked. Or I might interpret this as a suggestion that I am too weak or too lazy to carry my shopping back home. Or perhaps that this is an indirect request to view the beautiful flowers in my front garden, which is immediately next to my car. Or perhaps the assistant is trying to trick me into revealing my address so they can pass this on to their secret service handler. . . But more likely I will infer that the assistant assumes (incorrectly) that I have parked in the nearby car park, since this is what most shoppers do when they go shopping. Note that this is likely to require a novel inference – it is probably not a part of my shopping script, or of my previous experience with shopping that checkout assistants always assume that one's car is in the car park. But knowing how shops and shopping usually work (that shops usually have car parks, that shoppers usually use the car park and that assistants tend to be helpful rather than whimsical, rude or spies) enables me to rule out as highly unlikely a large proportion of potential mental states that I might ascribe to the checkout assistant.

Clearly, the constraints supplied by such structured representations of events, narratives and norms will usually require integration with other specific information about the current situation, and this will yield a situation model of the kind discussed earlier. Given the literature on discourse processing we should expect the recall and ad hoc elaboration of scripts to make demands upon general resources for memory and executive function. And indeed there is direct evidence of such processing costs from the social cognition literature, where participants under time pressure or cognitive load are more likely to make judgements reflecting stereotyped, script-based information, whereas participants with more time or resources make more nuanced judgements that take account of mitigating situational factors (e.g., Gilbert, 1998). We should expect the same to be the case for everyday, ad hoc mindreading inferences.

Importantly, even when time and resources are available for a reasonable level of integration between information from background knowledge and the current situation, the resulting model will remain relatively sparse, and when it comes to making a mindreading inference there is no guarantee that the inference that seems most probable on the basis of the current model of the situation is in fact the correct mental state to ascribe. Ascribing a misapprehension about where my car is parked may be my best bet, but the checkout assistant really might want to see my flowers!

Checking the faith that I should have in the mindreading inference that initially seems most probable might proceed in several ways. I might try elaborating my situation model (e.g., by integrating memories from my previous visits to the shop), or try out alternative assumptions within the model (e.g., what if the checkout assistant was being sarcastic?), and check the effects that this has on what mindreading inference seems most probable. And I might evaluate the most probable mindreading inference against other things that I already know about the target person (because these will not necessarily have been integrated into the relatively sparse situation model). Of course, these checking procedures will require further cognitive effort, and we should expect the effort that I devote to this to depend upon the time and cognitive resources that are available, my motivation, and the consequences of getting it wrong. At the shop checkout, when a mistake matters little, checking might amount to little more than a "double take", reflecting the fact that a simple mindreading inference was required to make sense of the situation. At the other extreme, as a juror in a court of law the normal expectation would be that a rather elaborate process of cross-checking and consideration of alternatives would be necessary for a critical decision, such as whether a defendant really knew the consequences of their actions. And indeed, this need for careful deliberation is institutionalized in the processes and procedures of a trial by jury.

Finally, the well-attested tendency for egocentric errors during mind-reading arises very naturally out of this view that flexible mindreading is based upon the construction of situation models, for two rather different reasons. Firstly, part of the job of the scripts and narratives that we use when constructing a situation model is to enable us to make background assumptions about the target for the mindreading inference. One obvious influence on such background assumptions is an assessment of the degree to which the target is similar to one's self (e.g., assessing the checkout assistant's similarity to me would help evaluate whether they would think it normal or strange that I chose to walk to the shop). However, although this may be a very valuable aid to filling in background information for the target, the problem is that we are notoriously prone to overestimate the similarity of another person's ideas and opinions to our own (e.g., Nickerson, 1999). So the basis on which we might make novel mindreading inferences will tend to be biased in an ego-centric direction.

Secondly, egocentric errors could arise because of the conflicting infor-mation represented in a situation model that includes the perspectives of others. As described in the last section, making a mindreading inference consists of constructing a model of "what is in the head" of the target other person, but this model is both related to *and* part of our larger model of the situation in which that person features. Thus, when evaluating the guilt of a defendant in the dock we need to model the reality of the situation in which they feature (including the fact that white powder they put in the deceased person's tea was lethal poison) and we also need to construct a linked model of what the defendant themselves knew about that situation (the defendant knew it was poison but thought it was non-lethal). Deciding whether the defendant knew he would kill the tea drinker requires us to take account of information from his model of the situation, but given that this model is derivative of our own model of the situation it seems highly plausible that our own privileged knowledge will be a strong competitor and will drive alternative interpretations that we may select incorrectly. It is easy to see how this might lead to a systematic tendency for egocentric errors that is only ameliorated by cognitively effortful cross-checking.

In summary, the frame problem or "problem of relevance" looms as large for mindreading as for any cognitive process. Although there is no agreed-upon solution to this problem, the literature suggests a variety of ways by which the imposition of soft processing constraints can enable a substantial degree of flexibility in mindreading without imposing an impossible cognitive burden. Mindreading inferences are not made in a vacuum. Our experience of everyday situations is structured by social scripts, narratives and knowledge of social norms, which help direct our limited processing resources towards the information that is most relevant in that context. Critically, what helps ensure that this highlighted information is relevant is that the set of knowledge guiding our own processing is largely shared with the person who we are trying to understand. These soft constraints help ensure that only a tiny subset of the logically possible information is actually likely to be considered when it comes to making a judgement about what someone in that situation thinks or knows.

Moreover, mindreading inferences result in the construction of a rather sparse model of "what is in the head" of the target person. And this model is contained within our own model of the situation, which is itself relatively sparse compared with our vast background knowledge. This view draws heavily from existing literatures on reasoning, discourse processing, and social cognition. What is, perhaps, surprising is that these lessons learned elsewhere have not always been applied to the particular case of mindreading.[11]

Taking this view of mindreading highlights several important points that relate to the questions with which I began. If something like this is correct then, although there is clearly a sense in which mindreading requires concepts about mental states, a large amount of the heavy lifting is performed by structured knowledge contained in scripts, narratives and social norms. Many of these are essentially social in origin, and variation in such knowledge over age or across individuals is likely to make a significant difference not only to general social skills but specifically to the accuracy of mindreading.

To the degree that mindreading works this way, it is best viewed as domain-general rather than domain-specific. Although mindreading clearly does depend on relatively specialized social knowledge, there is no reason to think that this knowledge is different in kind from any other knowledge. Indeed, I cannot see how a systematic distinction could be made. And moreover from this perspective there is no reason to think that this knowledge is deployed by anything other than wholly generic processes for forming situation models. Finally, to the degree that mindreading works this way it is no surprise at all that it makes demands on general cognitive resources for memory and executive function, with those demands being greatest when it is most important to be accurate. The current perspective clearly fits with the distinct demands identified at various points in the earlier chapters of working out "when and how" to make mindreading inferences, and to resist interference between self and other perspectives.

"Two systems" for mindreading

In the summary at the beginning of this chapter I pointed out the extensive contradictory evidence on the cognitive basis of mindreading, and suggested that these contradictions might be resolved in one of two ways: either one set of evidence would prove to be unsound, or the apparent contradictions actually reflect genuine diversity in the means by which mindreading is achieved. The latter view is strongly supported by the points discussed in the sections that followed. Mindreading poses some genuinely difficult problems for a cognitive system to solve because, on a normative account, mindreading requires abductive inferences, which place unlimited demands on information processing.

Cognitive science has yet to provide an account of how idealized abductive inferences could be possible. And the importance of this conclusion from a theoretical point of view should not be missed: it follows that the normative account of mindreading that is often taken for granted in theoretical accounts is almost certainly wrong as a description of what real mindreaders actually do.

Nonetheless, apparently unbounded information processing is a common problem in cognitive science, and two broad classes of solution have been proposed for limiting the kinds of information that gets processed. One solution places hard constraints on what information is ever considered or how it can ever be processed, and as a result gains high efficiency at the expense of low flexibility. Another kind of solution places soft constraints on information processing that vary in a context-sensitive manner. Such solutions make the opposite trade-off by being relatively flexible but making greater demands on general cognitive resources for attention, memory and executive control. The mindreading abilities of human adults require the virtues of both kinds of solution: they need to be both flexible enough for complex psychological reasoning and fast and efficient enough to get us through moment-by-moment social interactions. These dual requirements are not unique to mindreading, and for topics as diverse as social cognition (e.g., Gilbert, 1998), number cognition (e.g., Feigenson, Dehane & Spelke, 2004), and general reasoning (e.g., Evans, 2003), there is strong evidence that both kinds of solution are employed. I suggest that the same is true for mindreading (see Apperly and Butterfill, 2009).

A sketch of the mindreading architecture of human adults

If the foregoing discussion is even roughly correct then we are currently rather short on evidence for building a full information-processing model of adults' mindreading. What I want to do here is give a very simple and somewhat speculative sketch that captures the relationship between key points already discussed, and provides a structure for further investigations.

Figure 6.2 characterizes mindreading processes along two dimensions. The vertical dimension describes the nature of the constraints imposed on information processing. "Lower level" processes operate under hard information processing constraints. These constraints are most critical, but it follows that these processes are also likely to have a broadly modular

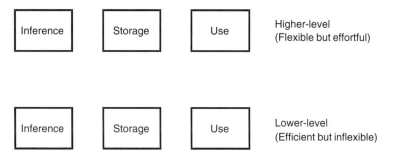

Figure 6.2 I suggest that it is useful to maintain distinctions between higher-level and lower-level mindreading processes, and that at each level it is useful to distinguish between the processes involved in mindreading inferences, in storing this information and in putting it to use.

character, tending to be fast but inflexible and make low demands on general processing resources. They will tend to resist strategic control (i.e., they will be relatively automatic) and may operate outside of awareness (i.e., they may be "implicit", sub-personal or unconscious). "Higher level" processes operate under soft information processing constraints. This enables them to be more flexible, both in terms of when they operate and the depth of processing that takes place. But this comes at the cost of being slower and more demanding of general processing resources, especially when more elaborate processing is required. As for verbal comprehension and everyday reasoning, these processes will operate within personal-level awareness; that is to say there will be a feeling of "oneself" actively and explicitly thinking, even if the mechanics of these processes remain opaque to introspection.

The horizontal dimension corresponds to potentially distinct sub-processes of mindreading. Based on the cases highlighted in earlier chapters it seems useful to distinguish between making mindreading inferences, storing this information and using this information in other processes. This captures important points that are sometimes overlooked, such as the fact that mindreading does not necessarily involve making inferences from behaviour, that effort may be involved just to hold in mind someone else's perspective, and inferring and holding in mind someone's perspective does not guarantee that this information will be used when necessary. By associating each of these sub-processes with a box in the diagram I am not suggesting that there must be complete separation between them, or that these are the only distinct sub-processes, or that mindreading always pro-gresses through these sub-processes in a serial fashion. But distinguishing between these sub-processes seems a useful starting point for asking systematic questions about how mindreading actually operates. To see how, I shall map some examples from earlier chapters onto this sketch.

On-line processes

Do different sub-processes make different requirements?

A standard, unexpected transfer false belief task (Figure 2.1) is usually taken to be a simple test of flexible mindreading, rather than the limited mindreading that might be possible in a module, and, consistent with this, the task makes demands on executive function and language. If it tests flexible mindreading then this task draws primarily upon "higher level" mindreading processes. As depicted in Figure 6.3a, the task typically requires participants to infer Sally's false belief and hold this information in mind long enough to be able to use it to predict her incorrect search. Many sources of evidence suggest the involvement of executive processes in this task, but it is clear from Figure 6.3a that we cannot tell whether they are necessary for inference, storage, use, or all three. Figure 6.3b depicts the variant on this standard task in which participants are asked to report Sally's belief, rather than use it to predict her action. Figure 6.3c depicts the variant in which participants are simply told Sally's false belief, plus what is really the case, and are then asked to report it back. By dividing mind-reading into different sub-processes it becomes very obvious that we should ask questions about development, and functional and neural bases separately for each potential sub-process. For example, the fact that all three of these variants on a standard false belief task pose a challenge for 3- to 4-year-old children suggests that storage may be an important limiting step in this age range,[12] but other sub-processes may be limiting factors at different ages.

Does information move between higher and lower levels?

Given that the main rationale for proposing lower-level processes is to achieve efficiency by placing hard constraints on information processing, we should expect strong restrictions on the exchange of information between levels. An example illustrating this comes from the developmental literature. The fact that infants have very limited access to language or executive resources suggests that their sensitivity to agents' beliefs, as manifest in their eye movements, is due to "lower-level" mindreading processes that make few demands on such resources and are systematically limited in the way that they process and share information. Figure 6.4 depicts one phenomenon that is a likely consequence of this inflexibility: the observation that the processes driving infants' "correct" eye movements on false belief tasks do not have outputs that are available for explicit report.[13] Of course this is just one instance, and it will be important for future research to ask whether there are circumstances when information can be exchanged on-line between higher-level and lower-level processes, or indeed between different lower-level processes. And in either case it will be important to ask what sub-processing steps permit such exchange.[14]

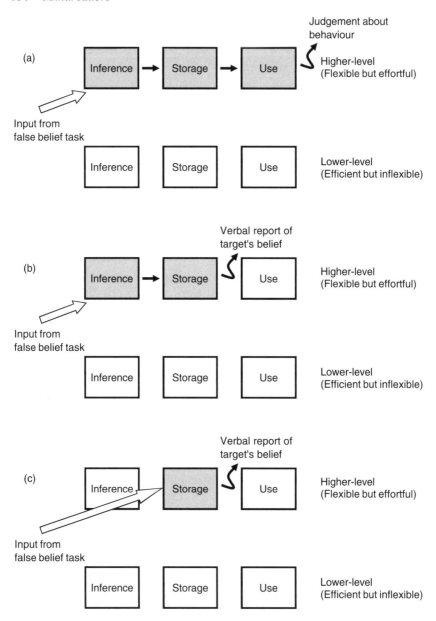

Figure 6.3 In panel (a) the scenario of the false belief task provides information about the background scenario, and the target character's access to what has happened, and this provides the basis for inferences about what the target thinks. This inference must then be held in mind and used to deduce what the character will do. In panel (b) the inference is held in mind and then reported directly. In panel (c) the false belief task directly supplies the target character's belief, obviating the need for inference, and the participant must simply report this back.

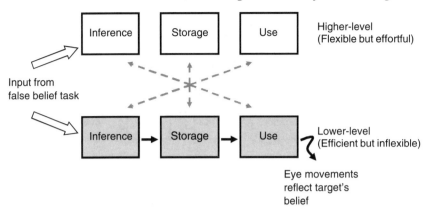

Figure 6.4 An infant who cannot yet make high-level inferences about false beliefs may nonetheless process information from the false belief task successfully using low-level processes. However, as indicated by the broken grey arrows, this information may not be able to transfer out of the lower-level system to become available for high-level processes, such as verbal report.

Change over time

Early development

As already discussed, the lower-level mindreading processes available to young infants will consist exclusively of original modules, which should develop relatively early, under relatively tight genetic and environmental constraints. A possible example that I have already mentioned is the capacity to track "Level-1-type" perspectives. However, this leaves open a range of important questions about how and when these developments occur: How many modules; To what degree does the development of one depend on the development of another; Are there intermediate stages when mindreading inferences are made and stored but not yet integrated for use in the ways they might be later in development?

Higher-level mindreading processes should develop more slowly, as the necessary cognitive resources become more available and as social experience increases. Important questions here are what role original modules might have in guiding development (e.g., as Leslie, 2000, has suggested, by directing children's attention to relevant information in the environment), and whether language, social experience and executive function might have unique roles in the construction of higher-level processes, in addition to lasting roles that they undoubtedly have in the mature system.

Later development

As higher-level mindreading processes take shape it becomes possible that repeated use of these processes to solve particular problems may lead to the

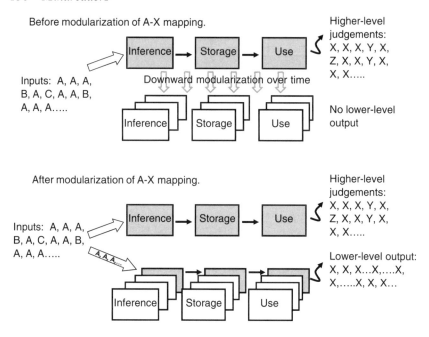

Figure 6.5 Schematic of the process of downward modularization. Initially (in the top panel) inputs A to D are incompatible with any lower-level mindreading modules, and must all be processed by the more effortful, high-level mindreading system. However, the mapping of input A to output X is both highly frequent and highly consistent (in contrast to inputs B and C, which both yield output Y, and are infrequent), making it a candidate for modularization. Downward modularization yields a new lower-level process (bottom panel), which only accepts A as input and only produces X as output. This input-output mapping is achieved efficiently by the low-level process, but the same stimuli can also still be processed via the more effortful higher-level route.

generation of new, specialized, low-level processes via downward modularization (see Figure 6.5). As discussed earlier, the output of such a process may go directly to influence other processes (such as a fencer making a counter-feint) or may provide a mindreading inference that is available for other, higher-level mindreading operations (such as an expert poker player inferring that his opponent is bluffing).

In summary, a human adult is likely to have many or all of the low-level mindreading processes developed in infancy, a more flexible and effortful high-level capacity for mindreading, and a further set of low-level mindreading processes modularized from heavily practised instances that were originally high-level. It can be seen from Figure 6.6 that the result of all of these processes is likely to be complicated! On the face of it, this should not be too surprising – on any analysis, mindreading is a complicated business. But it would be troubling if a solution of this complexity

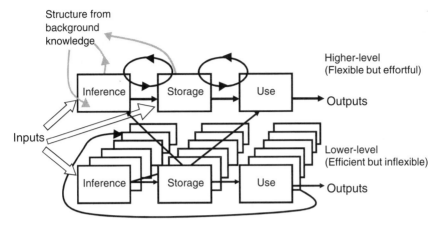

Figure 6.6 An indication of the complexity that follows from proposing multiple systems for mindreading. Higher-level processes integrate input with stored knowledge to make flexible, context-sensitive mindreading inferences, represented by the grey arrows. This information is likely to be repeatedly re-processed and elaborated, as represented by the oval arrows. There are likely to be multiple, distinct lower-level processes. In principle, distinct lower-level processes may exchange information with each other at any stage, and any stage may pass information to higher-level processes (for simplicity only arrows from the front-most lower-level process are shown). In practice these links will be relatively uncommon, in order to preserve the processing efficiency of the lower-level processes.

was unusual in comparison with other areas of cognition. In fact, I think the broader literature provides reassurance on this point, and I deal with this briefly in the final section of this chapter.

Is such a model unusual?

As I have already suggested, two-systems solutions have been proposed in a variety of cognitive domains including social cognition and general reasoning, and all of the phenomena discussed above have long pedigrees elsewhere. In Apperly and Butterfill (2009) we develop an analogy between mindreading and number cognition.[15] In the case of number cognition there is evidence for the existence of two original modules: one that enumerates small sets of objects with high precision; and one that estimates the size of large sets of objects. These modules are strictly limited in the kinds of calculations they can perform: the precise number module can only enumerate up to 3 or 4 items and the approximate number module delivers estimates that are more precise for smaller numbers than for larger numbers. They are also early-developing in human infants, appear to be shared with a variety of other species, and provide cognitively efficient processing of number in human adults (e.g., Feigenson, Dehane & Spelke, 2004). The limits on number cognition that are set by these modules are only overcome by learning an explicit, symbolic number system, which takes children years to achieve and continues to be cognitively effortful, even for adults. That is to say, flexible number cognition is a "high-level" process. However, high-level operations may become modularized over time if they are repeated with sufficient frequency. For example, LeFevre, Bisanz and Markonjic (1988) found that when adults are presented with a symbolic sum with which they will have had a great deal of practice (e.g., "6+4") they automatically compute the sum, even when they are not asked to, leading to interference with other number judgements.[16] Finally, the questions raised above about the developmental relationship between low-level and high-level abilities, and about the degree of information exchange between levels in on-line cognition have all been discussed (though not necessarily resolved!) in the literature on number cognition. Thus, my suggestions for how mindreading might operate are neither unusual nor outlandishly complex: they are similar to what we find if we look at other cognitive abilities that need to solve analogous problems.

Notes

1 Common coding may occur at the level of individual "mirror neurons" (e.g., Rizzolatti & Craighero, 2004; Rizzolatti, Fogassi & Gallese, 2001), and also at higher levels of description.

2 At first blush this conclusion seems at odds with recent neuroimaging evidence (e.g., Grezes, Frith & Passingham, 2004) indicating that judgements about agents lifting boxes with unexpected weights recruit regions of the social brain involved in mindreading inferences (already discussed in chapter 4). However, participants in Grezes et al.'s study were explicitly instructed to judge the mental states of the lifter, so such patterns of neural activity are not surprising and do not demonstrate that mental state inferences are necessary for some sensitivity to the lifter's surprise. Importantly, Grezes et al.'s study also showed activity in regions of premotor cortex, known to be involved not only in formulating one's own actions but also when viewing the actions of others, consistent with common coding of self and other action having a role in participants' judgements.

3 "Original" in the sense of original sin, and insofar as this was the first way in which modularity was conceptualized.

4 The existence of specialized functional and neural "modules" involved in reading is a good existence proof of this possibility, since reading is such a recent cultural invention that it is implausible that the emergence of reading modules falls under strong, specific genetic constraint.

5 Note that this is a fairly weak claim from a nativist perspective. Many people's views about modularity are determined by whether or not they assume cognitive abilities to be substantially innate. Fodor and Leslie are committed nativists, and most objections to their views about a modular basis for mindreading have been motivated by various objections to this nativism. In contrast, my assumption is only that genes and environment can be sufficiently constraining for the reliable development of modules that do some of the work of mindreading.

6 It is notable that others contest Fodor's strong conclusion about the impossibility of a modular account of "central" cognitive processes. For example, Barrett and Kurzban (2006), Carruthers (1996), Pinker (1997) and Sperber (2005) defend the idea that the mind is "massively modular", and propose various ways in which modules can overcome the inflexible limits imposed by informational encapsulation. But flexibility does not come for free, and in order to be flexible it seems that these accounts must give up much of the processing efficiency that is such a valuable property of a more traditional modular architecture. Massively modular accounts may offer one way of characterizing mindreading under "soft information processing constraints", discussed below. But I think it is useful to distinguish such accounts from the much narrower proposition that some, but by no means all, of the work of mindreading might be achieved by cognitively efficient but rather inflexible original modules.

7 A study by Sebanz and Shiffrar (2009) provides evidence that fits somewhere in between the two possibilities. Expert basketball players proved more accurate than novices at discriminating genuine versus bluffed passes from stimuli that presented the kinematics of the pass. In this case the input for the process was observed behaviour, but the output was an inference about a mental state, or, at least, whatever the direct output from the process actually was, it supported an explicit judgement about the deceptive intentions of the player.

8 Stich and Nichols (2003) are not explicit about how this updating is achieved but are clearly aware that such updating encounters the frame problem already discussed above. They do not claim to solve the frame problem, but assume that one's own cognitive system must itself have effected some kind of practical solution for updating its own beliefs, and this can be equally well applied to the model of the target's beliefs.

9 Or, of course, any other mindreading inference.

10 Clearly, different readers will arrive at different models, but a good outcome would be if they were just similar enough to entail approximately similar interpretations of the narrative.

11 Of course, in some cases they have, and in particular I have in mind Perner's (1991) account, which characterizes the development of children's mindreading in terms of the construction of increasingly sophisticated embedded mental models. The account I offer here is very much in the spirit of Perner's, but its direct motivation is rather different. Whereas Perner's primary concern is to characterize the form of thinking that is necessary for mindreading (and how such thinking develops through stages), mine is to identify how flexible mindreading can be possible without posing an impossible processing burden. And in my view, building such situation models is just one way (albeit an important way) in which people pull off the trick of mindreading.

12 By this I do not mean to suggest that children's difficulty is simply a matter of capacity: "storage" may not only entail the capacity to hold in mind someone else's perspective, but also the active resistance of interference from one's own knowledge.

13 In very young infants there may not even be a "higher-level" ability to reason about mental states. However, in 2- to 3-year-olds there surely is at least a limited ability of this kind, yet the evidence suggests that this does not have access to information driving the same children's eye movements.

14 Questions of exactly this nature are currently the topic of active investigation in other literatures, such as number cognition (e.g., Gilmore, McCarthy & Spelke, 2007).

15 There are, of course, many debates about the details of number cognition, which we summarize in our paper. Here I will skip over the ifs and buts to highlight the key points necessary to support the account of mindreading developed here.

16 This automaticity does not, in itself, guarantee informational encapsulation, or any other properties commonly associated with modules. However, there is evidence pointing to limits on what information may be processed in this way (i.e. evidence of encapsulation) insofar as the sums computed automatically are restricted to small numbers with which an individual is highly experienced.

7 Elaborating and applying the two-systems theory

Chapters 2–5 illustrated the complex and rather contradictory patterns of evidence about the mindreading abilities of children, adults and non-human animals, which provided the justification for a hard look, in chapter 6, at just what we mean by mindreading, and how such mindreading might ever be achieved by real cognitive systems. In chapter 6, I argued that human adults have two kinds of cognitive process for mindreading – "low-level" processes that are cognitively efficient but inflexible, and "high-level" processes that are highly flexible but cognitively demanding. And, equally importantly, I suggested that we also have a large amount of social and socially constructed knowledge, and a range of other cognitive processes that do not entail mindreading as such, but which underwrite a large proportion of everyday social cognition. I then sketched how these abilities might be organized, and the general kinds of question that this should lead us to ask. In this final chapter I want to pursue the implications of the model developed in chapter 6 in more concrete terms, before comparing it briefly with existing theoretical alternatives.

One very general objective is to explore the ability of the model to accommodate some of the existing empirical phenomena that appeared contradictory when discussed in earlier chapters, and to see how this leads to new questions. A second objective is to make the case that the model is more than a description. This is important for two reasons. Firstly, in proposing a relatively complex model it is always important to ask whether the model is *too* complex; whether there is any pattern of findings that it could not describe within its complexity. Secondly, there is more than a whiff of circularity about seeking to explain evidence for more or less cognitively efficient mindreading abilities in terms of the existence of low-level and high-level processes that are more or less cognitively efficient,[1] unless, of course, we can define some independent criteria for determining which processes are in use. My contention is that the necessary independent criteria come from the fact that low-level processes must be *limited*, and that examining the nature of these limits gives us a very powerful tool for investigating mindreading.

Low-level processes for mindreading

Recall from the last chapter that low-level mindreading processes achieve cognitive efficiency by placing hard constraints on the kinds of input that they will process and on the kinds of operations performed on that input. If we were to find evidence of such limits on the mindreading abilities of infants and non-human animals, or on the "cognitively efficient" abilities of adults, then we would have independent reasons – beyond the apparent cognitive efficiency of these abilities – for supposing that this mindreading was being achieved by low-level, modular processes. Moreover, if the limits observed are similar across different subject groups then we might infer that *the same* module is at work. A useful analogy, to which I shall keep returning, is the case of number processing, where there is very good evidence in human infants and adults, and non-human animals for the same two cognitive modules that process number information: one that allows efficient, precise enumeration of small sets of objects, but at the expense of a strict capacity limit of 3–4 items, and a second that allows efficient approximations of the number of objects in large sets at the expense of decreasing precision as set size increases (e.g., Apperly & Butterfill, 2009; Feigenson, Dehane & Spelke, 2004). How might these expectations about processing limitations be fulfilled for the case of mindreading, and what purchase could this give us on thorny questions about mindreading in adults, infants and non-human animals? Rather than describe hypothetical scenarios, I shall illustrate the way that this line of thinking could be developed using recent work that I have conducted with my collaborators and students as a case study.

Level-1 perspectives as a case study

Overview

Before tackling the details it may be useful to have a sense of where this argument is going. I shall begin by summarizing some new studies that extend the work on adults' "automatic" perspective processing presented in chapter 5. These suggest that automatic perspective processing is cognitively efficient, early-developing, and *limited* in that only simple, Level-1-type, perspectives can be processed. I shall then argue that there is a prima facie case that the abilities of human infants and non-human animals to process perception, knowledge and belief converge on similar limits. Finally, I shall explore how evidence regarding convergence adds to what we can say about the nature and origins of these processes. Future work may show the details of this case study to be wrong, but in any case, I hope it may serve as a template for thinking about how low-level mindreading can be studied systematically.

Processing characteristics in adults and children

Automatic and efficient?

In chapter 5, I described a series of recent experiments suggesting that human adults have a low-level process that supports processing of Level-1 visual perspectives. Recall that adults showed evidence of egocentrism in their explicit judgements about perspectives. But the critical evidence about automaticity came from the indirect, "implicit" effect of the avatar's perspective on participants' judgements about their own perspective. Samson et al.'s (in press) key finding was that adults found it more difficult to judge the number of dots that they could see on the walls of a cartoon room when the room included an avatar who saw fewer dots than them, compared with when the avatar saw all of the dots. This "altercentric" interference effect was observed even when adults never made explicit judgements about what was seen by avatar on any other trials of the experiment, and even though the repeated trials of the experiments gave participants the opportunity to use a strategy of ignoring the avatar. The fact that adults did not or could not use such a strategy, and so suffered interference from the avatar's irrelevant perspective when judging their own perspective, suggests that adults were processing the avatar's perspective in a relatively fast, relatively automatic manner. In addition to this, Qureshi et al.'s (2010) study, described later in chapter 5, suggested that processing the avatar's perspective was not only relatively automatic, but also cognitively efficient, insofar as participants' processing of the avatar's perspective was not interrupted by the simultaneous performance of a task that places demands on executive function. These characteristics fit with the possibility that, in addition to high-level perspective-taking abilities recruited for explicit judgements, adults also have a "low-level", modular mindreading process that is able to process at least simple contents for "what someone sees".

Original module or downward modularized process?

Importantly, evidence of a fast, automatic and efficient mindreading process in adults leaves open the question of provenance. As discussed in chapter 6, it could be that such effects observed in adults are due to an original module, which has underwritten efficient processing of Level-1 perspectives since infancy. Or it could be that Level-1 perspective-taking is an active and relatively demanding problem for infants and young children, but by the time we are adults we have had sufficient practice with visual perspective-taking for this to become modularized via downward modularization into an efficient, relatively encapsulated process. One way to distinguish between these hypotheses is to test whether young children also show automatic, implicit processing of simple visual perspectives: original modularity predicts that signs of automaticity should be observed at all ages, whereas modularization predicts that automaticity should increase with age.

In Surtees and Apperly (2010) we conducted a preliminary test of these predictions by adapting Samson et al.'s method to collect response-time data from children aged 6, 8 and 10 years, as well as from adults. Although older children and adults responded more quickly than younger children, equivalent "altercentric" effects were observed at all ages: that is to say, 6-year-olds' judgements of how many dots they themselves saw on the walls of the room suffered interference from the irrelevant perspective of the avatar, suggesting that they were processing the avatar's perspective in a similarly automatic manner to the older children and adults.

Of course, we cannot rule out the possibility that by 6 years of age children have already had sufficient experience with visual perspective-taking that this ability has been modularized. What we can say is that this study provides no evidence for modularization because we found no evidence of increasing automaticity with increasing age. This is therefore consistent with the possibility that the effects in children and adults are driven by an original module for perspective processing that has been present since infancy. A really strong test of this hypothesis will require the development of new methods suitable for detecting automatic perspective processing in younger children.

If future studies do provide clear evidence for an original module that supports Level-1 perspective processing, then this still leaves many open questions about how the module interfaces with other processes, and how this all develops. The possibility that I am describing is a relatively encapsulated process that might enable agents' "perceptions", "knowledge" and "beliefs" to be tracked in simple cases. As such it would clearly require inputs from prior "upstream" modular processes, which identify agents (in contrast to other objects), relevant parts of those agents (such as eyes and hands), and relevant relationships with the rest of the environment (such as where the eyes are looking or what the hands are touching). In this important sense I am not describing "a module for Level-1 perspective-taking", but rather a module that performs a specific and relatively late step in the efficient processing of social stimuli. Recall that I am not describing these processes as "modular" out of any particular commitment to nativism, but because modules are informationally encapsulated, and encapsulation is the way to avoid onerous burdens on memory and executive function. This is a critical constraint for explaining how infants (and perhaps non-human animals) manage to mindread, but it leaves plenty of room for developmental change in these abilities. As I describe below, the degree of genetic versus environmental constraint on this development is an empirical question, and moreover one that the current account should help to address.

Processing limits?

Modular processes gain efficiency at the expense of flexibility, and so if we are right to interpret the evidence described so far as evidence for a cognitively efficient module for processing perspectives, then we must expect to find distinct limits on the work that this module can do. If the only observable limits can be explained in terms of limits on an individual's knowledge, experience, or general cognitive capacity then this would count as clear evidence against a modular account. In Apperly and Butterfill (2009; Butterfill & Apperly, 2010) we discuss a variety of possible limits, among them the possibility that economy is achieved by representing the relationship between agents, objects and properties, rather than the more complicated business of representing relations between agents and propositions. This leads to the prediction that the low-level mindreading process would allow the processing of Level-1-type problems, which require representing what object or situation an agent sees (e.g., female agent sees a box – see Figure 2.2a). Indeed, it would also allow processing of the "knowledge" and "false belief" problems on which infants and non-human animals have shown precocious abilities. But it would not support the processing of Level-2-type problems, which require representing the particular way in which an agent sees an object or situation (e.g., female agent sees an upside-down box – see Figure 2.2b), because such representations require representing the relation between an agent and a proposition.

To investigate this prediction in adults we adapted Samson et al.'s method to make it into a Level-2 problem (Surtees, Apperly & Samson, 2010). We tested for the existence of egocentric interference on explicit judgements about the avatar's perspective, and, critically, for the existence of altercentric interference when participants judged their own perspective. The existence of the latter, altercentric, effect would indicate automatic processing of the avatar's perspective. As can be seen in Figure 7.1, the stimulus was a cartoon picture of a view into a room in which numerals could appear on the wall or on the table. An avatar was positioned behind the table facing out of the picture. His viewing angle meant that he saw digits on the table from the opposite point of view from the participant (i.e., under 180 degrees of rotation). Consequently, when the digit on the table read "9" from a participant's point of view it read "6" from the avatar's point of view, and vice versa. In contrast, rotationally symmetrical digits, such as 0 and 8 would be read as "0" and "8" from both points of view, so although the avatar and the participant had different viewing positions they would both "see" "0" or "8". These latter trials provided the baseline for assessing any interference that might occur between the participant's and the avatar's perspectives.

Our findings from children and from adults suggested that participants did indeed show egocentric interference when making explicit judgements about the avatar's perspective: they were slower and more error prone when their own perspective was different from that of the avatar (i.e., on "6" and "9" table trials, compared with "0" and "8" trials). So it seemed that the adapted paradigm was sensitive to such interference effects. Critically, however, we found no evidence of altercentric interference: when participants

**Perspective and
content cue**

Picture

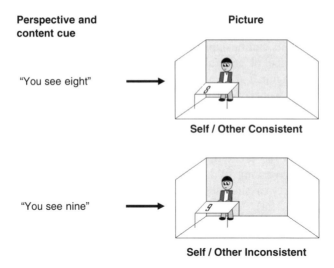

"You see eight"   ⟶

Self / Other Consistent

"You see nine"   ⟶

Self / Other Inconsistent

Figure 7.1 Level-2 visual perspective-taking task used by Surtees et al. (2010). On each trial a cue told participants the perspective (Self or Other) and the possible content for the perspective (illustration only shows Self trials). Participants then judged whether the Content cue accurately described what could be seen from that perspective in the picture.

judged their own perspective they were no slower to respond when the avatar's perspective was different from their own than when it was the same. That is to say, in contrast with our findings from the Level-1 task, we found no evidence here for implicit, automatic processing of the irrelevant perspective of the avatar, consistent with the hypothesis that the low-level process for perspective-processing does not support the propositional content needed for Level-2 perspectives.

The power of converging evidence on limits

The findings just described go some way to refining the notion of a low-level mindreading process, but of course there are many further questions, some rather specific, and others much more general and important. First of all, the findings from Surtees, Apperly and Samson (2010) deserve cautious interpretation because they only show limits on automatic perspective-processing in one paradigm. We would obviously like to be sure that the null result for automatic Level-2 perspective processing was not merely due to some wholly incidental feature of this task. More generally, we would like to know whether Level-2 perspective processing really falls outside of the capabilities of a low-level module that processes perspective, or whether Level-2 perspective processing just makes more memory and executive demands than Level-1 perspective processing, and so is not achieved sufficiently quickly to generate interference effects. Yet more general and important questions concern whether the low-level process responsible for altercentric interference effects in adults really is the same process responsible for the success of infants or non-human animals on mindreading tasks. And if it is, then we would like to know what are the relative contributions of genes and environment to the development of this module.

All of these questions can be addressed by examining the convergence of evidence across different methods used with children, adults, infants and non-human animals. I shall briefly describe the case of number cognition, where this strategy has been pursued with some success, before mapping this analogy to the case of mindreading.

Converging evidence for number modules, and what this tells us

As mentioned at the end of chapter 6, there is wide agreement that humans have a cognitively efficient process for enumerating small sets of objects,[2] which has a strict limit of 3–4 items. This limit is clearly not an artefact of one particular paradigm, because it has been identified using multiple methods in human adults, human infants and in non-human animals.[3] Nor is the limit set by the availability of working memory, executive function or other general cognitive processes, because the 3–4 item limit is invariant across human adults and human infants, who have very different processing capacities. Rather, the limit seems to be a fact about a modular process that gains cognitive efficiency by limiting its processing to a maximum of 4 items. This "signature limit" on processing makes it possible to identify when a participant's behaviour is being influenced by the module (because it will only be influenced by numbers up to 3–4) and when it is not (because it is not subject to this distinctive limit) (e.g., Spelke & Kinzler, 2007).

The identification of such a signature limit gives investigators purchase on difficult questions about the nature and origins of cognitive processes. For example, when the behaviour of a non-human species appears sensitive to number, it is of interest whether this sensitivity reflects an abstract enumeration process, or whether is the product of learned associations between an outcome (such as more versus fewer food items) and perceptual features that correlate with number (such as mass or surface area of the food). Importantly, if the same or very similar signature limits are observed in studies of non-human animals and in studies of efficient number processing in humans, and if the data from humans suggest that this reflects an abstract enumeration process, then the parsimonious conclusion is that the same, low-level cognitive process for enumeration is at work in non-human animals too (e.g., Feigenson et al., 2004).

Another difficult question is the relative importance of genes and environment in determining the structure of low-level cognitive processes. Here, the degree of similarity in the signature limit across individual humans and across different species is informative. If the signature limit is highly stable across individuals in very different environments, this suggests a high degree of genetic constraint.[4] Moreover, if it is also stable across species in very different niches, this would seem to point a genetic constraint that was relatively ancient in evolution. In the case of precise enumeration, there is a high degree of convergence on the signature limit of 3–4 items between humans (Feigenson, Dehane & Spelke, 2004), macaques (Hauser & Carey, 2003) and fish (Dadda, Piffer, Agrillo & Bisazza, 2009). It is far from clear what common environmental constraint could explain this convergence, making it seem more likely that the critical constraint is genetic in origin.[5]

Converging evidence for a mindreading module, and what this could tell us

Evidence from altercentric interference effects in adults leads to the working hypothesis that there might be a low-level mindreading module that supports processing of Level-1-type perspectives but not Level-2-type perspectives. How does this fit with evidence from other subject groups? In this respect, it is unfortunate that it is considered exciting to demonstrate previously unknown abilities in infants or non-human animals but often rather curmudgeonly to point out that these abilities are nonetheless limited. Researchers investigating mindreading in these subject groups have seldom directly sought evidence on the scope of any mindreading abilities, and this is unfortunate because both the surprising abilities, *and* the limits on these abilities are equally informative about cognitive processing.

Nonetheless, with all due caution about inferences based on the absence of evidence, the literature described in chapters 2 and 3 provides a good prima facie case for convergence between findings from non-human animals, human infants and adults. Recall that despite impressive evidence for mind-reading of some kind in human infants and in non-human animals, there is no evidence of sensitivity to Level-2 visual perspectives, or of any other ability that requires representation of *the particular way* in which someone thinks about something. Just to hammer the point, even the best evidence from studies of infants, which demonstrates success on simple false belief tasks, does not show that infants represent agents believing propositions; it would be sufficient for infants to be able to track a Level-1-type relationship between agents, objects and properties. So for the time being, let's grant that there is a prima facie case for convergence, in order to see what might be gained by thinking about low-level mindreading in this way.

First of all, this convergence provides some reassurance that Surtees et al.'s null findings for automatic Level-2 perspective processing may not have been an artefact of their particular task, because similar null findings for tasks that require similar sophistication have been obtained in infants and non-human animals using a very different range of tasks. Similarly, if there is such convergence across tasks and subject groups it suggests that the ability to support Level-1-type but not Level-2-type perspectives is not determined by the availability of general resources for memory or executive control, because the availability of such resources varies widely between human adults, human infants and non-human animals. Rather, it seems that being limited to representing Level-1-type perspectives might be a fact about how a modular process for perspective-processing manages to be cognitively efficient, by avoiding the complexities entailed by processing the relationship between agents and propositions. If so, then we may have a useful "signature limit", that allows us to tell when an individual's behaviour is being influenced by this module, because the influence will only extend to cases that can be solved with Level-1 perspective processing, and not to those that require Level-2.[6]

Secondly, a paradoxical effect of identifying signature limits in the abilities of infants or non-human animals is that this can provide powerful evidence against the most deflationary explanations of their mindreading abilities. Recall from chapter 3 that there is a fierce debate about whether the apparent mindreading abilities of human infants or non-human animals might in fact be due to sensitivity to observable behaviour rather than unobservable mental states, and so not count as mindreading at all (e.g., Penn & Povinelli, 2007; Perner, 2010; Povinelli & Giambrone, 1999).

One of the difficulties with this debate is with generating experiments suitable for infants or non-human animals that differentiate between the mindreading and behaviour-reading accounts. Convergence on signature limits can help with this problem by allowing conclusions from studies with other subject groups to be brought to bear on questions about non-human animals or human infants.

Recall that Povinelli, Perner and colleagues concede that human infants and non-human animals may reason in a sophisticated way about behaviour (i.e., they are "cognitive", not merely associative), but do not reason at all about mental content (i.e., they do not process "what is in the head" of the target of their reasoning). This may give an adequate account of current evidence from human infants and non-human animals, but it clearly cannot explain the findings of Samson et al. (in press) or the other related studies that indicate low-level processing of perspectives in adults. This is because the critical phenomenon in these studies is the interference that participants experience from the avatar's perspective when judging their own perspective, and this clearly entails that adults are processing "what is in the head" of the avatar.

Since the accounts of Povinelli and Perner were never intended to explain such evidence from adults, this might seem irrelevant for questions about infants or non-human animals. However, if such evidence from adults shows signature limits (in this case they apply to Level-1 but not Level-2 perspectives) that converge with those observed in infants or non-human animals, then this indicates that the very same cognitive module may be at work in these different subject groups. Thus, the evidence from adults also gives us good reasons for thinking that infants and non-human animals may in fact be processing "what is in the head" of target agents, rather than only processing behaviour. Crucially, this would mean that they *really are* mindreading, albeit in the limited way permitted by the modular process that is available to them.

Thirdly, as for the case of number, convergence on signature limits for mindreading provides purchase on tricky questions about the role of genes and environment in determining the structure of low-level mindreading processes. If these limits turn out to be highly consistent in the face of the very different learning environments of non-human animals and human adults, then this would indicate that they were based in similar cognitive processes, developed under strong genetic constraints. It really is an open question whether different species that show evidence of mindreading abilities will show the same signature limits. What is clear from the argument developed here is that limits should be expected, and the nature of those limits will be informative about the evolutionary origins of mindreading.

Finally, if we can identify signature limits for a mindreading module then we have a powerful tool for identifying the action of that module when children and adults perform tasks that might require mindreading. One obvious place to look for such effects is in communication, where speakers and listeners need to take rapid account of differences in their perspectives. As described in chapter 5, current evidence on adults' ability to take account of a speaker's visual perspective when interpreting what they say is decidedly mixed. A potential explanation for this inconsistent pattern is that adults are much faster and much less error-prone at taking account of the speaker's perspective when this work can be performed by a low-level module for perspective-taking, and the current discussion leads to the prediction that this should not be possible when Level-2 perspective processing is necessary.[7]

In summary, there are good reasons for thinking that human adults, human infants and some non-human animals might share a low-level mindreading process that supports the representation of Level-1-type but not Level-2-type perspectives. As I go on to explore in the next section, its effects are likely to be observed on "implicit", "indirect" measures, such as eye gaze, or interference effects in response-time paradigms, rather than when participants are asked to make explicit judgements. This hypothesis manages to integrate a surprising number of otherwise rather disparate findings from different methods and different types of experimental subject.

Importantly, however, the explanatory strategy pursued in this section would remain valid even if this specific hypothesis turned out to be wrong. This general strategy begins with the premise that, short of a cognitive miracle, cognitively efficient mindreading will come at the cost of inflexible limits on the kind of problem that can be solved. If we identify limits that cannot be explained in terms of a lack of general processing resources, or a lack of opportunities for learning, then this suggests the existence of a low-level, modular process. Identifying the nature of these limits is critical for understanding how cognitive efficiency is achieved by the low-level process.

But in addition, comparing the nature of these limits across different tasks and different subject groups is a powerful tool for interpreting apparent mindreading abilities in human infants and non-human animals, and for understanding the provenance of the low-level mindreading abilities of adults. The processing of Level-1 perspectives is just a case study. If we have such a capacity it would undoubtedly depend on other modules for input. But even if the specifics of this case study are wrong, I suspect that we may turn out to have other such original modules for mindreading.

Why don't 3-year-olds pass false belief tasks? Egocentrism and explicit mindreading judgements

If the foregoing discussion is correct, then human infants (as well as human adults and some non-human species) have a low-level module for mind-reading that represents relations between agents, objects and properties, and is sophisticated enough to explain evidence of sensitivity to false beliefs on tasks such as those used by Onishi and Baillargeon (2005). However, the expectation is that this module will turn out to be relatively inflexible, and will not support the diverse mindreading of which older children and adults are capable. This may be so, but it does not explain why 3-year-old children fail to respond correctly on standard mindreading tasks. In these tasks the target agent has exactly the same false belief about the location of an object as in Onishi and Baillargeon's study. This seems puzzling, and equally so when the question is put the other way around: how is it that infants manage to avoid the catastrophic tendency for egocentrism that dominates young children's responses on false belief tasks? Addressing this question seems critical for understanding the difference between putative low-level and high-level mindreading abilities.

One notable feature of the studies that have demonstrated precocious abilities in infants is that they use indirect measures, such as eye gaze or looking time, rather than requiring infants to make explicit judgements. The same is true in studies of adults. Samson et al.'s evidence of "auto-matic" processing of the avatar's perspective comes from the effect of the avatar's perspective on participants' judgements of their own perspective, not from participants' explicit judgements about the avatar. Likewise, evidence that listeners take rapid account of a speaker's perspective is apparent in their eye movements, rather than in their overt responses (e.g., Barr, 2008; Hanna & Brennan, 2007). And studies of 3-year-olds demonstrate a clear dissociation within the very same children between incorrect explicit answers on a standard false belief task, and a correct pattern of looking that anticipates the behaviour of an agent with a false belief (e.g., Clements & Perner, 1994; Ruffman et al., 2001).

On the strength of these findings it is tempting to conclude that the critical difference is that low-level mindreading abilities are "implicit" and so are not available for the explicit judgements required by standard mindreading tasks. However, while this may be an appropriate description of the phenomena, on its own this is clearly not an explanation for why low-level mindreading might be implicit, or why someone who is capable of implicit mindreading may nonetheless be stymied by egocentrism when they make explicit judgements about the very same mindreading problem. I think that the account developed in the last chapter provides ways of adding some explanatory power to this descriptive account.

Recall that low-level mindreading is achieved by placing hard restrictions on the kinds of information that is processed and on the operations performed on that information. It seems plausible that one of the benefits of modular processing behind such an informational firewall will be the absence of influence from knowledge that is generally available in the cognitive system. That is to say, modular mindreading may confer immunity from "egocentric bias" and, indeed, this may be one of the important ways in which the module manages to be cognitively efficient, by avoiding the need for executive processes to resist interference from other information. In contrast, flexible, high-level mindreading involves the construction of a model of the mental states of the target agent within a model of the wider situation. For the reasons described in the last chapter, it seems plausible that a consequence of this process of model construction will be a tendency for egocentric bias.

Now, let us make the plausible assumption that explicit judgements – as required by standard mindreading tasks – necessarily recruit high-level mindreading, even when the problem is simple enough to be dealt with by the low-level module. Then even for a simple problem, a successful explicit judgement will depend on the availability of the necessary cognitive resources, despite the fact that the low-level module may be able to process the agent's perspective correctly. This, I suggest, is the predicament of 3-year-olds in the studies by Clements, Perner, Ruffman and colleagues. The child's eye movements demonstrate successful processing of the agent's false belief by a mindreading module, but the child cannot muster the cognitive resources to resist egocentric interference in the high-level mindreading process that governs their explicit judgement, and so they judge incorrectly. Once again, the literature on number cognition provides some reassurance that this is not merely gratuitous speculation. The situation just described is analogous to similar dissociations observed between children's incorrect explicit judgements of cardinality (e.g., when counting out small numbers) and the "implicit" abilities observed in infants (e.g., Sarnecka & Lee, 2009).

Such cases, in which an individual seems quite literally to be "in two minds" about the correct answer seem very strange, and invite questions about why on earth we would bother with effortful and error-prone high-level processes if low-level processes would do the job effortlessly and accurately. But it is critical to recognize that these cases are really anomalies – informative anomalies, but anomalies nonetheless – in which the problem for explicit judgement falls within the relatively narrow range of problems that can also be processed successfully by a low-level processing module. In the case of mindreading, high-level processes may be effortful, and may open the door to egocentric interference, but they yield an enormous extension to the limited mindreading that can be achieved with modular processes. Understanding how they do so is critical for understanding the nature of mindreading in children and adults, and it is to the implications of my account of these high-level processes that I turn next.

High-level mindreading

High-level mindreading should feel like home territory. The vast majority of studies of mindreading in human children and adults have required participants to make explicit judgements about what others think or want, or what they will do as a consequence of having such beliefs and desires. However, the account developed in the last chapter recasts this familiar topic in a way that has consequences for how we interpret existing evidence, and for the kind of questions we should be asking in future research. I will explore some of these implications for each of the topic areas discussed in earlier chapters. But before doing so I want to re-emphasize a point made in the last chapter about the division of labour between high-level, low-level, and non-mindreading processes in everyday social cognition. The preponderance of studies that examine high-level mindreading can give the impression that this should be the primary subject matter for anyone interested in how we operate in a world of agents with minds of their own. I think that this is systematically misleading about the overall role of high-level mindreading.[8]

The traditional emphasis on high-level mindreading captures an important point: if we want to understand how we mindread in anything like the way described by the normative account of mindreading then we must understand mindreading as a high-level process. This, I contend, is the best hope we have of explaining how we manage to reason about highly diverse beliefs, desires and other mental states as inferences to the best explanation for people's behaviour. What is misleading is the presumption that high-level mindreading is the main thing that gets us through our social day. On the contrary, I think it likely that most of this work is underwritten by a combination of low-level mindreading processes and the rich endowment of social knowledge that we gain through development. This is possible because our everyday social lives include a high degree of regularity that can be exploited by inflexible modular processes, and captured in social scripts, schemas, roles and habits. Moreover, on the account developed in the last chapter, when we do engage in high-level mindreading this is only made possible by our possession of richly structured social knowledge. The following discussion of high-level mindreading should be viewed against this general back-drop.

Development

Thinking about children's mindreading has been dominated by the view that children's main problem is to acquire a certain set of concepts, such as "belief", "desire" and "knowledge". Indeed, this view is cemented in the very term "theory of mind", which is most commonly used to describe research on mindreading. An important consequence of the view developed in earlier chapters is to shift emphasis away from mindreading concepts. I do not doubt that there may be some sense in which it is meaningful to speak of changes in children's "concepts of mind". But describing children's mindreading development as the acquisition of concepts explains less than we might have hoped about mindreading because it remains unclear what it means to be the owner of such concepts, how we tell who has them, and how anyone puts these concepts to use in everyday mindreading. Moreover, since it is typically assumed that mindreading concepts are acquired in early to mid childhood, this approach offers little insight into the mindreading abilities of older children or adults. So what happens if we shift our emphasis away from concept possession, and focus instead on how children come to tackle the cognitive problems entailed by high-level mindreading in an adult-like manner?

Development in early childhood

In chapter 2, I discussed how the majority of developmental studies of mindreading concern children aged 2 to 6 years of age. Among other things these studies reveal that children's success on standard tests of mindreading is related to their success on tests of executive function, and various assessments of language and social experience. Although these factors may be inter-related I will discuss them separately here.

Executive function

The relationship between mindreading and executive function in 2- to 6-year-old children has been discussed extensively in the developmental literature, but little attention has been paid to findings from older children and adults (Apperly, Samson & Humphreys, 2009). I think this is surprising, because one of the most basic questions about development is whether executive function is involved in the developmental process itself (as suggested by "emergence accounts") or whether executive function is actually involved in mindreading per se (as suggested by executive "expression" or "competence" accounts). Clearly, evidence from the mature system of adults is relevant to this question.

In fact, the literature reviewed in earlier chapters provides strong evidence to suggest that executive function has a variety of roles in adults' mindreading, as predicted by expression and competence accounts. This does not rule out the possibility that executive function is also involved in the emergence of mindreading abilities. To gain positive evidence for the emergence hypothesis it would be necessary to show that executive function played a unique role in development that was not served in mature mind-reading. Such evidence does not exist currently, but it may be found. But what the evidence from adults clearly indicates is that at least one reason, and perhaps the only reason, why executive function is related to mind-reading abilities in young children is that executive function is an integral part of the mature mindreading abilities that children are in the process of developing.

So is the role of executive function to support mindreading expression or is it part of the underlying competence to mindread? In many ways, the discussion in the last two chapters was an extended rejection of the premise behind this question. Expression accounts presuppose that children already have mindreading concepts (either innately, or via some unspecified devel-opmental process), but hold that executive resources are necessary for children to put these concepts to use for mindreading. I hope it is clear that, while I think it likely that infants have early-developing mindreading abilities, I am doubtful about glossing these abilities in conceptual terms, and I am also doubtful that the only thing separating the abilities of infants from those of older children and adults is a shortage of executive resources.[9]

Instead, the account of high-level mindreading developed in the last chapter casts developments in executive function as critical enabling con-ditions for children's high-level mindreading. Crudely put, children will need to have big enough heads (executively speaking) to be able to maintain and elaborate a situation model that includes both the background situ-ation (whether this is "reality" or a fictional scenario) and the perspective of another person embedded within it. And they will need good enough control over their mental processes to be able to avoid interference between the background situation model and the embedded perspective while they keep this information in mind and when they put it to use. I think that this captures an insight worth retaining from the expression-competence dis-tinction, which is that executive function will serve a variety of roles in mindreading, some more central to the construction of the necessary situ-ation models, and others more important for using this information in a flexible way. But on this view children's high-level mindreading *consists in* the ability to build and manage situation models about other people's perspectives in a flexible way, and in this sense I am driven strongly to the conclusion that executive function is an integral part of children's mind-reading competence.

This proposal draws together elements from the rather different accounts of mindreading development offered by Perner (1991) and Russell (1996). Perner characterizes young children's increasingly sophisticated reasoning about minds in terms of their ability to create increasingly sophisticated mental models, but pays relatively little attention to how this ability might be underwritten by general cognitive processes. Russell suggests that thinking flexibly about alternative perspectives is at the very heart of our ability to understand the minds of others, as well as our own mind, but pays relatively little attention to the representational requirements of this ability. My own view is that high-level mindreading entails the construction of situation models of varying complexity, and that this ability is progressively enabled by a developing capacity for working memory and other aspects of executive control. Importantly, this means that the timetable for developing high-level mindreading abilities will be significantly constrained by the developmental timetable for relevant aspects of executive function, which are themselves under a variety of biological and environmental constraints.

What data from young children do and do not tell us

As mentioned in the last chapter, there is a lot of scope for future work to determine which aspects of executive function (e.g., working memory, inhibitory control) are involved in which aspects of high-level mindreading (e.g., inferring, holding in mind and using information about mental states). Data from young children are uniquely informative about whether these relationships change over developmental time, and so whether executive functions have a unique role in the emergence of mindreading. They can also tell us which aspect of executive function is the critical limit on children's mindreading at a particular point in time. But for precisely these reasons, data from young children need to be interpreted with caution as evidence about which aspects of executive processes are actually involved in mindreading. This is because examining relationships between a particular executive function and children's success or failure on a particular mindreading task can *only* tell us whether that executive function was the limiting factor on children's performance. It is perfectly possible for an executive function to be an integral part of children's mindreading ability, but not the critical factor that determines their success or failure on a given mindreading task. This is why data from young children should be viewed as just one among several sources of evidence about the cognitive basis of mindreading. And this is why data from adults are informative even if one's interest is only in the mindreading abilities of young children.

Language and social experience

The previous chapters provide two points for discussion about the role of language and social experience in young children's mindreading; one quite specific, the other much more general.

The specific question concerns the role of particular aspects of language in children's mindreading. In chapter 2, I described evidence that children's success on false belief tasks, in particular, is related to their performance on tests of syntax, semantics and pragmatics, and that there is evidence that, in whole or in part, language may be causally necessary for the development of mindreading. Importantly, these findings are subject to the same interpretive ambiguity as the relationship between mindreading and executive function discussed in the last section: from these developmental data alone it is not possible to say whether the role of language is in the emergence of mindreading, or whether language is part of the fabric of the mindreading ability that children are developing (see Apperly, Samson & Humphreys, 2009, for a more detailed discussion). Once again, data from adults are informative, though the conclusions are different from those for executive function. In chapter 4, I described evidence from studies of three patients whose brain injury led to severe impairments in their comprehension and production of grammatically well-formed language. In the case of PH (Apperly, Samson et al., 2006), we were able to show that these impairments extended to those aspects of syntax that might be particularly critical in children's developing mindreading. Despite these impairments to their language abilities, all three patients performed extremely well on a variety of rather complex mindreading tasks that could probably not be achieved without high-level mindreading. Thus, in adults, high-level mindreading does not appear to be critically dependent on the availability of grammatically structured language. This makes a real difference to how we should interpret studies of children, because it indicates that grammatically structured language may be involved in emergence; it may be part of the scaffolding for the development of mindreading, which can afterwards be removed without destroying the ability to mindread.

It remains hotly debated whether it is really possible to separate the effects of syntax on mindreading development from the effects of other aspects of language. And more broadly, it might be questioned whether language can be meaningfully separated from the more general effects of social interaction on mindreading development. As described in chapter 2, there is evidence that children's mindreading is influenced by the quality and quantity of their social relationships, and there seem good reasons for supposing that these effects are at least partially mediated through language. In any case, the general question that arises from earlier discussion is how language and social experience actually achieve their effects on children's mindreading.

The account developed in the last chapter suggests an alternative to the view that language and social interaction help children's acquisition of mindreading concepts. Instead I suggest that language and social interaction are essential means by which children become expert at understanding situations and scenarios, and, in particular, at understanding them in a similar way to the people around them. This is closely related to the existing view that children's mindreading consists in becoming familiar with their culture's social and narrative practices (e.g., Hutto, 2008, 2009), or with becoming enculturated into a "community of minds" (e.g., Nelson,

1996, 2005). But my suggestion does not reduce to this view. As already discussed, I do not doubt that such knowledge underwrites much of the everyday behaviour that is commonly misattributed to mindreading. And I do not doubt that some knowledge of the minds of others is actually encoded within the rich endowment of scripts and other memories that children gain from a typical upbringing. But I believe this endowment has a further role, not envisaged by these authors, in enabling children and adults to identify what information is likely to be relevant in a given situation. The social origins of much of this information ensure that there will normally be widespread interpersonal agreement on what is relevant in a given situation. This is the essential background for enabling the ad hoc ascription of mental states – i.e., high-level mindreading – without running into the brick wall of intractable information processing.

Summary

The development of executive function makes possible new forms of thinking about mental states by enabling the construction of increasingly sophisticated situation models. But it is the development of expertise in identifying what is relevant in a situation – a process of becoming "steeped in one's culture" that is mediated through language and social interaction – that makes it possible to put relevant information into those situation models without posing an impossible burden on information processing. Both of these processes are likely to be critical for understanding the development of mindreading in young children. And importantly, since there is also every reason to think that both executive function and socially mediated knowledge continue to change after the age of 6, these processes are also likely to be important for explaining continuing development in mindreading.

Changes in older children's mindreading

Remarkably little attention has been paid to how children's mindreading abilities might change after they start giving correct answers on the suite of "standard" mindreading tasks used with 2- to 6-year-old children. One exception is work that has examined changes in children's "folk epistemology" about the causes, consequences and justifications for holding beliefs and knowledge (e.g., Chandler, Boyes & Ball, 1990; Kuhn, 2009; Robinson & Apperly, 1998). But it is not clear that changes in these rarefied concepts will explain the everyday intuition that older children are simply *better* at mindreading than younger children. Work that has tried to capture this intuition has demonstrated improvements between 6 and 9 years of age in children's understanding of sarcasm and social faux pas – abilities that require an understanding of other people's mental states (e.g., Baron-Cohen et al., 1999; Happe, 1994b). The difficulty with these findings is that they are not readily interpretable if one adopts the common view that the engine of mindreading development is conceptual change. It is just not clear that you need a more sophisticated concept of mental states to understand sarcasm and faux pas than you do to succeed on the mindreading tasks passed by 6 years. Indeed, it is not at all clear what would count as a more sophisticated concept of mental states than the concept of beliefs as mental representations that is routinely ascribed to young children who pass false belief tasks. As ever, I am not denying that mindreading development has a conceptual flavour. But standard conceptual change accounts offer little for understanding changes in the mindreading abilities of older children.

Besides it seeming self-evidently true that children's mindreading abilities continue to develop beyond 6 years of age, there are at least three specific reasons for expecting this to be the case. Firstly, the neural systems implicated in mindreading abilities in chapter 4, particularly medial prefrontal cortex, and temporo-parietal regions, are among the very latest to reach maturity, with structural changes continuing through adolescence and into early adulthood (Blakemore, 2008; Blakemore et al., 2007; Giedd et al., 1999; Paus, Evans & Rapoport, 1999; Reiss, et al., 1996). Of course, we should be cautious in assuming that these late neural changes are causes rather than consequences of late cognitive changes. But at the very least this provides converging evidence for the existence of late developmental change. Secondly, general cognitive capacities for executive control and processing speed, which seem closely involved in the mindreading of young children and adults, show continued development throughout later childhood and adolescence (e.g., Luna et al., 2004). And thirdly, it seems obvious that children over the age of 6 continue their social apprenticeship, improving their ability to make sense of an increasingly wide range of social situations. If I am right to suggest that this expertise plays a critical role in mindreading then it seems reasonable to think this will be an engine of developmental change.

Evidence of late developmental change on simple mindreading tasks

No studies have directly addressed the role of social expertise in later mindreading development. Thus, the preliminary studies I review here are informative about the effects of general cognitive changes on simple mindreading abilities.

One of the practical difficulties with testing older children is that they pass standard mindreading tasks. However, this is just the same problem encountered when trying to test adults, and, in chapter 5, I described a number of paradigms that solve this problem. These studies demonstrate that adults show a variety of errors, biases and response time costs, particularly on mindreading problems involving conflicting perspectives, which young children find most difficult. In recent work researchers have begun adapting such tasks to study older children (e.g., Epley, Morewedge &

Keysar, 2004; Nilsen & Graham, 2009). The important point is that these tasks examine mindreading that clearly falls within the conceptual abilities of older children to understand false beliefs or differences in visual perspective, but they measure the speed and accuracy with which these abilities can be deployed.

Figure 7.2 summarizes some results from two recent studies that have assessed older children's mindreading on a test of explicit Level-1 perspective-taking (Surtees & Apperly, 2010) and a test of belief-desire reasoning

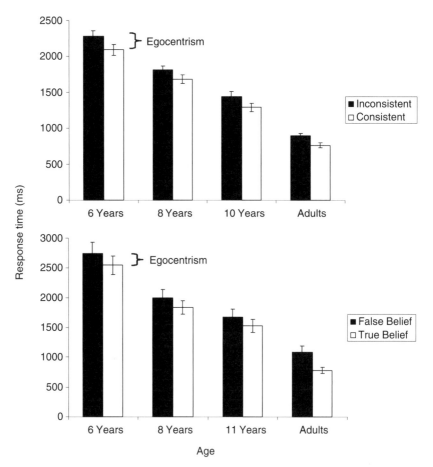

Figure 7.2 Summary charts from two studies of mindreading in older children and adults redrawn to allow comparison of age-related changes: Lower panel, speed of true belief and false belief judgements from Apperly, Warren et al.'s (in press) study of belief-desire reasoning; Upper panel, Speed of explicit Level-1 visual perspective judgements when one's own perspective is either consistent or inconsistent with the target's (Surtees & Apperly, 2010). Both studies show strong evidence of age-related improvement in speed of responses, and much less evidence of a reduction in egocentrism, as indexed by the difference between conditions.

(Apperly, Warren et al., in press). There are three notable features of these findings. Firstly, there is dramatic age-related improvement in speed of correct responses.[10] Secondly, conditions that young children pass later (conflicting perspectives, false belief) continue to be the most demanding throughout development into adulthood. Finally, there is little evidence of disproportionate improvement on these "harder" problems.[11] Instead, developmental change consists primarily in overall improvements in speed and accuracy. This means that older children and adults may indeed be less "egocentric" than younger children, but this does not come from a specific reduction in egocentrism. Children do not just improve on probems where egocentrism is possible, but improve across all sorts of mindreading problem.

Finding that older children are generally faster and more accurate on mindreading tasks than younger children probably will not strike anyone as particularly surprising. But I think it is easy to underestimate the significance of these changes. Most of the literature on children's mindreading has worked hard to develop the most sensitive tasks in order to identify the youngest ages at which mindreading abilities can be demonstrated. This is clearly a worthwhile enterprise, but it also distracts attention from the equally important point that a mindreading ability that is only manifest in the most favourable of circumstances is unlikely to be much practical use. Most obviously, mindreading must be achieved *in time for it to be useful* in an on-going task.

For example, imagine that Sam is listing his plans for next weekend, but has not yet mentioned his birthday party. Since you have been invited to the party, it would be very natural for you to mention it as a further activity in which Sam will obviously be involved. However, you might also reason that Sam's surprising omission is a clue that he doesn't know about the party, and that it has, perhaps, been kept deliberately secret. Now, the important point here is not whether you are able *in principle* to make a guess about Sam's ignorance; but whether you can do this quickly enough to guide your conversation with Sam away from revealing the surprise. I strongly suspect that increasing speed of children's high-level mindreading has significant consequences for how far these abilities are integrated with other activities, and therefore how much they are actually used.

Individual differences in mindreading: typical and atypical variability

The everyday intuition that some people are just rather better at mindreading than others has been investigated in general terms by using a questionnaire that aims to identify a personality factor corresponding to an individual's tendency to "empathize" with others (e.g., Baron-Cohen, Richler, Bisarya, Gurunathan & Wheelwright, 2003). Items on this questionnaire are quite diverse, ranging from ones that seem to ask directly about mindreading (e.g.,

"Other people tell me that I am good at telling how they are feeling and what they are thinking") to others that seem more directed at social motivation rather than mindreading per se (e.g., "I really enjoy caring for other people"). This may well be an advantage for gaining a general index of someone's general "sociability", but it makes it difficult to reach any clear conclusions about the functional basis of individual differences in mindreading. Instead I am going to draw on the foregoing discussion to identify possible factors that may operate at a functional level. I shall begin with individual variability in the typical population, and then briefly consider the case of autism.

What is the difference between a "good" and a "bad" mindreader?

Low-level mindreading

To date there is no evidence concerning variability in low-level mindreading within typically-developing individuals. To the degree that the architecture and processing characteristics of low-level mindreading processes are tightly constrained by genetic and environmental input, we might expect these processes to be ubiquitous in the typical population, and the level of individual variability in these processes to be low. However, the case of number cognition suggests that variability may exist, even in a cognitive process that is universal in humans and shared with many non-human species. Recall that one of the two low-level processes for number cognition allows the efficient estimation of the magnitude of large sets of items. Although this process always yields an estimation, the accuracy of the estimation does vary across individuals and, moreover, this variability is related to performance on "high-level" symbolic number problems (Gilmore & Inglis, 2009). It may well be that similar effects will be found for mindreading.

High-level mindreading

High-level mindreading is heavily dependent upon general cognitive resources, including those for executive control. It is well established that there are individual differences in executive function (e.g., Miyake et al., 2000; Rabbitt, 1997), and it would be surprising if these did not have consequences for mindreading. But these relationships are likely to be complex, because both executive function and mindreading are multi-faceted abilities.

The range and depth of an individual's social experience and expertise will also clearly make a difference to the ease with which they make mindreading inferences by helping them to identify what information is likely to be "relevant" in different situations. If you have ever visited a country with a very different culture then you are likely to have experienced an extreme illustration of how dependent we are upon such social knowledge. We can presume that people in all cultures operate on the same fundamental principles – we are all sentient, we all have knowledge, beliefs, desires and intentions, and these mental states interact in essentially similar ways. But this does not stop us from feeling totally disorientated if we are unfamiliar with a culture's everyday knowledge, norms and background assumptions: everything seems as if it should make sense but for some reason things just don't connect.

The sharing of a joke provides a nice illustration, because this is an activity that depends acutely upon agreeing about what is relevant. I was once in a park in an expensive area of London, and was amused to hear a very well-spoken child called Matilda ask: "Mummy, can I have some more brioche to feed the ducks?". Without saying anything I exchanged a humorous glance with someone else who overheard, and assumed that they found it funny, and for the same reasons as me: only here would one hear a child with a posh voice, called Matilda, who would think it normal to feed ducks with brioche! It seemed so obvious to me, but there are surely other reasons why this might be funny for different people. It could be funny if we supposed that Matilda had made a mistake, and meant to say "bread" instead of "brioche", and this could be more funny because we were in an expensive area of London where children might be presumed to know better. Or it might not be seen as funny at all: someone might see the very idea of feeding expensive brioche to ducks as rather offensive given that there were undoubtedly homeless people on streets not so very far away. My presumption of a shared joke actually assumed much about the other person: that they shared local knowledge, that they recognized a "posh" accent, that they knew Matilda was a "posh" name and, of course, that they shared typically British class prejudices and a tendency for mordant humour.

It is no surprise, therefore, that jokes tend not to travel very well. But we don't have to be very exotic in our travels to experience changes in culture. On a given day we will negotiate our way through a variety of micro-cultures, such as home, public transport, the coffee shop and different kinds of work meeting. Each of these micro-cultures has its own scripts and norms, and therefore its own criteria for what would be considered "relevant" by two people in that situation. Jokes from work often do not seem so funny at home. Of course, jokes are just one illustration of the need for intricate alignment to underwrite our everyday social interactions. I suspect that individual variability in experience and sensitivity to these different situations will make a substantial difference to how well we mindread.

Finally, we should not overlook the possibility of variation in people's motivation for mindreading. I already mentioned briefly the attempts of Baron-Cohen and colleagues (2003) to identify a personality factor for "empathizing" that varies between individuals. Although only some of the items on the Empathising Questionnaire (EQ) ask directly about mind-reading, other more general questions may pick up relevant variability in people's social motivation, and therefore their propensity to pay attention to the minds of others and to have appropriate 1st person emotive responses to situations imagined from the other person's point of view. However, what is puzzling from the current perspective is that participants' score on the EQ is contrasted by these authors with their score on a questionnaire designed to test for a tendency to "systematize"; that is, their motivation to find structure and order in the world. Yet, on many accounts, the whole purpose of our mindreading abilities is to use mental states as a means of systematizing the world of agents by providing explanations, predictions and justifications for their behaviour (e.g., Davidson, 1989, 1995; Dennett, 1987). From this perspective we might expect the best mindreaders to show a propensity for both empathizing and systematizing. Thus, although I think this work highlights the possibility that individual differences in cognitive style may impact on mindreading, it would be informative to unpick the constructs of "empathizing" and "systematizing" to identify more clearly what the underlying factors might be.

Mindreading in autism

As mentioned in chapter 2, many researchers now doubt that a deficit in mindreading could be a general explanation of autism. One reason is that it is far from clear how a mindreading deficit could explain a variety of other distinctive characteristics of autism, such as limited interests and repetitive behaviours. Another reason is that it is common for high-functioning people with autism to pass standard laboratory tests of mindreading. I would not argue with this general view. Nevertheless, pervasive impairments in social interaction and communication remain distinctive characteristics of autism, and clearly require explanation. Can any light be cast by the account developed here?

Low-level mindreading in autism

Autism has strong heritability, and mindreading in autism is impaired out of proportion to general intellectual abilities. Cognitive modules can have strong genetic constraints on their architecture, and operate with substantial independence from other cognitive abilities. It seems compelling to ask whether people with autism might have impairment to a mindreading module, and this, of course, was the insight behind the original work on mindreading in autism (e.g., Baron-Cohen, Leslie & Frith, 1985; Leslie & Thaiss, 1992). From all of the foregoing discussion it should be clear that I think there are compelling reasons for rejecting modularity as a general account of mindreading, but this does not rule out a role for modular processes, or the possibility that damage to a cognitive module specialized for mindreading might explain the mindreading deficit in autism.

Until recently, this hypothesis did not look very viable. As described in chapter 2, there is good evidence that the difficulty that people with autism often have on standard mindreading tasks is not as specific as it at first appeared, and actually extends to well-matched control tasks that make similar demands on language and executive function. However, two recent studies have found evidence that people with autism also show impairment on an "implicit" false belief task that has shown precocious mindreading competence in typically developing 2-year-olds (Senju, Southgate, White & Frith, 2009; Senju et al., 2010). It seems unlikely that impairment on this task is due to impairments in language or executive function, since the task is fully non-verbal, and measures eye movements rather than explicit responses. This interpretation is reinforced by the finding that higher-functioning adults with autism were impaired on this task while, at the same time, showing typical performance on a battery of standard mindreading tasks, which are known to make substantial demands on language and executive function. So it seems very plausible that these studies show a deficit in a relatively low-level process related to mindreading.[12] However, it is equally striking that this deficit did not prevent success on standard mindreading tasks, suggesting that these low-level and high-level abilities are at least partially dissociable.

High-level mindreading in autism

The findings of Senju and colleagues add to the already puzzling observation that high-functioning people with autism may pass standard mind-reading tasks yet continue to show distinctive social and communicative impairments. One possible interpretation of this surprising pattern is that the social and communicative impairments are all a direct consequence of a primary impairment in mindreading identified on the implicit false belief task (Senju et al., 2009). On this interpretation, "success" on standard mindreading tasks reflects the use of a coping strategy that sufficiently able individuals might use to "hack out" a correct answer via an atypical route (e.g., Happe, 1995).

The account developed here is clearly compatible with this possibility, but also suggests a further factor that may contribute to the difficulties experienced by high-functioning individuals. On the account developed here high-level mindreading draws on wholly generic processes for constructing situation models. There is every reason to think that intelligent individuals with autism will be fully capable of such thinking, and to this extent, that their high-level mindreading abilities might not be atypical. However, on this account, high-level mindreading also depends heavily upon an individual being expert in identifying "relevant" information in situations, an ability that is the accumulated result of extensive social engagement with others. It does not seem much of a stretch to suppose that differences in quite basic social abilities and social motivation in people with autism will change their "social apprenticeship" and make it less likely that they converge with the people around them on what is relevant in any given situation. Moreover, given the substantial heritability of autism, this may be compounded by serving one's social apprenticeship among parents and siblings who themselves have social traits that might fall on the autistic spectrum. If so, then we should expect this to have quite severe conse- quences for the ease with which high-level mindreading is possible outside of relatively common, relatively well-structured situations. I wonder whether it might be this, rather than an inability to "conceptualize" mental states, and in addition to any direct, on-line effect of an impaired low-level process, that explains why even highly intelligent people with autism report difficulty with "getting the point" behind what other people do or say.

Implications for the cognitive neuroscience of mindreading

Discussion of mindreading in the cognitive neuroscience literature has been dominated by two related questions, firstly about the role of different parts of the brain in mindreading, and secondly about whether parts of the brain are actually specialized for mindreading.

Multiple contributions to high-level mindreading

High-level mindreading requires the construction of a situation model of the situation of the target for mindreading and, within this, a model of "what is in their head". This constructive process depends upon information about the situation and target being interpreted through the lens of background knowledge (of scripts, episodic memories, social norms and narrative practices), judgements about the target (e.g., similarity to self), and upon an open-ended process of monitoring, evaluation and correction that will clearly make a variety of demands on executive function and memory. Viewed this way, it is really not surprising that mindreading would recruit a range of functional and neural systems.[13]

This list of functions accords well with functions associated with some of the neural regions involved in mindreading. As discussed in chapter 4, the temporal poles are implicated in processing high-level semantic knowledge such as scripts and social norms. Medial prefrontal cortex has been impli- cated in a variety of high-level processes that involve construction of ad hoc representations, including novel problem-solving, episodic memory and introspection. More lateral prefrontal regions are implicated in executive inhibitory control, and bilateral TPJ is implicated in switching attention away from stimuli that are currently salient (besides any more specific role – as discussed below). It seems reasonable to suppose that these regions are part of a network that allows the flexible construction of situation models that is necessary for high-level mindreading.

Of course, this does not entail that all regions are equally critical for solving any given mindreading task. For example, in chapter 4, I discussed the striking case study of a patient with extensive damage to mPFC who nonetheless passes a variety of standard mindreading tasks. I think this can be understood if we suppose that a critical role of mPFC is in managing the "ill-structured" nature of many everyday mindreading situations, which require cycles of integration and cross-checking between new and stored information. In contrast, as discussed in chapter 6, standard mindreading tasks are carefully constructed to help constrain possible interpretations. Success on these tasks might be possible without the functions served by mPFC, even if mPFC is often recruited in healthy brains when participants perform these tasks.

Likewise, the proposition that high-level mindreading requires several neural regions does not entail that all of these neural regions will show significant activation in a given neuroimaging study. Whether or not activation is observed will depend firstly upon whether the particular mindreading task requires the function served by that region, and secondly upon whether the control task also requires the same function to the same degree. For example, in chapter 4, I drew attention to the fact that activity was not observed in temporal poles in studies that contrasted activation while participants read simple stories about false beliefs compared with "false" photographs. If the role of temporal poles in mindreading is to provide high-level semantic information about scripts and social norms, then we can generate two hypotheses about the surprising absence of temporal pole activity in these studies. Either the simple stories used in these studies do not require integration with stored high-level semantic information for their interpretation, or both false belief and "false" photograph trials require similar integration to similar degrees. These hypotheses can be tested with fMRI methods by varying the need for integration of story material with stored knowledge independently of whether or not the task requires mindreading.[14]

Importantly, this is just one instance of a more general point. If we accept the conclusion from chapter 6, that high-level mindreading is unlikely to be modular at either a functional or a neural level, then the primary question for research is not how we can distinguish neural regions that are the seat of mindreading per se from those that offer peripheral support. Rather, it is to understand how multiple functions, and the neural structures that support them, combine to enable the rather complex, emergent phenomenon of mindreading. This question should lead us to use both neuroimaging and neuropsychological methods to test hypotheses about the roles of different neural regions in mindreading by varying the need for a putative function (such as social scripts or introspection) within well-matched mindreading and non-mindreading tasks.

Selective activity in TPJ: Tips of the cognitive iceberg or spuriously activated modules?

What, then, are we to make of the impressive body of evidence summarized in chapter 4 suggesting that R-TPJ shows selective activation for stimuli involving mental states such as beliefs and desires, and the currently rather smaller body of evidence that L-TPJ shows selective activation for stimuli involving perspective differences? Such findings, particularly for R-TPJ, have been interpreted as evidence for a mindreading module with its own neural seat (e.g., Leslie, 2005). The account developed here suggests two alternative interpretations (for simplicity I will focus on R-TPJ from here on, but similar arguments can be made for L-TPJ).

One interpretation assumes that R-TPJ activity reflects the demands of high-level mindreading. If so, then it is clear that the function of R-TPJ is not mindreading per se because there are ample reasons for thinking that high-level mindreading is a complex function that is achieved by a large network of neural regions. It is just not the case that you can peel away these other functions to reveal the core essence of mindreading: what is left may be specific to mindreading, but it will not *be* mindreading. So if we suppose that "false" photograph or false sign control conditions make it possible to peel away the majority of functions involved in mindreading from a false belief task, what is left? One, rather literal, interpretation of this subtraction is that this leaves the need to represent abstract semantic knowledge about mental states such as beliefs and desires.[15] Another, discussed in chapter 4, is that selective activation for mindreading in R-TPJ reflects an effect of social content modulating the pattern of activation observed during the execution of a more generic function, such as shifting attention between more and less salient information. Identifying whether one of these, or some other, interpretation is correct will be informative about the cognitive and neural basis of high-level mindreading. But the general point is that this will be telling us about the tip of the cognitive iceberg, which is composed largely of processes that are essential for mindreading but shared with structurally similar non-mindreading tasks, such as "false" photograph tasks, false sign tasks, and many other activities.

A quite different interpretation of selective activation in R-TPJ during mindreading tasks is that this reflects the activity of a low-level module for mindreading. However, this interpretation is much less straightforward than it might at first appear. It is certainly the case that if there are one or more low-level, original modules for mindreading then this leads quite naturally to the hypothesis that these modules will be neurally localised, even though this is not a strong requirement (see e.g., Coltheart, 1999). It would be very interesting to investigate whether there were unique neural regions associated with mindreading that showed signs of being automatic, implicit or inflexible, and therefore signs of being low-level, modular processes. But these are clearly not the characteristics of the tasks that have shown the best evidence of selective activation in R-TPJ: these tasks require explicit responses to verbal stories and the associated neural activity shows no sign of automaticity (e.g., Saxe, Schulz & Jiang, 2006). So if selective activity in R-TPJ is indeed due to a low-level mindreading module, then it seems most likely that the module is being triggered by stimuli that it cannot process in the way required by the task. A direct analogy for such an effect comes from functional and neural evidence that the low-level system for estimating the magnitude of large number sets is recruited when subjects solve mathematical problems with precise large numbers, even though the low-level system is too imprecise to solve these problems (e.g., Dehane, 2009). A first step in unpicking this potentially complex pattern is to identify the neural correlates of low-level mindreading. This enterprise is likely to benefit from the use of methods with better temporal resolution than fMRI.

New directions: The time-course of mindreading processes

Adults' response times in mindreading tasks are usually less than one or two seconds and often of the order of a few hundred milliseconds. Contrast this with the temporal resolution of fMRI, which is of the order of several seconds, and it becomes clear that fMRI is rather limited as a tool for investigating when information is processed in different parts of the brain during a mindreading task.

In contrast, Electroencephalography (EEG) records scalp potentials that result from co-ordinated neural activity, giving this method millisecond temporal resolution. EEG is much less accurate than fMRI at localising activity in specific brain areas, but this difficulty is partially overcome by the fact that existing fMRI studies give strong a priori reasons for expecting separate sources in frontal, temporal and parietal neural regions. The other main reason why EEG has not been used more widely to study mindreading is that high temporal resolution only becomes useful once there are tasks that locate processes of interest precisely in time. The kind of mindreading tasks with which fMRI studies of mindreading were pioneered – involving rather complex stories or cartoons – are not very suitable because it is just not clear when to "start the clock" for recording event-related potentials (ERPs).

In a study that broke some of this difficult ground, Sabbagh and Taylor (2000) employed short stories about false beliefs and "false" photographs, rather like those in Figure 4.2, and began recording scalp potentials at the point when participants were asked to respond to a question about the story. The results showed that scalp potentials differed between the false belief and "false" photograph conditions within just a few hundred milliseconds of the response stimulus. Moreover, the locations for these differences also bore some correspondence to the data from fMRI studies in that significant differences were observed both in left frontal and (less reliably) left parietal locations.

This study succeeds in identifying differences in scalp potentials between a mindreading task and a well-matched control condition. However, there are limits on what the method employed can tell us about the time-course of mindreading, because it is not at all clear what participants actually had to do during the test question, when the ERP signal was recorded. One possibility is that participants had to infer the mental state of the character described in the story. However, as discussed in chapters 5 and 6, participants are likely to make spontaneous mindreading inferences in many circumstances, raising the possibility that differences observed during the test question reflected the recall of information about the character's mental state that had already been inferred and encoded. If so, this would still be interesting, but the point is that the method employed by Sabbagh and Taylor (2000; see also Liu, Sabbagh, Gehring & Wellman, 2009) does not make it possible to distinguish between these interesting possibilities.

In chapter 5, I described a variety of behavioural methods that are beginning to tease apart different sub-processes of mindreading, making it easier to identify precise moments in time when participants are making a mindreading inference, encoding mindreading information, holding this information in mind and using it to guide further judgements. Combining methods of this kind with EEG[16] has a great deal of potential for extending understanding of how and when different brain regions contribute to mindreading, and this in turn may be informative about the time course of the mindreading processes themselves.

Other theories

As described in chapter 1, researchers usually distinguish between two kinds of theoretical account of mindreading: simulation-theory and theory-theory. It is also common to discuss modularity theories separately, because even though they may be viewed as a species of theory-theory, they make rather distinct assumptions about the nature and origins of mindreading. I shall discuss these theories below. But I start by distinguishing the account I have developed here from others that have discussed multiple systems for mindreading.

Other "two-systems" accounts

A desire to explain the mindreading abilities of infants and non-human animals on the one hand, and the abilities of older children and adults on the other, has led many researchers to posit some sort of two-systems account. Given this, it is reasonable to ask whether the account developed here is really new. In Apperly and Butterfill (2009), Stephen Butterfill and I suggested three ways in which existing accounts differed from the kind that I have been discussing: superficial resemblance; different targets for each system; and underspecification.

Superficial resemblance

Accounts developed over many years by Leslie and colleagues (e.g., Leslie, 1987, 1994a, 1994b, 2000, 2005), and more recently by Baillargeon and colleagues (e.g., Onishi & Baillargeon, 2005; Song & Baillargeon, 2008; Song et al., 2008) describe different "sub-systems" of a "theory of mind" module. Different sub-systems perform different mindreading tasks, and infants' early mindreading improves as new sub-systems come on-line during very early development (for a related view see Baron-Cohen, 1995). These are very interesting ideas, and are compatible with the view developed here, insofar as I think it highly likely that infants have at least one and most likely more than one low-level mindreading process. None-theless, because these accounts only characterize multiple low-level mind-reading processes, they are fundamentally "one-system" accounts, and so bear only superficial resemblance to the one developed here. The reason why this matters is that, as described over the last two chapters and in the section on modular accounts below, I think that such one-system accounts cannot offer anything like a full explanation of our mindreading abilities.

Different targets for each system

Other accounts propose two (or more) mindreading systems, but each is directed at entirely different target problems. For example, Tager-Flusberg and Sullivan (2000) distinguish between systems for "social cognition" (including mindreading) and systems for "social perception", which include processing of biological motion and faces for social information. Gergely and Csibra (2003) distinguish between a system for mindreading and a system that makes sense of goal-directed action without ascribing any mental states at all. Singer (2006) distinguishes between a system for mind-reading and a system for empathy. These accounts clearly have independent merit, but they do not describe two kinds of system for ascribing the same mental states and so they are quite different from the two-systems account proposed here. The reason why this matters is that, whatever their merits, such accounts give no purchase whatsoever on the problem of explaining how the ascription of mental states can be cognitively efficient on the one hand and highly flexible on the others. Of course, this is not their fault, as they were never intended to do so.

Underspecification

Finally, perhaps the most informative type of existing account is a range of suggestions for two-systems accounts that describe different ways in which mindreading might be achieved, but which are underspecified with respect to how this actually enables mindreading to be both flexible and efficient.

In the existing literature, authors have suggested a variety of contrasting properties for different kinds of mindreading: implicit versus explicit (e.g., Dienes & Perner, 1999), intuitive versus reflective (e.g., Keysers & Gazzola, 2007), lower versus higher levels of consciousness (e.g., Zelazo, 2004), and different levels of representations (e.g., Karmiloff-Smith, 1992). Many of these descriptions could readily be applied to the contrasting properties I have given to lower-level versus higher-level mindreading processes in the previous pages, raising the question of whether my account is different. And this question is made particularly important by recent criticisms of two-systems accounts of human reasoning (e.g., Gigerenzer, 2009; Keren & Schul, 2009). The charge of these critiques is that two-systems explanations typically amount to little more than a ". . . yin-yang list of dichotomies . . .", given as a pseudo-explanation once empirical investigations have already revealed a particular psychological phenomenon to be either yin or yang (Gigerenzer, 2009). Put another way, this is the same worry about circular explanations with which I began this chapter. Applied to my account, this questions whether the theoretical proposition of more or less efficient processes for mindreading can count as an explanation of empirical evidence of more or less efficient mindreading performance, or whether it is mere description.

I hope by now to have convinced you that my account does not fall foul of such criticisms because it specifies independent criteria – in the form of signature limits on low-level processes – that make it possible to determine whether a particular instance of mindreading is being performed by a low-level or a high-level process. Importantly, this follows directly from a theoretical analysis of the problems posed by mindreading. The analysis, presented in chapter 6, argues that cognitively efficient mindreading is achieved by trading high efficiency for low flexibility, and low flexibility is manifest in signature limits. Thus, the two-systems account that I have proposed is not another descriptive dichotomy, but is a potential *explanation* of why we observe the contrasting range of empirical phenomena that I described in previous chapters.

It is in this important sense that the existing accounts described above are underspecified. It may well be that the processes I have described as low-versus high-level are also divided along the dichotomies of explicitness, consciousness or levels of representation, and I hope it is obvious that these accounts have been a substantial influence on my thinking. But whatever their descriptive virtues, these accounts fail to specify *how* explicitness, consciousness or levels of representation affect the processing of information for mindreading. For this reason, they lack the explanatory power of the account developed here.

Modular accounts of mindreading

It should be clear from the foregoing chapters that I think it very likely that some of the work of mindreading is achieved by cognitive processes that are modular, in the sense that they have hard limits on the kinds of input that they will process and on the operations performed on that input. A further gain achieved by this "informational encapsulation" is that the mindreading that they perform may be relatively fast, relatively automatic, and relatively independent of general cognitive resources. It is also quite likely that some modules for mindreading have strong genetic constraints on their form (others are likely to be the product of late-developing modularization), and it remains plausible that they might have distinct, localised, neural implementation. Thus, although my primary motivation for taking the modularity thesis seriously was because informational encapsulation presented one kind of solution to the computational intractability of idealized mindreading, I think it likely that mindreading modules have many of the characteristics commonly associated with a Fodorian account of modularity (e.g., Coltheart, 1999; Fodor, 1983, 2000).

However, modularity theories are generally assumed to be much more ambitious than the role I have given to modules, and are frequently discussed as a general account of mindreading. In chapter 6, I argued that this is very unlikely to be correct: modules – as generally understood – have exactly the wrong kinds of properties for a general account because a module cannot support (or even approximate) the kinds of open-ended, context-sensitive processing that is necessary for many kinds of mindreading. Thus, although I think that modules may be an important part of a cognitive account of mindreading, other kinds of process are required to explain how mindreading manages to approximate to the normative account of our everyday ability to reason about the mental states of others.

One caveat to this rejection of a wholly modular account of mindreading comes from recent proposals of a wholly modular account of other high-level cognitive processes, including those that require very flexible processing, such as general abductive reasoning, imagination and creativity (e.g., Barrett & Kurzban, 2006; Carruthers, 2006; Pinker, 1997; Sperber, 2005). The common theme in these suggestions is that although any individual module must be limited in what information it accesses, and what it does with that information, these limitations would not matter if one had a large collection of modules with complementary restrictions on function and information access. Especially so if it was easy for the outputs from modules to become the inputs for further rounds of modular processing. In this way, it is claimed that information processing might end up being highly flexible and responsive to a very wide range of information, even though each processing step was modular and inflexible. Interestingly, in the most detailed account of such "massive modularity", Carruthers (2006) actually ascribes the function of mindreading to a single module. For the reasons already discussed, I think this cannot work. Nonetheless, in principle, massive modularity might offer a way in which high-level mindreading could be achieved via wholly or largely modular processes.

However, it is critical to see that a move to massive modularity does not escape the fundamental trade-off that cognitive processes must make between flexibility and efficiency. Flexible processing in a massively modular architecture requires repeated cycles of information processing through a variety of modules. Although the operation of each module may be cognitively efficient, the overall product will take time to achieve, will require some medium of domain-general memory for the free exchange of information between modules, and most likely will require some domain-general executive processes for controlling the effects of the output. Thus, mindreading in a massively modular architecture may provide an account of how mindreading can be flexible, but it does not provide an account of how mindreading is efficient. Of course, the natural move from this theoretical perspective is to say that we have the ability to mindread flexibly by integrating the processing of many different modules, *and* we have one or more specialized mindreading modules that perform a limited amount of mindreading in a very efficient manner. In principle I see no problem with this move; the only challenge is to use it to generate empirical predictions that are distinct from those of a non-modular account of flexible, high-level mindreading. But my point here is that this is a world away from the claim that mindreading *per se* is the task of a domain-specific, innate cognitive module (e.g., Baron-Cohen, 1995; Leslie, 1987, 1994a, 2005; Segal, 1995). This view has dominated discussion of modularity in relation to mind-reading, and for the reasons described above and in earlier chapters, I think it is unlikely to be correct.

Simulation-theory and theory-theory

In chapter 1, I set aside the two dominant theoretical accounts of mind-reading – simulation-theory and theory-theory – as not particularly useful to my purpose of developing an account of how mindreading is actually achieved in the cognitive system. Here I revisit them briefly, in light of the last seven chapters. The two theories are summarized schematically in Figure 7.3.

"Theory-theories" hold that mindreading depends on our having mental state concepts and principles that describe their interactions (see e.g., Davies & Stone, 1995a, 1995b for extensive discussions of theory-theory and simulation theory). An episode of mindreading requires us to martial a variety of initial information about the state of the world (real or fictional) and the state of the target agent. But the defining feature of theory-theories is that this information is run through a series of reasoning steps that use our concepts and principles about mental states to deduce a prediction about what it is that the target will think, want or do. Such theories obviously contain some interesting insights, and subscribers to these theories might take some comfort from the fact that the current account sees high-level mindreading as just another kind of reasoning problem, albeit with particular form and content. And, consistent with theory-theories, I think there is clearly a sense in which humans (at least) have a conceptual grasp of mental states, even if the nature of these concepts is difficult to pin down.

"Simulation theories" hold that although mindreading may depend, in part, on concepts, it does not require mindreaders to have a fully specified

Theory-Theory

Initial information about target other:
- There is beer in the cupboard
- Target thinks there is beer in the fridge
- Target wants beer

General mindreading principles:
- People seek things they desire
- People act according to their beliefs, not objective reality
- People are unhappy when their desires are not fulfilled

Prediction about target other:
- Target will go to the fridge
- Target will be disappointed

Simulation-Theory

Figure 7.3 Schematic representation of Simulation-Theory and Theory-Theory accounts of mindreading, adapted from Apperly (2008). Theory-Theory: Starting with initial information about the target's beliefs and desires, the agent uses general mindreading principles to generate a prediction about the target's future mental states and behaviour. Simulation-Theory: The agent first takes their own decision-making system off-line from its usual role in guiding the agent's behaviour. Starting with initial information about the target's beliefs and desires, this information is fed into the agent's own decision-making system, which generates a decision or behavioural output that can be taken as a prediction of the decision or behaviour of the target other.

Whereas Theory-Theory requires that the General mindreading principles constitute an exhaustive account of the causal workings of the mind, Simulation-Theory holds that at least some of these principles can remain implicit in the processes for Self decision-making. Both theories require the agent to have appropriate initial information about the target. In either case, specifying this initial information requires participants to identify what is "relevant", and as discussed in chapters 6 and 7, this is a computationally difficult problem to solve and should not be taken for granted.

theory of the mind because we can use our own minds to simulate the minds of others. As in theory-theories, an episode of mindreading requires us to martial information about the state of the target agent, and if the target agent is in a different situation to us (i.e., anything other than being right here, right now) we must also martial information about that situation. The defining feature of simulation theories is that this information is then fed into our very own cognitive systems for judgement and decision-making, which produce judgements and decisions on behalf of the target in just the same way as we would produce them for ourselves. Because our own mind instantiates a working mind this obviates the need for an exhaustive "theory" of how minds work. Subscribers to these theories might take comfort from the current account's emphasis upon high-level mindreading as a process of counterfactual or "imaginative" reasoning, which allows the business of mindreading to inherit any of one's own background knowledge as potential content.[17]

So both theory-theorists and simulation-theorists might find the account developed here at least somewhat amenable to their ideas about mind-reading. In one way this might suggest that we are all barking up the right tree, even if we think we are barking at something different at the top of it. Perhaps. But I think it would be disappointing if this were the only conclusion. Theory-theorists and simulation-theorists have spent a lot of effort trying to generate distinctive empirical predictions with rather limited success (see e.g., Carruthers & Smith, 1995; Saxe, 2005; Stich & Nichols, 1997). Adding a further theory that converged on the same common ground would not be much of an advance. In fact, I think these points of convergence are important, but only a part of the story.

My reason for avoiding simulation- and theory-theory accounts through-out the book is that I think they obscure or ignore one of the most psychologically critical problems that a mindreader must solve. The debate between simulation and theory-theory has focused on the middle stage diagrammed in Figure 7.3, where the question is most often whether we process information about the target agent's starting state by theory-driven reasoning or imagination.[18] Little consideration is given to the problem that these accounts share, which is how it is possible to engage in reasoning or imagination about other people's mental states (or anything else) without running into the gnarly computational problems discussed in chapter 6. Recall that the appearance of simplicity for these reasoning problems is highly deceptive. It is just not clear that a target who thinks there's beer in the fridge and wants a beer will necessarily go to the fridge: logically speaking she could do almost anything. This problem is compounded once we notice that even before we get to the focal episode of mindreading, corresponding to the middle stage of Figure 7.3, we need to identify the "starting state" of the agent and the situation in which they find themselves. Beyond the confines of experiments where this information is supplied, identifying the starting conditions surely poses just the same kinds of problem of identifying what is plausible and relevant,[19] yet these starting conditions are usually taken for granted by simulation- and theory-theories. The fact that it seems "obvious" what the starting conditions should be and what the target will do is a testament to our ability to identify potentially relevant information and ignore other logically possible information when mindreading, but the fact that it seems obvious is no explanation of how this is achieved. My general contention is that an account of how we do this should be at the centre of our psychological account of mindreading. My objection to most simulation- and theory-theory accounts is that they dupe us into thinking that this is not a problem at all.

In summary, this highlights the features that, I think, distinguish my account from simulation- and theory-theories, and that do not follow directly from these theories. On my account we should be extremely worried by the potentially intractable computational problems posed by mindreading. Facing up to these problems leads to the expectation that people use two general kinds of cognitive process for high-level and low-level mindreading that make mindreading tractable in quite different ways. I hope that the previous sections and chapters have shown this view to be a powerful new way of interpreting existing empirical findings, and for making predictions for future research.

Notes

1 I am grateful to Guenther Knoblich, in particular, for forcing me to wriggle on this uncomfortable hook.

2 A very similar case can be made for a separate, cognitively efficient process for estimating large sets of objects, but I focus on precise enumeration for simplicity.

3 There may also be converging evidence from comparative linguistics. Many languages encode number in their syntax. English distinguishes singular from plural, but other languages have obligatory grammatical marking for singular, dual and plural; or singular, dual, trial and plural. It would be an amazing coincidence if the limits on how number is grammatically marked in languages just happened to be the same as the limits on efficient number cognition. More likely, the limits in what numbers ever become obligatorily marked in language reflect the more basic cognitive limits that we share with non-linguistic species. It would be interesting to ask whether the same might be true for the relationship between evidential marking and mindreading. Many languages (not including English) oblige speakers to mark grammatically the source of evidence for what they say (for example, if I said that "the house was on fire" I would be obliged to use a grammatical formulation that expressed whether I saw that it was on fire, whether someone told me, or whether I worked it out via an indirect inference) (e.g., Papafragou, Li, Choi & Han, 2007). On analogy with the case of number, it might be that this indicates a set of distinctions that are automatically encoded by a non-linguistic low-level process.

4 Note, this is not to rule out a critical role for environmental input in the development of the module; it is just that the environment would not have a critical role in constraining the architecture of the module to a particular signature limit.

5 Of course, this will not always be the case. As described at the end of chapter 6,

there is evidence from human adults of an automatic tendency to calculate the sum of symbolic number strings (e.g., "4+6"), but this effect is heavily dependent upon practice, and nobody would expect to find it in untrained infants or non-human animals. In this case, the nature of the limits point clearly to modul-arization, rather than original modularity.

6 In all likelihood, the Level-1/Level-2 distinction will not cut precisely at the joints, and there may well be further, wholly arbitrary, limits on what can be processed by a cognitively efficient mindreading process (we discuss this in more detail in Apperly & Butterfill, 2009, and Butterfill & Apperly, 2010). Identifying the precise characteristics of these limits is an important project, but the Level-1/ Level-2 distinction is sufficient for my current purpose of illustrating how such limits can be a useful tool for understanding mindreading.

7 It is important to note that the Level-1/Level-2 distinction clearly cannot explain the difference between existing studies where listeners appear to succeed at taking rapid account of the speaker's perspective, and studies where they do not succeed, since almost all of the studies only require Level-1 perspective-taking (see chapter 5). The systematic difference between these studies is that participants are much more successful when the number of objects in common and privileged ground is small. An interesting possibility is that rapid, on-line perspective-taking is supported by a module that is not only limited to Level-1 problems, but also has a capacity limit of just a few items.

8 Such suggestions about the critical, but limited role for high-level mindreading processes are not new (see, e.g., concluding comments in Perner, 1991), but often seem to get lost in discussions about mindreading.

9 Of course, children might fail a particular task because they lack the executive resources for performing that task rather than because they lack the mindreading ability that the task was designed to measure. This is the more modest claim of some performance accounts of children's errors on false belief tasks (see, e.g., Bloom & German, 2000). But this has no bearing whatsoever on the bigger question about where children's mindreading ability actually comes from.

10 I have selected speed because it was the variable in which differences were most clearly seen for each study, but in fact both speed and accuracy showed analogous, or at least non-contradictory, effects in both studies.

11 An exception is in Dumontheil, Apperly & Blakemore (2010) who did find a disproportionate reduction in egocentrism between the oldest adolescents and the adult group.

12 Whether this process is actually a module for mindreading, or whether performance on the mindreading task is being affected by impairment of some other low-level process remains an open question.

13 This may appear circular, since, in chapter 4, I reviewed the diversity of brain regions recruited for mindreading and the diversity of their other functions, and used this as part of the argument that mindreading was, in part, a "high-level" process. Of course, this is partly true. But other chapters provide a large amount of evidence converging on the same view, and chapter 6 provides conceptual motivation for this view that is independent of specific pieces of evidence. So I think it legitimate to take the general conclusions from previous chapters and apply them to questions about the neural basis of mindreading.

14 As reviewed in chapter 4, Saxe and colleagues have already begun work that examines the effect of factors such as the need for integration of background material, and the congruency of a character's traits with the participants' traits. But so far, this work has only examined the effects of these manipulations in neural regions pre-identified by the false belief-false photograph localiser, which means that neural regions not identified by the localiser (such as temporal poles) would not be considered.

15 If this turned out to be correct I imagine that some people would claim it as support for the theoretical proposal that mindreading amounts to our having a "theory of other minds". From the current perspective this would be a mistake, because such abstract knowledge would, itself, be largely useless for mind-reading, without the ability to use it in a flexible, context-sensitive way which depends on other functional and neural systems.

16 Not only EEG, but also magnetoencephalography (MEG), which assesses the magnetic component of the signal measured by EEG, and Trans-cranial Magnetic Stimulation, which can disrupt neural processing with high temporal precision.

17 In fact I think there is a real muddle contained in this point, which means this may be rather false comfort. Some simulation theorists argue that if mindreading entails a process of imagination (or counterfactual reasoning) about what the other person would think, and if this imaginative process draws upon my own 1st person knowledge in order to make 3rd person mindreading judgements, then this is evidence that I am mindreading via simulation (e.g., Currie & Ravenscroft, 2002; Mitchell, Currie & Ziegler, 2009). The account of high-level mindreading presented here is clearly compatible with this view of simulation. But I can see nothing in this characterization with which a theory-theorist should disagree: it is perfectly compatible with the view that mindreading depends upon mindreading concepts and mindreading principles to suppose that these concepts and principles operate over content that draws upon our own 1st person knowledge. Indeed it is difficult to see where else this content would come from. Goldman (2006) recognizes this problem and is careful to distinguish such "theory-driven simulation" from "process-driven simulation". Process-driven simulation exploits the fact (or rather, the reasonable assumption) that my own processes for judgement and decision-making operate according to the same general principles as yours, and so whatever content I plug into these processes, irrespective of whether that content is derived from assuming that you have similar knowledge to me or by some other means, I will successfully simulate the same judgement or decision as you would have arrived at if you had processed the same content. I don't doubt that this kind of simulation is open to us (for example, when we judge whether someone else will think a particular sentence is grammatical or ungrammatical), but I doubt that this characterizes the majority of mindreading activity, and, as I describe in the main text, process-driven simulation still begs critical questions about how we identify the starting conditions for the simulation in the first place.

18 For simplicity I'm ignoring process-driven simulation here (see note 17). Process-driven simulation does not fall foul of the problem of relevance as long as one limits focus to the middle stage diagrammed in Figure 7.3. But as I go on to argue, the problem of relevance is also encountered in identifying the "starting conditions" for an episode of mindreading, and process-driven simulation falls foul of this as much as any other account.

19 Recall that this is just the kind of problem we think might be at the heart of patient PF's mindreading difficulties (Samson et al., 2007).

Coda

The scope of this book is at once unusually broad and unusually narrow. One of the things I have always found most exciting about research on mindreading is its broad, cross-disciplinary nature. Researchers have often worked with non-human animals as well as human children, drawn upon evidence from both atypical and typical development, and collaborated with philosophers and linguists to define theoretically interesting questions. In recent years the range of methods and participant groups has expanded yet further to include research with infants, and research using methods from cognitive neuroscience and cognitive psychology with adult participants. In the process, the base of empirical evidence has become richer, but also more complicated and confusing, resulting in bitter debates about who can mindread, how they might mindread and how we can tell.

Difficult as these questions may be, I think that, if anything, we have underestimated the scale of the problems. In particular, we have paid little attention to how mindreaders pull off the cognitive trick of making abductive inferences about mental states, let alone how they might do this in time for mindreading to play a role in fast-moving social interactions. Yet it is clear that these problems loom as large for mindreading as for any cognitive ability, and so an adequate account of mindreading must explain how these problems are solved. I hope to have convinced you that progress can be made on all of these questions by looking at the bigger picture that emerges from the many fields that contribute to research on mindreading, and by drawing upon lessons learned from research in other topic areas.

Converging evidence is valuable because findings that appear to be anomalies when viewed in a local context can turn out to be part of a broader pattern. For example, it might seem most sensible to view evidence of mindreading in human infants as anomalous, when seen against the background of extensive research showing that language and executive function – which infants lack – are necessary for the development of mindreading in older children. But this evidence looks less anomalous when viewed alongside evidence of cognitively efficient mindreading in non-human animals and human adults.

Recognizing that there are many sources of evidence that bear on questions about mindreading is also important when evaluating the trade-off between the parsimony of a theory and its power to explain the evidence. I have proposed a "two-systems" view, suggesting that mindreading in humans is achieved by a combination of high-level and low-level processes that make complementary trade-offs between flexibility and efficiency. However, a preference for parsimonious explanations should lead us to ask whether a "one-system" account might be better.

I think that when each area of the literature is viewed separately one might judge that a one-system account covered enough of the available data to make it preferable. But the problems with one-system accounts become clear when the different areas of the literature are combined. Not only does the stack of "anomalous" findings become uncomfortably large, but also, the kind of one-system account that we would devise for infants or for non-human animals would be very different from the one we would devise for human adults, making one-system approaches look less parsimonious after all. My contention is that when viewed in the round, the loss of parsimony in positing a two-systems account of mindreading is more than compensated by the gain in explanatory power across the diverse literatures where mindreading is studied. Moreover, it should be reassuring that when we look outside of mindreading to other topic areas in psychology, we find that similar proposals for two-system solutions are very common.

It is important to note that other authors have already posited different forms of two-system account for social cognition (see Apperly & Butterfill, 2009 for a discussion). But as discussed in chapter 7, many of these distinguish between processes involved in mindreading *as such*, and processes involved in other aspects of social cognition, such as the perception of faces or eye gaze, the capacity for empathy, or the ability to make predictions about an agent's behaviour without mindreading at all. These authors are of course correct to suppose that there is much more to social cognition than the ascription of mental states. But critically, in the account I have developed here I suggest that even if we restrict ourselves to mindreading as such, and moreover, even if we restrict ourselves to epistemic mental states, such as perceptions, knowledge and beliefs, the tension between demands for flexibility and efficiency does not go away, and so the case for a two-systems account remains. In this respect, the narrowness of my focus on such mental states is critical to the development of my account.

On the other hand, we should be concerned that this focus is actually too narrow for anything like a general account of mindreading. It is critical to acknowledge that there are large tracts of the literature on mindreading that I have not mentioned at all. I have discussed perceptions, knowledge and belief, but have hardly mentioned desires and intentions. Likewise, some researchers would make a basic distinction between the "cognitive" mental states that have been my focus, and "affective" mental states, such as emotions (Shamay-Tsoory & Aharon-Peretz, 2007). Not only is there evidence that different mental states are understood at different times by infants and children, but also that they are understood to varying degrees by non-human animals, and have cognitive and neural bases that may be only partially similar to epistemic mental states. What is the effect of ignoring all these on the account I have developed here?

It is obviously true that emotions, intentions, desires, not to mention enduring personality traits and other vital information about persons are all essential for a full account of mindreading. So in this important sense the account developed here is significantly incomplete. There is a much richer story to be told about the evolutionary, developmental, cognitive and neural bases of mindreading that takes account of all of the mental states, and how it is that we manage (or fail!) to integrate them into a coherent way of explaining, predicting and justifying behaviour. However, the critical question is whether my simplifying strategy is in danger of leading us to the wrong conclusions about the cognitive basis of mindreading, and here I think the answer is a straightforward "no".

Firstly, the rather contradictory pattern of mindreading success and failure observed in children, infants and non-human animals holds just as surely for desires, intentions and emotions as it does for epistemic mental states. So my focus has not overestimated the complexity of the phenomena that need to be explained. Secondly, from a more theoretical perspective, the cognitive problems entailed by mindreading desires, intentions, emotions and other mental states are directly analogous to those for perceptions, knowledge and beliefs. In all cases there are competing demands to be both highly flexible and fast and efficient, and there is no more reason to think that we pull off a cognitive miracle for mental states that I have not discussed than for those that I have.

Of course, the low-level mechanisms for mindreading intentions or emotions might be quite different from those involved in mindreading epistemic mental states. For example, the rapidly emerging literature on mirror neurons and the "mirror system" in humans and non-human animals is providing candidate mechanisms for low-level processing of intentions and emotions in a way that is cognitively efficient. But, despite some ambitious claims, it is clear that these mechanisms do not have the capacity to explain the full richness and complexity of our everyday thinking about these mental states (e.g., Decety & Grezes, 2006; Gallese & Goldman, 1998).

Thus, I think there is every reason to suppose that the arguments for a two-system account of mindreading developed here for the particular case of epistemic mental states will hold for mindreading in general. Needless to say, there is room for a good deal of future work investigating how it is that different components of mindreading are integrated into an ability that both meets the rigorous demands of on-going social activity, and approximates to the richness and complexity entailed by the normative account of mindreading.

In the preface, I described the various literatures on mindreading as building the walls of a tower but omitting to put in the floors. I still think the analogy is accurate: the edifice of research on mindreading will be more sound when we have an account of its cognitive basis. I hope to have laid a few floorboards.

References

Aichhorn, M., Perner, J., Kronbichler, M., Staffen, W., & Ladurner, G. (2006). Do visual perspective tasks need theory of mind? *Neuroimage, 30(3)*, 1059–1068.

Aichhorn, M., Perner, J., Weiss, B., Kronbichler, M., Staffen, W., & Ladurner, G. (2009). Temporo-parietal junction activity in theory-of-mind tasks: Falseness, beliefs, or attention? *Journal of Cognitive Neuroscience, 21*, 1179–1192.

Andrews, G., Halford, G. S., Bunch, K. M., Bowden, D., & Jones, T. (2003). Concept of mind and relational complexity. *Child Development, 74(5)*, 1476–1499.

Andrews, K. (2008). It's in your nature: a pluralistic folk psychology. *Synthese, 165*, 13–29.

Andrews, K. (2009). Understanding norms without a theory of mind. *Inquiry, 52(5)*, 433–448.

Apperly, I. A. (2008). Beyond Simulation-Theory and Theory-Theory: Why social cognitive neuroscience should use its own concepts to study "Theory of Mind". *Cognition, 107*, 266–283.

Apperly, I. A. (2009). Alternative routes to perspective-taking: Imagination and rule-use may be better than simulation and theorising. *British Journal of Developmental Psychology, 27(3)*, 545–553.

Apperly, I. A., Back, E., Samson, D., & France, L. (2008). The cost of thinking about false beliefs: Evidence from adult performance on a non-inferential theory of mind task. *Cognition, 106*, 1093–1108.

Apperly, I. A., & Butterfill, S. A. (2009). Do humans have two systems to track beliefs and belief-like states? *Psychological Review. 116(4)*, 953–970.

Apperly, I. A., Carroll, D. J., Samson, D., Qureshi, A., Humphreys, G. W., & Moffatt, G. (in press). Why are there limits on theory of mind use? Evidence from adults' ability to follow instructions from an ignorant speaker. *Quarterly Journal of Experimental Psychology*.

Apperly, I. A., Riggs, K. J., Simpson, A., Chiavarino, C., & Samson, D. (2006). Is belief reasoning automatic? *Psychological Science, 17(10)*, 841–844.

Apperly, I. A., & Robinson, E. J. (1998). Children's mental representation of referential relations. *Cognition, 63*, 287–309.

Apperly, I. A., & Robinson, E. J. (2001). Children's difficulties handling dual identity. *Journal of Experimental Child Psychology, 78*, 374–397.

Apperly, I. A., & Robinson, E. J. (2002). Five year olds' handling of reference and description in the domains of language and mental representation. *Journal of Experimental Child Psychology, 83*, 53–75.

Apperly, I. A., & Robinson, E. J. (2003). When can children handle referential opacity? Evidence for systematic variation in 5–6 year old children's reasoning about beliefs and belief reports. *Journal of Experimental Child Psychology, 85(4)*, 297–311.

Apperly, I. A., Samson, D., Carroll, N., Hussain, S., & Humphreys, G. W. (2006). Intact 1st and 2nd order false belief reasoning in a patient with severely impaired grammar. *Social Neuroscience, 1(3–4)*, 334–348 (Special issue on theory of mind).

Apperly, I. A., Samson, D., Chiavarino, C., & Humphreys, G. W. (2004). Frontal and temporo-parietal lobe contribution to Theory of Mind: Neuropsychological evidence from a false belief task with reduced language and executive demands. *Journal of Cognitive Neuroscience, 16(10)*, 1773–1784.

Apperly, I. A., Samson, D., Chiavarino, C., Bickerton, W., & Humphreys, G. W. (2007). Testing the domain-specificity of a theory of mind deficit in brain-injured patients: Evidence for consistent performance on non-verbal, "reality-unknown" false belief and false photograph tasks. *Cognition, 103*, 300–321.

Apperly, I. A., Samson, D., & Humphreys, G. W. (2005). Domain-specificity and theory of mind: Evaluating evidence from neuropsychology. *Trends in Cognitive Sciences, 9(12)*, 572–577.

Apperly, I. A., Samson, D., & Humphreys, G. W. (2009). Studies of adults can inform accounts of theory of mind development. *Developmental Psychology, 45(1)*, 190–201.

Apperly, I. A., Warren, F., Andrews, B. J., Grant, J., & Todd, S. (in press). Error patterns in the belief-desire reasoning of 3- to 5-year-olds recur in reaction times from 6 years to adulthood: evidence for developmental continuity in theory of mind.

Astington, J. W., & Baird, J. A. (2005). Introduction. In J. W. Astington, & J. A. Baird (Eds.), *Why language matters for theory of mind* (pp. 3–25). New York: Oxford University Press.

Back, E., & Apperly, I. A. (2010). Two sources of evidence on the non-automaticity of true and false belief ascription. *Cognition, 115(1)*, 54–70.

Bargh, J. A. (1994). The Four Horsemen of automaticity: Awareness, efficiency, intention, and control in social cognition. In R. S. Wyer, Jr., & T. K. Srull (Eds.), *Handbook of social cognition* (2nd ed., pp. 1–40). Hillsdale, NJ: Erlbaum.

Baron-Cohen, S. (1995). *Mindblindness: an essay on autism and theory of mind.* MIT Press: Bradford Books.

Baron-Cohen, S. (2000). Theory of mind and autism: a fifteen year review. In S. Baron-Cohen, H. Tager-Flusberg and D. Cohen (Eds.), *Understanding other minds: Perspectives from developmental cognitive neuroscience* (pp. 3–20). Oxford: Oxford University Press.

Baron-Cohen, S., Leslie, A. M., & Frith, U. (1985). Does the autistic child have a "theory of mind"? *Cognition, 21*, 37–46.

Baron-Cohen, S., O'Riordan, M., Stone, V., Jones, R., & Plaisted, K. (1999). Recognition of faux pas by normally developing children and children with Asperger Syndrome or high-functioning autism. *Journal of Autism and Developmental Disorders, 29*, 407–418.

Baron-Cohen, S., Richler, J., Bisarya, D., Gurunathan, N., & Wheelwright, S. (2003). The Systemising Quotient (SQ): An investigation of adults with Asperger Syndrome or High Functioning Autism and normal sex differences. *Philosophical*

Transactions of the Royal Society, Series B. Special issue on "Autism: Mind and Brain", *358*, 361–374.

Baron-Cohen, S., Tager-Flusberg, H., & Cohen, D. J. (2000). *Understanding other minds. Perspectives from developmental cognitive neuroscience* (2nd ed.). Oxford: Oxford University Press.

Barr, D. J. (2008). Pragmatic expectations and linguistic evidence: Listeners anticipate but do not integrate common ground. *Cognition, 109(1)*, 18–40.

Barrett, H. C., & Kurzban, R. (2006). Modularity in cognition: Framing the debate. *Psychological Review, 113(3)*, 628–647.

Bartsch, K., & Wellman, H. M. (1989). Young children's attribution of action to beliefs and desires. *Child Development, 60*, 946–964.

Bartsch, K., & Wellman, H. M. (1995). *Children talk about the mind*. New York: OUP.

Bayliss, A. P., Paul, M. A., Cannon, P. R., & Tipper, S. P. (2006). Gaze cueing and affective judgments of objects: I like what you look at. *Psychonomic Bulletin & Review, 13(6)*, 1061–1066.

Beck, S. R., Robinson, E. J., Carroll, D. J., & Apperly, I. A. (2006). Children's thinking about counterfactuals and future hypotheticals as possibilities. *Child Development, 77(2)*, 413–426.

Bennett, J. (1978). Some remarks about concepts. *Behavioural and Brain Sciences, 1*, 557–560.

Birch, S. A. J., & Bloom, P. (2007). The curse of knowledge in reasoning about false beliefs. *Psychological Science, 18(5)*, 382–386.

Bird, C. M., Castelli, F., Malik, O., Frith, U., & Husain, M. (2004). The impact of extensive medial frontal lobe damage on "theory of mind" and cognition. *Brain, 127(4)*, 914–928.

Blakemore, S.-J. (2008). The social brain in adolescence. *Nature Reviews Neuroscience, 9*, 267–277.

Blakemore, S.-J., den Ouden, H., Choudhury, S., & Frith, C. (2007). Adolescent development of the neural circuitry for thinking about intentions. *Social Cognitive and Affective Neuroscience, 2*, 130–139.

Blakemore, S.-J., Winston, J., & Frith, U. (2004). Social Cognitive Neuroscience: where are we heading? *Trends in Cognitive Science, 8*, 216–222.

Bloom, P., & German, T. P. (2000). Two reasons to abandon the false belief task as a test of theory of mind. *Cognition, 77*, B25–B31.

Bowler, D. M., Briskman, J., Gurvidi, N., & Fornells-Ambrojo, M. (2005). Understanding the mind or predicting signal-dependent action? Performance of children with and without autism on analogues of the false-belief task. *Journal of Cognition and Development, 6*, 259–283.

Boysen, S. T., & Berntson, G. G. (1995). Responses to quantity: Perceptual versus cognitive mechanisms in Chimpanzees (Pan Troglodytes). *Journal of Experimental Psychology: Animal Behavior Processes, 21(1)*, 82–86.

Bräuer, J., Call, J., & Tomasello, M. (2007). Chimpanzees really know what others can see in a competitive situation. *Animal Cognition, 10*, 439–448.

Bräuer, J., Call, J., & Tomasello, M. (2008). Chimpanzees do not take into account what others can hear in a competitive situation. *Animal Cognition, 11*, 175–178.

Breheny, R. (2006). Communication and folk psychology. *Mind & Language, 21(1)*, 74–107.

Brennan, S. E., & Clark, H. H. (1996). Conceptual pacts and lexical choice in conversation. *Journal of Experimental Psychology: Learning, Memory, and Cognition*, *22*, 1482–1493.

Brothers, L. (1990). The social brain: a project for integrating primate behavior and neurophysiology in a new domain. *Concepts in Neuroscience*, *1*, 27–51.

Brunet, E., Sarfati, Y., Hardy-Bayle, M. C., & Decety, J. (2000). A PET investigation of the attribution of intentions with a nonverbal task. *Neuroimage*, *11*, 157–166.

Bull, R., Phillips, L. H., & Conway, C. A. (2008). The role of control functions in mentalizing: Dual-task studies of Theory of Mind and executive function. *Cognition*, *107*, 663–672.

Burgess, P. W., Gilbert, S. J., Okuda, J., & Simons, J. S. (2005). Rostral prefrontal brain regions (area 10). A gateway between inner thought and the external world? In W. Prinz, & N. Sebanz (Eds.), *Disorders of volition* (pp. 373–395). Cambridge, MA: MIT Press.

Buttelmann, D., Carpenter, M., & Tomasello, M. (2009). Eighteen-month-old infants show false belief understanding in an active helping paradigm. *Cognition*, *112(2)*, 337–342.

Butterfill, S., & Apperly, I. A. (2010). Minimal theory of mind. Manuscript under submission.

Byrne, R. M. J. (2005). *The rational imagination: How people create alternatives to reality*. Cambridge, MA: MIT Press.

Call, J., & Tomasello, M. (1999). A nonverbal false belief task: The performance of children and great apes. *Child Development*, *70*, 381–395.

Call, J., & Tomasello, M. (2008). Does the chimpanzee have a theory of mind? 30 years later. *Trends in Cognitive Sciences*, *12(5)*, 187–192.

Cantor, N., Mischel, W., & Schwartz, J. C. (1982). A prototype analysis of psychological situations. *Cognitive Psychology*, *14*, 45–77.

Carey, S. (2004). Bootstrapping and the origin of concepts. *Daedalus*, 59–68.

Carlson, S., Mandell, D., & Williams, L. (2004). Executive function and theory of mind: Stability and prediction from ages 2 to 3. *Developmental Psychology*, *40*, 1105–1122.

Carlson, S. M., & Moses, L. J. (2001). Individual differences in inhibitory control and children's theory of mind. *Child Development*, *72*, 1032–1053.

Carlson, S. M., Moses, L. J., & Breton, C. (2002). How specific is the relation between executive function and theory of mind? Contributions of inhibitory control and working memory. *Infant and Child Development*, *11*, 73–92.

Carlson, S. M., Moses, L. J., & Claxton, L. J. (2004). Individual differences in executive functioning and theory of mind: An investigation of inhibitory control and planning ability. *Journal of Experimental Child Psychology*, *87*, 299–319.

Carlson, S. M., Davies, A. C., & Leach, J. G. (2005). Less is more: Executive function and symbolic representation in preschool children. *Psychological Science*, *16(8)*, 609–616.

Carpendale, J. I. M., & Lewis, C. (2006). *How children develop social understanding*. Oxford: Blackwell Publishers.

Carrington, S. J., & Bailey, A. J. (2009). Are there theory of mind regions in the brain? A review of the neuroimaging literature. *Human Brain Mapping*, *30(8)*, 2313–2335.

Carroll, D. J., Apperly, I. A., & Riggs, K. J. (2007). The executive demands of strategic reasoning are modified by the way in which children are prompted to think about the task: Evidence from 3- to 4-year-olds. *Cognitive Development*, *22(1)*, 142–148.

Carruthers, P. (1996). *Language, thought and consciousness: an essay in philosophical psychology*. Cambridge: CUP.

Carruthers, P. (2002). The cognitive functions of language. *Behavioral and Brain Sciences*, *25*, 657–674.

Carruthers, P. (2006). *The architecture of the mind: Massive modularity and the flexibility of thought*. Oxford: Oxford University Press.

Carruthers, P., & Smith, P. K. (Eds.) (1995). *Theories of theories of mind*. Cambridge: Cambridge University Press.

Cassidy, K. W. (1998). Three- and four-year-old children's ability to use desire- and belief-based reasoning. *Cognition*, *66*, B1–B11.

Castelli, F., Happe, F., Frith, U., & Frith, C. D. (2000). Movement and mind: A functional imaging study of perception and interpretation of complex intentional movement pattern. *Neuroimage*, *12*, 314–325.

Chandler, M., Boyes, M., & Ball, L. (1990). Relativism and stations of epistemic doubt. *Journal of Experimental Child Psychology*, *50*, 370–395.

Channon, S., & Crawford, S. (2000). The effects of anterior lesions on performance on a story comprehension test: Left anterior impairment on a theory of mind-type task. *Neuropsychologia*, *38*, 1006–1017.

Clark, H. H., & Marshall, C. R. (1981). Definite reference and mutual knowledge. In A. K. Joshi, I. A. Sag, & B. L. Webber (Eds.), *Elements of discourse understanding* (pp. 10–63). Cambridge: Cambridge University Press.

Clayton, N. S., Dally, J. M., & Emery, N. J. (2007). Social cognition by food-caching corvids. The western scrub-jay as a natural psychologist. *Philosophical Transactions of the Royal Society B*, *362*, 507–552.

Clements, W. A., & Perner, J. (1994). Implicit understanding of belief. *Cognitive Development*, *9*, 377–397.

Cohen, A. S., & German, T. C. (2010). A reaction time advantage for calculating beliefs over public representations signals domain specificity for "theory of mind". *Cognition*, *115(3)*, 417–425.

Coltheart, M. (1999). Modularity and cognition. *Trends in Cognitive Sciences*, *3(3)*, 115–120.

Corbett, A. T., & Dosher, B. A. (1978). Instrument inferences in sentence encoding. *Journal of Verbal Learning and Verbal Behaviour*, *17*, 479–491.

Corbetta, M., & Shulman, G. L. (2002). Control of goal-directed and stimulus-driven attention in the brain. *Nature Reviews Neuroscience*, *3*, 201–15.

Costall, A., & Leudar, I. (2007). Getting over "the problem of other minds": Communication in context. *Journal of Infant Behavior and Development*, *30*, 289–295.

Csibra, G., & Gergely, G. (2007). "Obsessed with goals": Functions and mechanisms of teleological interpretation of actions in humans. *Acta Psychologica*, *124*, 60–78.

Currie, G., & Ravenscroft, I. (2002). *Recreative minds: Imagination in philosophy and psychology*. New York: Oxford University Press.

Dadda, M., Piffer, L., Agrillo, C., & Bisazza, A. (2009). Spontaneous number representation in mosquitofish. *Cognition*, *112*, 343–348.

Dally, J. M., Emery, N. J., & Clayton, N. S. (2004). Cache protection strategies by western scrub-jays (Aphelocoma californica): hiding food in the shade. *Proceedings of the Royal Society London: Biology Letters, 271*, S387–S390.

Dally, J. M., Emery, N. J., & Clayton, N. S. (2005). Cache protection strategies by western scrub-jays: Implications for social cognition. *Animal Behaviour, 70*, 1251–1263.

Davidson, D. (1989). The conditions of thought. In J. Brandl, & W. Gombocz (Eds.), *The mind of Donald Davidson*. Amsterdam: Rodopi.

Davidson, D. (1995). Could there be a science of rationality? *International Journal of Philosophical Studies, 3(1)*, 1–16.

Davies, M., & Stone, T. (Eds.). (1995a). *Folk psychology: The theory of mind debate*. Oxford: Blackwell.

Davies, M., & Stone, T. (Eds.). (1995b). *Mental simulation: Evaluations and applications*. Oxford: Blackwell.

Davis, H. L., & Pratt, C. (1996). The development of children's theory of mind: The working memory explanation. *Australian Journal of Psychology, 47*, 25–31.

Decety, J., & Grezes, J. (2006). The power of simulation: Imaging one's own and other's behaviour. *Brain Research, 1079*, 4–14.

Decety, J., & Lamm, C. (2007). The role of the right temporoparietal junction in social interaction: How low-level computational processes contribute to meta-cognition. *The Neuroscientist, 13*, 580–593.

Dehane, S. (2009). Origins of mathematical intuitions: the case of arithmetic. *Annals of the New York Academy of Science, 1156*, 232–259.

Dennett, D. (1978). Beliefs about beliefs. *Behavioral & Brain Sciences, 1(4)*, 568–570.

Dennett, D. (1987). *The intentional stance*. Cambridge, MA: MIT Press.

de Villiers, J. G., & de Villiers, P. A. (2000). Linguistic determinism and false belief. In P. Mitchell, & K. Riggs (Eds.), *Children's reasoning and the mind*. Hove, UK: Psychology Press.

de Villiers, J. G., & Pyers, J. E. (2002). Complements to cognition: A longitudinal study of the relationship between complex syntax and false-belief understanding (pp. 191–228). *Cognitive Development, 17*, 1037–1060.

Dienes, Z., & Perner, J. (1999). A theory of implicit and explicit knowledge. *Behavioral and Brain Sciences, 22(5)*, 735–808.

Doherty, M. J. (2009). *Theory of mind: How children understand others' thoughts and feelings*. Hove, UK: Psychology Press.

Driver, J., Davis, G., Kidd, P., Maxwell, E., Ricciardelli, P., & Baron-Cohen, S. (1999). Gaze perception triggers reflexive visuospatial orienting. *Visual Cognition, 6(5)*, 509–540.

Dumontheil, I., Apperly, I., & Blakemore, S.-J. (2010). Online usage of theory of mind continues to develop in late adolescence. *Developmental Science, 13(2)*, 331–338.

Dunn, J., & Brophy, M. (2005). Communication, relationships, and individual differences in children's understanding of mind. In J. W. Astington & J. A. Baird (Eds.), *Why language matters for theory of mind* (pp. 50–69). New York: Oxford University Press.

Dunn, J., Brown, J., Slomkowski, C., Tesla, C., & Youngblade, L. (1991). Young children's understanding of other people's feelings and beliefs: Individual differences and their antecedents. *Child Development, 62*, 1352–1366.

Elman, J. L., Bates, E. A., Johnson, M. H., Karmiloff-Smith, A., Parisi, D., &

Plunkett, K. (1996). *Rethinking innateness: A connectionist perspective on development*. Cambridge, MA: MIT Press.

Emery, N. J. (2004). Are corvids "feathered apes"? Cognitive evolution in crows, jays, rooks and jackdaws. In S. Watanabe (Ed.), *Comparative analysis of minds* (pp. 181–213). Tokyo: Keio University Press.

Emery, N. J., & Clayton, N. S. (2001). Effects of experience and social context on prospective caching strategies by scrub jays. *Nature, 414*, 443–446.

Emery, N. J., & Clayton, N. S. (2004). The mentality of crows: Convergent evolution of intelligence in corvids and apes. *Science, 306*, 1903–1907.

Emery, N. J., & Clayton, N. S. (2007). How to build a scrub-jay that reads minds. In S. Itakura & K. Fujita (Eds.), *Origins of the social mind: Evolutionary and developmental perspectives*. Tokyo: Springer.

Emery, N. J., & Clayton, N. S. (2009). Comparative social cognition. *Annual Review of Psychology, 60*, 87–113.

Epley, N., Keysar, B., Van Boven, L., & Gilovich, T. (2004). Perspective taking as egocentric anchoring and adjustment. *Journal of Personality and Social Psychology, 87*, 327–339.

Epley, N., Morewedge, C., & Keysar, B. (2004). Perspective taking in children and adults: Equivalent egocentrism but differential correction. *Journal of Experimental Social Psychology, 40*, 760–768.

Evans, J. St. B. T. (2003). In two minds: dual-process accounts of reasoning. *Trends in Cognitive Sciences, 7(10)*, 454–459.

Fauconnier, G. (1985). *Mental spaces: Aspects of meaning construction in natural language*. Cambridge, MA: MIT Press.

Feigenson, L., Dehane, S., & Spelke, E. S. (2004). Core systems of number. *Trends in Cognitive Sciences, 8(7)*, 307–314.

Fernyhough, C. (2008). Getting Vygotskian about theory of mind: Mediation, dialogue, and the development of social understanding. *Developmental Review, 28*, 225–262.

Ferreira, F., & Patson, N. D. (2007). The "good enough" approach to language comprehension. *Language and Linguistics Compass, 1/1–2*, 71–83.

Fine, C., Lumsden, J., & Blair, R. J. R. (2001). Dissociation between "theory of mind" and executive functions in a patient with early left amygdala. *Brain, 124*, 287–298.

Fiske, S. T., & Taylor, S. E. (1984). *Social cognition*. New York: Random House.

Flavell, J. (1974). The development of inferences about others. In T. Mischel (Ed.), *Understanding other persons* (pp. 66–116). Oxford: Blackwell.

Flavell, J. H., Everett, B. A., Croft, K., & Flavell, E. R. (1981). Young children's knowledge about visual-perception – further evidence for the Level 1-Level 2 distinction. *Developmental Psychology, 17*, 99–103.

Flavell, J. H., Flavell, E. R., Green, F. L., & Moses, L. J. (1990). Young children's understanding of fact beliefs versus value beliefs. *Child Development, 61*, 915–928.

Fletcher, P. C., Happe, F., Frith, U., Baker, S. C., Dolan, R. J., Frackowiak, R. S., & Frith, C. D. (1995). Other minds in the brain: A functional imaging study of "theory of mind" in story comprehension. *Cognition, 57*, 109–128.

Flombaum, J. I., & Santos, L. R. (2005). Rhesus monkeys attribute perceptions to others. *Current Biology, 15*, 447–452.

Fodor, J. (1975). *The language of thought*. Cambridge, MA: Harvard University Press.

Fodor, J. (1983). *The modularity of mind: An essay on faculty psychology.* Cambridge, MA: MIT Press.

Fodor, J. (1992). A theory of the child's theory of mind. *Cognition, 44(3)*, 283–296.

Fodor, J. (2000). *The mind doesn't work that way: The scope and limits of computational psychology.* Cambridge, MA: MIT Press.

Frege, G. (1892). Über Sinn und Bedeutung. *Zeitschrift für Philosophie und philosophische Kritik, 100*, 25–50. Translated as: "On sense and reference," in P. Geach, & M. Black (Eds.) (1960), *Translations from the philosophical writings of Gottlob Frege.* Oxford: Basil Blackwell.

Friedman, O., & Leslie, A. M. (2004). Mechanisms of belief-desire reasoning: Inhibition and bias. *Psychological Science, 15*, 547–552.

Friston, K. J., & Henson, R. N. (2006). Commentary on: Divide and conquer; a defence of functional localisers. *NeuroImage, 30(4)*, 1097–1099.

Friston, K. J., Rotshtein, P., Geng, J. J., Sterzer, P., Henson, R. N. (2006). A critique of functional localisers. *NeuroImage, 30(4)*, 1077–1087.

Frith, C. D. (2004). Schizophrenia and theory of mind. *Psychological Medicine, 34(3)*, 385–389.

Frith, C. D. (2007). The social brain? *Philosophical Transactions of the Royal Society B-Biological Sciences, 362(1480)*, 671–678.

Frith, C. D., & Frith, U. (2006). The neural basis of mentalizing. *Neuron, 50(4)*, 531–534.

Frith, U. (2003), *Autism: Explaining the enigma.* Oxford: Blackwell.

Frith, U., & Frith, C. D. (2003). Development and neurophysiology of mentalising. *Philosophical Transactions of the Royal Society of London. Series B, Biological Sciences, 358*, 459–473.

Frye, D., Zelazo, P. D., & Palfai, T. (1995). Theory of mind and rule-based reasoning. *Cognitive Development, 10*, 483–527.

Funnell, E. (2001). Evidence for scripts in semantic dementia. Implications for theories of semantic memory. *Cognitive Neuropsychology, 18*, 323–341.

Gallagher, H. L., & Frith, C. D. (2003). Functional imaging of "theory of mind". *Trends in Cognitive Science, 7*, 77–83.

Gallagher, H. L., Happe, F., Brunswick, N., Fletcher, P. C., Frith, U., & Frith, C. D. (2000). Reading the mind in cartoons and stories: An fMRI study of "theory of mind" in verbal and nonverbal tasks. *Neuropsychologia, 38*, 11–21.

Gallagher, H. L., Jack, A. I., Roepstorff, A., & Frith, C. D. (2002). Imaging the intentional stance in a competitive game. *Neuroimage, 16*, 814–821.

Gallese, V., & Goldman, A. (1998). Mirror neurons and the simulation theory of mind-reading. *Trends in Cognitive Sciences, 2*, 493–501.

Gallistel, C. R., & Gelman, R. (2000). Non-verbal numerical cognition: from reals to integers. *Trends in Cognitive Sciences, 4*, 59–65.

Garnham, A. (1987). *Mental models as representations of discourse and text.* Chichester: Ellis Horwood.

Garnham, W. A., & Perner, J. (2001). Actions really do speak louder than words – but only implicitly: Young children's understanding of false belief in action. *British Journal of Experimental Psychology, 19(3)*, 413–432.

Garnham, W. A., & Ruffman, T. (2001). Doesn't see, doesn't know: Is anticipatory looking really related to understanding of belief? *Developmental Science, 4(1)*, 94–100.

Gelman, R., & Gallistel, C. R. (1978). *The child's understanding of number.* Cambridge, MA: Harvard University Press.

Gelman, R., & Gallistel, C. R. (2004). Language and the origin of numerical concepts. *Science, 306,* 441–443.

Gergely, G., & Csibra, G. (2003). Teleological reasoning in infancy: The naive theory of rational action. *Trends in Cognitive Sciences, 7,* 287–292.

German, T. P., & Hehman, J. A. (2006). Representational and executive selection resources in "theory of mind": Evidence from compromised belief-desire reasoning in old age. *Cognition, 101,* 129–152.

Gernsbacher, M. A. (1990). *Language comprehension as structure building.* Hillsdale, NJ: Lawrence Erlbaum Associates, Inc.

Giedd, J. N., Blumenthal, J., Jeffries, N. O., Castellanos, F. X., Liu, H., Zijdenbos, A., Paus, T., Evans, A. C., & Rappaport, J. L. (1999). Brain development during childhood and adolescence: a longitudinal MRI study. *Nature Neuroscience, 2,* 861–863.

Gigerenzer, G. (2009). Surrogates for theory. *APS Observer, 22,* 21–23.

Gilbert, D. T. (1998). Ordinary personology. In D. T. Gilbert, S. T., Fiske, & G. Lindzey (Eds.), *The handbook of social psychology* (4th ed., pp. 89–150). New York: McGraw Hill.

Gilbert, D. T., Pelham, B. W., & Krull, D. S. (1988). On cognitive busyness: When person perceivers meet persons perceived. *Journal of Personality and Social Psychology, 54,* 733–740.

Gilbert, S. J., Frith, C. D., & Burgess, P. W. (2005). Involvement of rostral prefrontal cortex in selection between stimulus-oriented and stimulus-independent thought. *European Journal of Neuroscience, 21,* 1423–1431.

Gilbert, S. J., Williamson, I. D. M., Dumontheil, I., Simons, J. S., Frith, C. D., & Burgess, P. W. (2007). Distinct regions of medial rostral prefrontal cortex supporting social and nonsocial functions. *Social Cognitive and Affective Neuroscience, 2,* 217–226.

Gilmore, C. K., & Inglis, M. (2009). Automatic access to numerosity in symbolic arithmetic. Manuscript submitted for publication.

Gilmore, C. K., McCarthy, S. E., & Spelke, E. (2007, May 31). Symbolic arithmetic knowledge without instruction. *Nature, 447,* 589–591.

Goel, V., & Grafman, J. (2000). The role of the right prefrontal cortex in ill-structured problem solving. *Cognitive Neuropsychology, 17(5),* 415–436.

Goel, V., Grafman, J., Sadato, N., & Hallett, M. (1995). Modeling other minds. *Neuroreport, 6,* 1741–1746.

Goldman, A. I. (2006). *Simulating minds: The philosophy, psychology, and neuroscience of mindreading.* New York: Oxford University Press.

Gopnik, A., & Meltzoff, A. N. (1997). *Words, thoughts, and theories.* Cambridge, MA: MIT Press.

Gopnik, A., Slaughter, V., & Meltzoff, A. N. (1994). Changing your views: How understanding visual perception can lead to a new theory of the mind. In C. Lewis, & P. Mitchell (Eds.), *Origins of a theory of mind* (pp. 157–181). New Jersey: Erlbaum.

Graesser, A. C., Millis, K. K., & Zwaan, R. A. (1997). Discourse comprehension. *Annual Review of Psychology, 48,* 163–189.

Graesser, A. C., Singer, M., & Trabasso, T. (1994). Constructing inferences during narrative text comprehension. *Psychological Review, 101(3),* 371–395.

Grant, C., Riggs, K., & Boucher, J. (2004). Counterfactual and mental state reasoning in children with autism. *Journal of Autism and Developmental Disorders, 34*, 177–188.

Grezes, J., Frith, C. D., & Passingham, R. E. (2004). Inferring false beliefs from the actions of oneself and others: an fMRI study. *Neuroimage, 21*, 744–750.

Grice, P. (1957). Meaning. *The Philosophical Review, 66*, 377–388.

Grice, P. (1989). *Studies in the way of words.* Cambridge, MA: Harvard University Press.

Gusnard, D. A., Akbudak, E., Shulman, G. L., & Raichle, M. E. (2001). Medial prefrontal cortex and self-referential mental activity: Relation to a default mode of brain function. *Proceedings of the National Academy of Sciences, U.S.A., 98*, 4259–4264.

Hadwin, J., & Perner, J. (1991). Pleased and surprised: Children's cognitive theory emotion. *British Journal of Developmental Psychology, 9*, 215–234.

Hanna, J. E., & Brennan, S. E. (2007). Speakers' eye gaze disambiguates referring expressions early during face-to-face conversation. *Journal of Memory and Language, 57(4)*, 596–615.

Hanna, J. E., Tannenhaus, M. K., & Trueswell, J. C. (2003). The effects of common ground and perspective on domains of referential interpretation. *Journal of Memory and Language, 49*, 43–61.

Happe, F. G. E. (1994a). *Autism: An introduction to psychological theories.* London: UCL Press.

Happe, F. G. E. (1994b). An advanced test of theory of mind: Understanding of story characters' thoughts and feelings by able autistic, mentally handicapped, and normal children and adults. *Journal of Autism and Developmental Disorders, 24*, 129–154.

Happe, F. G. E. (1995). The role of age and verbal ability in the theory of mind task performance of subjects with autism. *Child Development, 66*, 843–855.

Happe, F., Brownell, H., & Winner, E. (1999). Acquired "theory of mind" impairments following stroke. *Cognition, 70*, 211–240.

Happe, F., Malhi, G. S., & Checkley, S. (2001). Acquired mind-blindness following frontal lobe surgery? A single case study of impaired "theory of mind" in a patient treated with stereotactic anterior capsulotomy. *Neuropsychologia, 39*, 83–90.

Happe, F., & Ronald, A. (2008). The "fractionable autism triad": A review of evidence from behavioural, genetic, cognitive and neural research. *Neuropsychology Review, 18(4)*, 287–304.

Hare, B., Call, J., Agnetta, B., & Tomasello, M. (2000). Chimpanzees know what conspecifics do and do not see. *Animal Behaviour, 59*, 771–785.

Hare, B., Call, J., & Tomasello, M. (2001). Do chimpanzees know what conspecifics know and do not know? *Animal Behaviour, 61*, 139–151.

Hare, B., Call, J., & Tomasello, M. (2006). Chimpanzees deceive a human competitor by hiding. *Cognition, 101(3)*, 495–514.

Harris, P. L. (2005). Conversation, pretense, and theory of mind. In J. W. Astington, & J. A. Baird (Eds.), *Why language matters for theory of mind* (pp. 70–83). Oxford: Oxford University Press.

Harris, P. L., German, T., & Mills, P. (1996). Children's use of counterfactual thinking in causal reasoning. *Cognition, 61*, 233–259.

Harris, P., Johnson, C. N., Hutton, D., Andrews, G., & Cooke, T. (1989). Young children's theory of mind and emotion. *Cognition and Emotion, 3*, 379–400.

Hauser, M. D., & Carey, S. (2003). Spontaneous representations of small numbers of objects by rhesus macaques: Examinations of content and format. *Cognitive Psychology, 47*, 367–401.

Herrmann, E., Call, J., Lloreda, M., Hare, B., & Tomasello, M. (2007). Humans have evolved specialized skills of social cognition: The cultural intelligence hypothesis. *Science, 317*, 1360–1366.

Hill, E. L. (2004). Executive dysfunction in autism. *Trends in Cognitive Sciences, 8(1)*, 26–32.

Hogrefe, G. J., Wimmer, H., & Perner, J. (1986). Ignorance versus false belief: A developmental lag in attribution of epistemic states. *Child Development, 57*, 567–582.

Hood, B. M. (1995). Gravity rules for 2- to 4-year olds? *Cognitive Development, 10*, 577–598.

Hood, B. M., Carey, S., & Prasada, S. (2000). Predicting the outcomes of physical events: Two-year-olds fail to reveal knowledge of solidity and support. *Child Development, 71(6)*, 1540–1554.

Hughes, C. (1998). Finding your marbles: Does preschoolers' strategic behavior predict later understanding of mind? *Developmental Psychology, 34*, 1326–1339.

Hughes, C. (2002). Executive functions and development: Emerging themes. *Infant and Child Development, 11*, 201–210.

Hughes, C., & Ensor, R. (2007). Executive function and theory of mind: Predictive relations from ages 2 to 4. *Developmental Psychology, 43(6)*, 1447–1459.

Hughes, C., & Russell, J. (1993). Autistic children's difficulty with mental disengagement from an object: Its implications for theories of autism. *Developmental Psychology, 29*, 498–510.

Hulme, S., Mitchell, P., & Wood, D. (2003). Six-year-olds' difficulties handling intensional contexts. *Cognition, 87*, 73–99.

Hutto, D. D. (2008). *Folk psychological narratives: The sociocultural basis of understanding reasons.* MIT Press: Bradford Books.

Hutto, D. D. (2009). Folk psychology as narrative practice. *Journal of Consciousness Studies, 16*(6–8), 9–39.

Jenkins, A. C., & Mitchell, J. P. (2009). Mentalizing under uncertainty: Dissociated neural responses to ambiguous and unambiguous mental state inferences. *Cerebral Cortex, 21(8)*, 1560–1570.

Johnson-Laird, P. N. (1983). *Mental models: Towards a cognitive science of language, inference, and consciousness.* Cambridge: Cambridge University Press.

Just, M. A., & Carpenter, P. A. (1992). A capacity theory of comprehension: Individual differences in working memory. *Psychological Review, 99(1)*, 122–149.

Kaminski, J., Bräuer, J., Call, J., & Tomasello, M. (2009). Domestic dogs are sensitive to a human's perspective. *Behaviour, 146*, 979–998.

Kaminski, J., Call, J., & Tomasello, M. (2004). Body orientation and face orientation: two factors controlling apes' begging behavior from humans. *Animal Cognition, 7(4)*, 216–223.

Kaminski, J., Call, J., & Tomasello, M. (2006). Goats' behaviour in a competitive food paradigm: Evidence for perspective taking? *Behaviour, 143(11)*, 1341–1356.

Kaminski, J., Call, J., & Tomasello, M. (2008). Chimpanzees know what others know but not what they believe. *Cognition, 109(2)*, 224–234.

Karin-D'Arcy, M., & Povinelli, D. J. (2002). Do chimpanzees know what each other see? A closer look. *International Journal of Comparative Psychology*, *15*, 21–54.

Karmiloff-Smith, A. (1992). *Beyond modularity*. Cambridge, MA: MIT press.

Keren, G., & Schul, Y. (2009). Two is not always better than one: A critical evaluation of two-system theories. *Perspectives on Psychological Science*, *4(6)*, 533–550.

Keysar, B., Barr, D. J., Balin, J. A., & Brauner, J. S. (2000). Taking perspective in conversation: The role of mutual knowledge in comprehension. *Psychological Sciences*, *11*, 32–38.

Keysar, B., Lin, S. H., & Barr, D. J. (2003). Limits on theory of mind use in adults. *Cognition*, *89(1)*, 25–41.

Keysers, C., & Gazzola, V. (2007). Integrating simulation and theory of mind: from self to social cognition. *Trends in Cognitive Sciences*, *11(5)*, 194–196.

Knoblich, G., & Sebanz, N. (2006). The social nature of perception and action. *Current Directions in Psychological Science*, *15*, 99–104.

Kochanska, G., Murray, K., Jacques, T. Y., Koenig, A. L., & Vandegeest, K. A. (1996). Inhibitory control in young children and its role in emerging internalization. *Child Development*, *67*, 490–507.

Krueger, F., Barbey, A. K., & Grafman, J. (2009). The medial prefrontal cortex mediates social event knowledge. *Trends in Cognitive Sciences*, *13(3)*, 103–109.

Kuhn, D. (2009). The importance of learning about knowing: Creating a foundation for development of intellectual values. *Child Development Perspectives*, *3(2)*, 112–117.

Leekam, S., & Perner, J. (1991). Does the autistic child have a metarepresentational deficit? *Cognition*, *40*, 203–218.

Leekam, S., Perner, J., Healey, L., & Sewell, C. (2008). False signs and the non-specificity of theory of mind: Evidence that preschoolers have general difficulties in understanding representations. *British Journal of Developmental Psychology*, *26*, 485–497.

LeFevre, J.-A., Bisanz, J., & Markonjic, L. (1988). Cognitive arithmetic: Evidence for obligatory activation of arithmetic facts. *Memory & Cognition*, *16*, 45–53.

Legrand, D., & Ruby, P. (2009). What is self-specific? Theoretical investigation and critical review of neuroimaging results. *Psychological Review*, *116(1)*, 252–282.

Leslie, A. M. (1987). Pretense and representation: The origins of "theory of mind". *Psychological Review*, *94*, 412–426.

Leslie, A. (1994a). ToMM, ToBY, and agency: Core architecture and domain specificity. In L. Hirschfeld, & S. Gelman (Eds.), *Mapping the mind: Domain specificity in cognition and culture* (pp. 119–148). Cambridge: Cambridge University Press.

Leslie, A. M. (1994b). Pretending and believing: Issues in the theory of ToMM. *Cognition*, *50*, 211–238.

Leslie, A. M. (2000). "Theory of Mind" as a mechanism of selective attention. In M. Gazzaniga (Ed.), *The new cognitive neurosciences* (pp. 1235–1248). Cambridge, MA: MIT Press.

Leslie, A. M. (2005). Developmental parallels in understanding minds and bodies. *Trends in Cognitive Sciences*, *9(10)*, 459–462.

Leslie, A. M., Friedman, O., & German, T. P. (2004). Core mechanisms in "theory of mind". *Trends in Cognitive Sciences*, *8(12)*, 528–533.

Leslie, A. M., German, T. P., & Polizzi, P. (2005). Belief-desire reasoning as a process of selection. *Cognitive Psychology, 50*, 45–85.

Leslie, A. M., & Polizzi, P. (1998). Inhibitory processing in the false belief task: two conjectures. *Developmental Science, 1*, 247–253.

Leslie, A. M., & Thaiss, L. (1992). Domain specificity in conceptual development: Neuropsychological evidence from autism. *Cognition, 43*, 225–251.

Leudar, I., & Costall, A. (2009). *Against theory of mind.* Basingstoke: Palgrave Macmillan.

Lewis, C. N., Freeman, N. H., Kryiakidou, C., Maridaki-Kassotaki, K., & Berridge, D. M. (1996). Social influences on false belief access: Specific sibling influences or general apprenticeship? *Child Development, 67*, 2930–2947.

Lieberman, M. D. (2007). Social cognitive neuroscience: A review of core processes. *Annual Review of Psychology, 58*, 259–289.

Liversedge, S. P., & Findlay, J. M. (2000). Saccadic eye movements and cognition. *Trends in Cognitive Sciences, 4(1)*, 6–14.

Liu, D., Sabbagh, M. A., Gehring, W. J., & Wellman, H. M. (2009). Neural correlates of children's theory of mind development. *Child Development, 80(2)*, 318–326.

Lohmann, H., & Tomasello, M. (2003). The role of language in the development of false-belief understanding: A training study. *Child Development, 74*, 1130–1144.

Luna, B., Garver, K. E., Urban, T. A., Lazar, N. A., & Sweeney, J. A. (2004). Maturation of cognitive processes from late childhood to adulthood. *Child Development, 75(5)*, 1357–1372.

Luo, Y., & Baillargeon, R. (2007). Do 12.5-month-old infants consider what objects others can see when interpreting their actions? *Cognition, 105*, 489–512.

Macrae, C. N., Bodenhausen, G. V., Schloerscheidt, A. M., & Milne, A. B. (1999). Tales of the unexpected: Executive function and person perception. *Journal of Personality and Social Psychology, 76(2)*, 200–213.

Masangkay, Z. S., McCluskey, K. A., McIntyre, C. W., Sims-Knight, J., Vaughn, B. E., & Flavell, J. H. (1974). The early development of inferences about the visual precepts of others. *Child Development, 45*, 357–366.

Maylor, E. A., Moulson, J. M., Muncer, A.-M., & Taylor, L. A. (2002). Does performance on theory of mind tasks decline with age? *British Journal of Psychology, 93*, 465–485.

McCloskey, M. (1983). Intuitive physics. *Scientific American, 248*, 114–122.

McCloskey, M., Washburn, A., & Felch, L. (1983). Intuitive physics: The straight-down belief and its origin. *Journal of Experimental Psychology: Learning, Memory, and Cognition, 9*, 636–649.

McKinnon, M. C., & Moscovitch, M. (2007). Domain-general contributions to social reasoning: Theory of mind and deontic reasoning re-explored. *Cognition, 102(2)*, 179–218.

McKoon, G., & Ratcliff, R. (1998). Memory-based language processing: Psycholinguistic research in the 1990s. *Annual Review of Psychology, 49*, 25–42.

McKoon, G., & Ratcliff, R. (1986). Inferences about predictable events. *Journal of Experimental Psychology: Learning, Memory and Cognition, 12(1)*, 82–91.

McLeod, P., Reed, N., & Dienes, Z. (2003). Psychophysics: How fielders arrive in time to catch the ball. *Nature, 426*, 244–245.

Meins, E., Fernyhough, C., Wainwright, R., Das Gupta, M., Fradley, E., & Tuckey,

M. (2002). Maternal mindmindedness and attachment security as predictors of theory of mind understanding. *Child Development*, *73*, 1715–1726.

Melis, A. P., Call, J., & Tomasello, M. (2006). Chimpanzees (Pan troglodytes) conceal visual and auditory information from others. *Journal of Comparative Psychology*, *120*, 154–162.

Mevorach, C., Humphreys, G. W., & Shalev, L. (2006). Opposite biases in salience-based selection for the left and right posterior parietal cortex. *Nature Neuroscience*, *9*, 740–742.

Milligan, K., Astington, J. W., & Dack, L. A. (2007). Language and theory of mind: Meta-analysis of the relation between language ability and false-belief understanding. *Child Development*, *78(2)*, 622–646.

Mitchell, J. P. (2008). Activity in right temporo-parietal junction is not selective for theory-of-mind. *Cerebral Cortex*, *18(2)*, 262–271.

Mitchell, J. P., Banaji, M. R., & Macrae, C. N. (2005). The link between social cognition and self-referential thought in the medial prefrontal cortex. *Journal of Cognitive Neuroscience*, *17*, 1306–1315.

Mitchell, J. P., Macrae, C. N., & Banaji, M. R. (2006). Dissociable medial prefrontal contributions to judgments of similar and dissimilar others. *Neuron, 50*, 655–663.

Mitchell, P. (1996). *Acquiring a conception of mind. A review of psychological research and theory*. Hove, UK: Psychology Press.

Mitchell, P., Currie, G., & Ziegler, F. (2009). Two routes to perspective: Simulation and rule-use as approaches to mentalizing. *British Journal of Developmental Psychology*, *27(3)*, 513–543.

Mitchell, P., Robinson, E. J., Isaacs, J. E., & Nye, R. M. (1996). Contamination in reasoning about false belief: An instance of realist bias in adults but not children. *Cognition*, *59*, 1–21.

Miyake, A., Friedman, N. P., Emerson, M. J., Witzki, A. H., Howerter, A., & Wager, T. D. (2000). The unity and diversity of executive functions and their contributions to complex frontal lobe tasks: A latent variable analysis. *Cognitive Psychology*, *41*, 49–100.

Moll, H., & Tomasello, M. (2006). Level 1 perspective-taking at 24 months of age. *British Journal of Developmental Psychology*, *24*, 603–613.

Moll, H., & Tomasello, M. (2007). How 14- and 18-month-olds know what others have experienced. *Developmental Psychology*, *43(2)*, 309–317.

Moore, C., Pure, K., & Furrow, D. (1990). Children's understanding of the modal expression of speaker certainty and uncertainty and its relation to the development of a representational theory of mind. *Child Development*, *61*, 722–730.

Moors, A., & De Houwter, J. (2006). Automaticity: A theoretical and conceptual analysis. *Psychological Bulletin*, *132(2)*, 297–326.

Muldoon, K., Lewis, C., & Freeman, N. (2009). Why set-comparison is vital in early number learning. *Trends in Cognitive Sciences*, *13(5)*, 203–208.

Nadig, A. S., & Sedivy, J. C. (2002). Evidence for perspective-taking constraints in children's on-line reference resolution. *Psychological Science*, *13*, 329–336.

Narvaez, D., van den Broek, P., & Ruiz, A. B. (1999). The influence of reading purpose on inference generation and comprehension in reading. *Journal of Educational Psychology*, *91(3)*, 488–496.

Nelson, K. A. (1996). *Language in cognitive development: The emergence of the mediated mind.* Cambridge: Cambridge University Press.

Nelson, K. A. (2005). Language pathways into the community of minds. In J. W. Astington, & J. A. Baird (Eds.), *Why language matters for theory of mind* (pp. 26–49). New York: Oxford University Press.

Newton, A. M., & de Villiers, J. G. (2007). Thinking while talking: Adults fail nonverbal false belief reasoning. *Psychological Science, 18(7)*, 574–579.

Nickerson, R. S. (1999). How we know – and sometimes misjudge – what others know: Imputing one's own knowledge to others. *Psychological Bulletin, 125*, 737–759.

Nilsen, E. S., & Graham, S. A. (2009). The relations between children's communicated perspective-taking and executive functioning. *Cognitive Psychology, 58(2)*, 220–249.

Norman, D. A., & Shallice, T. (1986). Attention to action: willed and automatic control of behaviour. In G. E. Schwartz, & D. Shapiro (Eds.), *Consciousness and self-regulation, Vol. 4.* New York: Plenum Press.

Olson, I. R., Plotzker, A., & Ezzyat, Y. (2007). The enigmatic temporal pole: A review of findings on social and emotional processing. *Brain, 130(7)*, 1718–1731.

O'Neill, D. K. (1996). Two-year-old children's sensitivity to a parent's knowledge state when making requests. *Child Development, 67*, 659–677.

Onishi, K. H., & Baillargeon, R. (2005). Do 15-month-old infants understand false beliefs? *Science, 308(8)*, 255–258.

Ozonoff, S., Pennington, B. F., & Rogers, S. J. (1991). Executive function deficits in high-functioning autistic individuals: Relationship to theory of mind. *Journal of Child Psychology and Psychiatry, 32*, 1081–1105.

Papafragou, A., Li, P., Choi, Y., & Han, C. (2007). Evidentiality in language and cognition. *Cognition, 103*, 253–299.

Parkin, L. J. (1994). Children's understanding of misrepresentation. Unpublished doctoral thesis, University of Sussex, Brighton, UK.

Paus, T., Evans, A. C., & Rapoport, J. L. (1999). Brain development during childhood and adolescence: A longitudinal MRI study. *Nature Neuroscience, 2*, 861–863.

Pellicano, E. (2007). Links between theory of mind and executive function in young children with autism: clues to developmental primacy. *Developmental Psychology, 43*, 974–990.

Penn, D. C., & Povinelli, D. J. (2007). On the lack of evidence that non-human animals possess anything remotely resembling a "theory of mind". *Philosophical Transactions of the Royal Society B, 362(1480)*, 731–744.

Perner, J. (1991). *Understanding the representational mind.* Brighton: Harvester.

Perner, J. (2010). Who took the cog out of Cognitive Science? Mentalism in an era of anti-cognitivism. In P. A. Frensch, et al. (Eds.), *ICP 2008 Proceedings.* Hove, UK: Psychology Press.

Perner, J., Aichhorn, M., Kronbichler, M., Staffen, W., & Ladurner, G. (2006). Thinking of mental and other representations: The roles of left and right temporo-parietal junction. *Social Neuroscience, 1(3)*, 245–258.

Perner, J., & Howes, D. (1992). "He thinks he knows": And more developmental evidence against the simulation (role-taking) theory. *Mind & Language, 7*, 72–86.

Perner, J., & Lang, B. (1999). Development of theory of mind and executive control. *Trends in Cognitive Sciences, 3(9)*, 337–344.

Perner, J., & Lang, B. (2000). Theory of mind and executive function: Is there a developmental relationship? In S. Baron-Cohen, H. Tager-Flusberg, & D. Cohen (Eds.), *Understanding other minds: Perspectives from autism and developmental cognitive neuroscience* (pp. 150–181). Oxford, UK: Oxford University Press.

Perner, J., & Leekam, S. (2008). The curious incident of the photo that was accused of being false: Issues of domain specificity in development, autism and brain imaging. *Quarterly Journal of Experimental Psychology, 61(1),* 76–89.

Perner, J., Leekam, S. R., & Wimmer, H. (1987). Three-year olds' difficulty with false belief: The case for a conceptual deficit. *British Journal of Developmental Psychology, 5,* 125–137.

Perner, J., & Ruffman, T. (2005, April 8). Infant's insight into the mind: How deep? *Science, 308,* 214–216.

Perner, J., Ruffman, T., & Leekam, S. (1994). Theory of mind is contagious: You catch it from your sibs. *Child Development, 65,* 1228–1238.

Perner, J., Sprung, M., Zauner, P., & Haider, H. (2003). Want that is understood well before say that, think that, and false belief: A test of de Villiers' linguistic determinism on German-speaking children. *Child Development, 74,* 179–188.

Perner, J., & Wimmer, H. (1985). "John thinks that Mary thinks that": Attribution of second-order beliefs by 5- to 10-year-old children. *Journal of Experimental Child Psychology, 39,* 437–471.

Peterson, D., & Riggs, K. J. (1999). Adaptive modelling and mindreading. *Mind & Language, 14,* 80–112.

Peterson, C. C., & Siegal, M. (2000). Insights into theory of mind from deafness and autism. *Mind & Language, 15,* 123–145.

Pickering, M. J., & Garrod, S. (2004). Towards a mechanistic psychology of dialogue. *Behavioral and Brain Sciences, 27,* 169–226.

Pillow, B. H. (1989). Early understanding of perception as a source of knowledge. *Journal of Experimental Child Psychology, 47,* 116–129.

Pinker, S. (1997). *How the mind works.* London: Penguin Press.

Povinelli, D. J., & Eddy, T. J. (1996). What young chimpanzees know about seeing. *Monographs of the Society for Research in Child Development, 61* (2, Serial No. 247).

Povinelli, D. J., & Giambrone, S. (1999). Inferring other minds: Failure of the argument by analogy. *Philosophical Topics, 27,* 167–201.

Povinelli, D. J., & Vonk, J. (2004). We don't need a microscope to explore the chimpanzee's mind. *Mind & Language, 19,* 1–28.

Pratt, C., & Bryant, P. E. (1990). Young children's understanding that looking leads to knowing (so long as they are looking into a single barrel). *Child Development, 61,* 973–982.

Premack, D., & Woodruff, G. (1978). Does the chimpanzee have a theory of mind? *Behavioural and Brain Sciences, 1,* 515–526.

Pylyshyn, Z. W. (1978). When is the attribution of beliefs justified? *Behavioural and Brain Sciences, 1,* 592–593.

Pylyshyn, Z. W. (Ed.). (1987). *The robot's dilemma.* New York: Ablex.

Pylyshyn, Z. W. (1996). The frame problem blues. Once more, with feeling. In K. M. Ford, & Z. W. Pylyshyn (Eds.), *The robot's dilemma revisited: The frame problem in artificial intelligence.* New York: Ablex.

Qureshi, A. (2009). The cognitive basis of mental state reasoning in adults. Unpublished doctoral thesis, University of Birmingham, UK.

Qureshi, A., Apperly, I. A., & Samson, D. (2010). Executive function is necessary for perspective-selection, not Level-1 visual perspective-calculation: Evidence from a dual-task study of adults. Manuscript under submission.

Quine, W. V. (1953). *From a logical point of view* (1st ed.). Cambridge, MA: Harvard University Press.

Rabbitt, P. (1997). Introduction: Methodologies and models in the study of executive function. In P. Rabbitt (Ed.), *Methodology of frontal and executive function* (pp. 1–37). Hove, UK: Psychology Press.

Rakoczy, H., Warneken, F., & Tomasello, M. (2008). The sources of normativity: Young children's awareness of the normative structure of games. *Developmental Psychology, 44(3)*, 875–881.

Reddy, V. (1991). Teasing, joking and mucking about: Playing with others' expectations. In A. Whiten (Ed.), *Natural theories of mind* (pp. 143–158). Oxford: Blackwell.

Reddy, V. (2003). On being an object of attention: Implications for self-other-consciousness. *Trends in Cognitive Sciences, 7(9)*, 397–402.

Reiss, A. L., Abrams, M. T., Singer, H. S., Ross, J. L., & Denckla, M. B. (1996). Brain development, gender and IQ in children. A volumetric imaging study. *Brain, 119*, 1763–1774.

Riggs, K. J., Peterson, D. M., Robinson, E. J., & Mitchell, P. (1998). Are errors in false belief tasks symptomatic of a broader difficulty with counterfactuality? *Cognitive Development, 13*, 73–90.

Riggs, K. J., & Peterson, D. M. (2000). Counterfactual thinking in pre-school children: Mental state and causal inferences. In P. Mitchell, & K. J. Riggs (Eds.), *Children's reasoning and the mind* (pp. 87–99). Hove, UK: Psychology Press.

Rizzolatti, G., & Craighero, L. (2004). The mirror-neuron system. *Annual Reviews of Neuroscience, 27*, 169–192.

Rizzolatti, G., Fogassi, L., & Gallese, V. (2001). Neurophysiological mechanisms underlying the understanding and imitation of action. *Nature Reviews Neuroscience, 2*, 661–670.

Robinson, E. J., & Apperly, I. A. (1998). Adolescents' and adults' views about the evidential basis for beliefs: Relativism and determinism re-examined. *Developmental Science, 1*, 279–290.

Robinson, E. J., & Beck, S. R. (2000). What is difficult about counterfactual reasoning. In P. Mitchell, & K. J. Riggs (Eds.), *Children's reasoning and the mind* (pp. 101–119). Hove, UK: Psychology Press.

Royzman, E. B., Cassidy, K. W., & Baron, J. (2003). "I know, you know": Epistemic egocentrism in children and adults. *Review of General Psychology, 7(1)*, 38–65.

Ruffman, T., Perner, J., & Parkin, L. (1999). How parenting style affects false-belief understanding. *Social Development, 8*, 395–411.

Ruffman, T., Perner, J., Naito, M., Parkin, L., & Clements, W. A. (1998). Older (but not younger) siblings facilitate false belief understanding. *Developmental Psychology, 32*, 40–49.

Ruffman, T., Slade, L., Rowlandson, K., Rumsey, C., & Garnham, A. (2003). How language relates to belief, desire, and emotion understanding. *Cognitive Development, 18*, 139–158.

Ruffman, T., Garnham, W., Import, A., & Connolly, D. (2001). Does eye gaze indicate knowledge of false belief: Charting transitions in knowledge. *Journal of Experimental Child Psychology*, *80*, 201–224.

Rugg, M. D., Fletcher, P. C., Chua, P. M. L., & Dolan, R. J. (1999). The role of the prefrontal cortex in recognition memory and memory for source: An fMRI study. *NeuroImage*, *10*, 520–529.

Runeson, S., & Frykholm, G. (1983). Kinematic specification of dynamics as an informational basis for person- and-action perception: Expectation, gender recognition, and deceptive intention. *Journal of Experimental Psychology: General*, *112*, 585–615.

Russell, J. (1987). "Can we say . . .?" Children's understanding of intensionality. *Cognition*, *25*, 289–308.

Russell, J. (1996). *Agency: Its role in mental development*. Hove: Erlbaum.

Russell, J. (1997). *Autism as an executive disorder*. Oxford: Oxford University Press.

Russell, J., Jarrold, C., & Potel, D. (1994). What makes strategic deception difficult for children – the deception or the strategy? *British Journal of Developmental Psychology*, *12*, 301–314.

Russell, J., Mauthner, N., Sharpe, S., & Tidswell, T. (1991). The "windows task" as a measure of strategic deception in preschoolers and autistic subjects. *British Journal of Developmental Psychology*, *9*, 331–349.

Sabbagh, M. A., Bowman, L. C., Evraire, L. E., & Ito, J. M. B. (2009). Neuro-developmental correlates of theory of mind in preschool children. *Child Development*, *80(4)*, 1147–1162.

Sabbagh, M. A., Moses, L. J., & Shiverick, S. (2006). Executive functioning and preschoolers' understanding of false beliefs, false photographs and false signs. *Child Development*, *77*, 1034–1049.

Sabbagh, M. A., & Taylor, M. (2000). Neural correlates of the theory-of-mind reasoning: An event-related potential study. *Psychological Science*, *11*, 46–50.

Sabbagh, M., Xu, F., Carlson, S., Moses, L., & Lee, K. (2006). The development of executive functioning and theory-of-mind: A comparison of Chinese and U.S. preschoolers. *Psychological Science*, *17*, 74–81.

Saltmarsh, R., Mitchell, P., & Robinson, E. (1995). Realism and children's early grasp of mental representation: Belief-based judgments in the State Change task. *Cognition*, *57*, 297–325.

Samson, D., Apperly, I. A., & Humphreys, G. W. (2007). Error analysis in brain damaged patients with perspective taking deficits: A window to the social mind and brain. *Neuropsychologia*, *45(11)*, 2561–2569.

Samson, D., Apperly, I. A., Braithwaite, J., Andrews, B., & Bodley Scott, S. E. (in press). Seeing it their way: Evidence for rapid and involuntary computation of what other people see. *Journal of Experimental Psychology: Human Perception and Performance*.

Samson, D., Apperly, I. A., Kathirgamanathan, U., & Humphreys, G. W. (2005). Seeing it my way: A case of selective deficit in inhibiting self-perspective. *Brain*, *128*, 1102–1111.

Samson, D., Apperly, I. A., Chiavarino, C., & Humphreys, G. W. (2004). The left temporo-parietal junction is necessary for representing someone else's belief. *Nature Neuroscience*, *7(5)*, 449–500.

Sanford, A. J., & Garrod, S. C. (1998). The role of scenario mapping in text comprehension. *Discourse Processes*, *26*, 159–190.

Sarnecka, B. W., & Lee, M. D. (2009). Levels of number knowledge during early childhood. *Journal of Experimental Child Psychology*, *103(3)*, 325–337.

Savage-Rumbaugh, E. S., Murphy, J., Sevcik, R. A., Brakke, K. E., Williams, S. L., & Rumbaugh, D. M. (1993). Language comprehension in ape and child. *Monographs for the Society for Research in Child Development*, *58*, 1–256.

Saxe, R. (2005). Against simulation: the argument from error. *Trends in Cognitive Sciences*, *9*, 174–179.

Saxe, R. (2006). Uniquely human social cognition. *Current Opinion in Neurobiology*, *16*, 235–239.

Saxe, R., Brett, M., & Kanwisher, N. (2006). Divide and conquer: A defense of functional localizers. *Neuroimage*, *30*, 1088–1096.

Saxe, R., Carey, S., & Kanwisher, N. (2004). Understanding other minds: Linking developmental psychology and functional neuroimaging. *Annual Review of Psychology*, *55*, 87–124.

Saxe, R., & Kanwisher, N. (2003). People thinking about thinking people. The role of the temporo-parietal junction in "theory of mind". *Neuroimage*, *19*, 1835–1842.

Saxe, R., Moran, J., Scholz, J., & Gabrieli J. (2006). Overlapping and non-overlapping brain regions for theory of mind and self reflection in individual subjects. *Social Cognitive and Affective Neuroscience*, *1*, 229–234.

Saxe, R., & Powell, L. (2006). It's the thought that counts: Specific brain regions for one component of Theory of Mind. *Psychological Science*, *17*, 692–699.

Saxe, R., Schulz, L. E., & Jiang, Y. V. (2006). Reading minds versus following rules: Dissociating theory of mind and executive control in the brain. *Social Neuroscience*, *1(3–4)*, 284–298.

Saxe, R., & Wexler, A. (2005). Making sense of another mind: The role of the right temporo-parietal junction. *Neuropsychologia*, *43*, 1391–1399.

Schank, R. C. (1982). *Dynamic memory: A theory of reminding and learning in computers and people.* Cambridge, UK: Cambridge University Press.

Schank, R. C., & Abelson, R. (1977). *Scripts, plans, goals, and understanding.* Hillsdale, NJ: Erlbaum Associates.

Sebanz, N., & Shiffrar, M. (2009). Detecting deception in a bluffing body: the role of expertise. *Psychonomic Bulletin & Review*, *16(1)*, 170–175.

Segal, G. (1995). The modularity of theory of mind. In P. Carruthers, & P. Smith (Eds.), *Theories of theories of mind* (pp. 141–158). Cambridge: Cambridge University Press.

Senju, A., Southgate, V., White, S., & Frith, U. (2009). Mindblind eyes: An absence of spontaneous theory of mind in Asperger syndrome. *Science*, *325*, 883–885.

Senju, A., Southgate, V., Miura, Y., Matsui, T., Hasegawa, T., Tojo, Y., Osanai, H., & Csibra, G. (2010). Absence of spontaneous action anticipation by false belief attribution in children with autism spectrum disorder. *Development and Psychopathology*, *22*, 353–360.

Shallice, T., & Burgess, P. W. (1996). The domain of supervisory processes and the temporal organisation of behaviour. *Philosophical Transactions of the Royal Society of London B*, *351*, 1405–1412.

Shamay-Tsoory, S. G., & Aharon-Peretz, J. (2007). Dissociable prefrontal networks for cognitive and affective theory of mind: A lesion study. *Neuropsychologia*, *45(13)*, 3054–3067.

Shaw, P., Lawrence, E. J., Radbourne, C., Bramham, J., Polkey, C. E., & David, A.

S. (2004). The impact of early and late damage to the human amygdala on "theory of mind" reasoning. *Brain, 127(7)*, 1535–1548.

Shillito, D. J., Shumaker, R. W., Gallup, G. G. Jr., & Beck, B. B. (2005). Understanding visual barriers: evidence for Level 1 perspective taking in an orang-utan, *Pongo pygmaeus. Animal Behaviour, 69(3)*, 679–687.

Siegal, M., & Beattie, K. (1991). Where to look first for children's understanding of false beliefs. *Cognition, 38*, 1–12.

Siegal, M., Carrington, J., & Radel, M. (1996). Theory of mind and pragmatic understanding following right hemisphere damage. *Brain and Language, 53*, 40–50.

Simpson, A., Riggs, K. J., & Apperly, I. A. (2000). Belief ascription in adults: Evidence from text processing for off-line inferences rather than on-line encoding. Unpublished manuscript.

Simpson, A., Riggs, K. J., & Simon, M. (2004). What makes the windows task difficult for young children: Rule inference or rule use? *Journal of Experimental Child Psychology, 87(2)*, 155–170.

Singer, T. (2006). The neural basis and ontogeny of empathy and mind reading: Review of literature and implication for future research. *Neuroscience and Biobehavioral Reviews, 30*, 855–863.

Smith, M., Apperly, I. A., & White, V. (2003). False belief reasoning and the acquisition of relative clause sentences. *Child Development, 74*, 1709–1719.

Sodian, B., Thoermer, C., & Metz, U. (2007). Now I see it but you don't: 14-month-olds can represent another person's visual perspective. *Developmental Science, 10(2)*, 199–204.

Song, H., & Baillargeon, R. (2008). Infants' reasoning about others' false perceptions. *Developmental Psychology, 44(6)*, 1789–1795.

Song, H., Onishi, K. H., Baillargeon, R., & Fisher, C. (2008). Can an actor's false belief be corrected by an appropriate communication? Psychological reasoning in 18.5-month-old infants. *Cognition, 109*, 295–315.

Southgate, V., Senju, A., & Csibra, G. (2007). Action anticipation through attribution of false belief by two-year-olds. *Psychological Science, 18*, 587–592.

Spelke, E. S., & Kinzler, K. D. (2007). Core knowledge. *Developmental Science, 10(1)*, 89–96.

Sperber, D. (2005). Modularity and relevance: How can a massively modular mind be flexible and context sensitive? In P. Carruthers, S. Laurence, & S. Stich (Eds.), *The innate mind: Structure and content*. Oxford: Oxford University Press.

Sperber, D., & Wilson, D. (1995). *Relevance: communication and cognition* (2nd ed.). Oxford: Basil Blackwell.

Sperber, D., & Wilson, D. (2002). Pragmatics, modularity & mindreading. *Mind and Language, 17*, 3–23.

Sprung, M., Perner, J., & Mitchell, P. L. (2007). Opacity and embedded perspectives: object identity and object properties. *Mind & Language, 22(3)*, 215–245.

Starkey, P., & Cooper, R. G. Jr. (1980). Perception of numbers by human infants. *Science, 210*, 1033–1035.

Stich, S., & Nichols, S. (1992). Folk psychology: Simulation or tacit theory. *Mind & Language, 7(1)*, 35–71.

Stich, S., & Nichols, S. (1997). Cognitive penetrability, rationality, and restricted simulation. *Mind and Language, 12*, 297–326.

Stich, S., & Nichols, S. (2003). *Mindreading: An integrated account of pretence, self-awareness and understanding other minds.* Oxford: Oxford University Press.

Stone, V. E., Baron-Cohen, S., & Knight, R. T. (1998). Frontal lobe contributions to theory of mind. *Journal of Cognitive Neuroscience, 10,* 640–656.

Stone, V. E., Baron-Cohen, S., Calder, A., Keane, J., & Young, A. (2003). Acquired theory of mind impairments in individuals with bilateral amygdala lesions. *Neuropsychologia, 41,* 209–220.

Stone, V. E., & Gerrans, P. (2006). What's domain-specific about theory of mind? *Social Neuroscience, 1(3–4),* 309–319.

Stulp, G., Emery, N. J., Verhulst, S., & Clayton, N. S. (2009). Western scrub-jays conceal auditory information when competitors can hear but cannot see. *Biology Letters, 5,* 583–585.

Sullivan, K., Zaitchik, D., & Tager-Flusberg, H. (1994). Preschoolers can attribute 2nd order beliefs. *Developmental Psychology, 30,* 395–402.

Surian, L., Caldi, S., & Sperber, D. (2007). Attribution of beliefs by 13-month-old infants. *Psychological Science, 18(7),* 580–586.

Surian, L., & Siegal, M. (2001). Sources of performance on theory of mind tasks in right hemisphere-damaged patients. *Brain and Language, 78,* 224–232.

Surtees, A., & Apperly, I. A. (2010). Egocentrism and automatic perspective-taking in children and adults. Manuscript under submission.

Surtees, A., Apperly, I. A., & Samson, D. (2010). Automatic processing of Level-1 but not Level-2 visual perspectives. Manuscript in preparation.

Tager-Flusberg, H., & Josef, R. M. (2005). How language facilitates the acquisition of false-belief understanding in children with autism. In J. W. Astington, & J. A. Baird (Eds.), *Why language matters for theory of mind* (pp. 298–318). Oxford: Oxford University Press.

Tager-Flusberg, H., & Sullivan, K. (2000). A componential view of theory of mind: Evidence from Williams syndrome. *Cognition, 76,* 59–89.

Tolstoy, L. N. (1954). *Anna Karenin* (R. Edmonds, Trans.). Harmondsworth, Middlesex: Penguin Classics.

Tomasello, M., Call, J., & Hare, B. (2003). Chimpanzees understand psychological states – the question is which ones and to what extent. *Trends in Cognitive Science, 7,* 153–156.

Tomasello, M., & Haberl, K. (2003). Understanding attention: 12- and 18-month-olds know what is new for other persons. *Developmental Psychology. 39,* 906–912.

Uttal, W. R. (2001). *The new phrenology. The limits of localizing cognitive processes in the brain.* Cambridge MA: MIT Press.

Van Boven, L., & Loewenstein, G. (2003). Projection of transient drive states. *Personality and Social Psychology Bulletin, 29,* 1159–1168.

Varley, R., & Siegal, M. (2000). Evidence for cognition without grammar from causal reasoning and "theory of mind" in an agrammatic aphasic patient. *Current Biology, 10,* 723–726.

Varley, R., Siegal, M., & Want, S. C. (2001). Severe impairment in grammar does not preclude theory of mind. *Neurocase, 7,* 489–493.

Vlamings, P. H. J. M., Uher, J., & Call, J. (2006). How the great apes (*Pan troglodytes, Pongo pygmaeus, Pan paniscus,* and *Gorilla gorilla*) perform on the reversed contingency task: The effects of food quantity and food visibility. *Journal of Experimental Psychology: Animal Behaviour Processes, 32(1),* 60–70.

Vogeley, K., Bussfeld, P., Newen, A., Herrmann, S., Happe, F., Falkai, P., Maier,

W., Shah, N. J., Fink, G. R., & Zilles, K. (2001). Mind reading: Neural mechanisms of theory of mind and self-perspective. *Neuroimage, 14*, 170–181.

Vogeley, K., May, M., Ritzl, A., Falkai, P., Zilles, K., & Fink, G. R. (2004). Neural correlates of first-person perspective as one constituent of human self-consciousness. *Journal of Cognitive Neuroscience, 16*, 817–827.

von Bayern, A. M. P., & Emery, N. J. (2009). Jackdaws are sensitive to human attentional and communicative gestures in different contexts. *Current Biology, 19*, 602–606.

Wellman, H. (1990). *The child's theory of mind.* Cambridge, MA: MIT Press.

Wellman, H. M., & Bartsch, K. (1988). Young children's reasoning about beliefs. *Cognition, 30*, 239–277.

Wellman, H., Cross, D., & Watson, J. (2001). Meta-analysis of theory of mind development: The truth about false-belief. *Child Development, 72(3)*, 655–684.

Wellman, H. M., & Liu, D. (2004). Scaling of theory-of-mind tasks. *Child Development, 75*, 523–541.

Wimmer, H., & Perner, J. (1983). Beliefs about beliefs: Representation and constraining function of wrong beliefs in young children's understanding of deception. *Cognition, 13*, 103–128.

Winner, E., Brownell, H., Happe, F., Blum, A., & Pincus, D. (1998). Distinguishing lies from jokes: Theory of mind deficits and discourse interpretation in right hemisphere brain-damaged patients. *Brain and Language, 62*, 89–106.

Woolfe, T., Want, S. C., & Siegal, M. (2002). Signposts to development: Theory of mind in deaf children. *Child Development, 73(3)*, 768–778.

Wynn, K. (1996). Infants' individuation and enumeration of actions. *Psychological Science, 7*, 164–169.

Xu, F., & Spelke, E. S. (2000). Large number discrimination in 6-month old infants. *Cognition, 74*, B1–B11.

Young, L., Camprodon, J., Hauser, M., Pascual-Leone, A., & Saxe, R. (2010). Disruption of the right temporo-parietal junction with transcranial magnetic stimulation reduces the role of beliefs in moral judgment. *Proceedings of the National Academy of Science, 107(15)*, 6753–6758.

Young, L., Cushman, F., Hauser, M., & Saxe, R. (2007). The neural basis of the interaction between theory of mind and moral judgment. *Proceedings of the National Academy of Science, 104(20)*, 8235–8240.

Young, L., & Saxe, R. (2008). The neural basis of belief encoding and integration in moral judgment. *Neuroimage, 40*, 1912–1920.

Zacks, J. M., Vettel, J. M., & Michelon, P. (2003). Imagined viewer and object rotations dissociated with event-related fMRI. *Journal of Cognitive Neuroscience, 15*, 1002–1018.

Zaitchik, D. (1990). When representations conflict with reality: The preschooler's problem with false beliefs and "false" photographs. *Cognition, 35*, 41–68.

Zelazo, P. D. (2004). The development of conscious control in childhood. *Trends in Cognitive Sciences, 8(1)*, 12–17.

Zelazo, P. D., Frye, D., & Rapus, T. (1996). An age-related dissociation between knowing rules and using them. *Cognitive Development, 11*, 37–63.

Zwaan, R. A., & Radvansky, G. A. (1998). Situation models in language comprehension and memory. *Psychological Bulletin, 123*, 162–185.

Author index

Subject index